HAND BOOK ON RAJPUTS

HAND BOOK ON RAJPUTS

CAPTAIN A H BINGLEY

Low Price Publications

2010

First Published 1899

Reprinted in LPP 1999, 2002, 2006, 2010

ISBN 10: 81-7536-524-2
ISBN 13: 978-81-7536-524-7

Published by
Low Price Publications
A-6, Second Floor, Nimri Commercial Centre,
Ashok Vihar Phase-IV, Delhi 110 052
Phone: 011 27302453
e-mail: info@Lppindia.com
website: www.Lppindia.com

Printed at
IIP Printers
Delhi

PRINTED IN INDIA

LIST OF SOME OF THE PRINCIPAL AUTHORITIES CONSULTED IN THE PREPARATION OF THIS WORK.

Hindu Tribes and Castes—Sherring.

Ethnographical Handbook for the North-West Provinces and Oudh —Crooke.

Notes on the Hindu Religion—Newell.

Notes on Rájpúts—Newell.

Notes on Rájpútána Rájpúts—Prior.

Notes on Hinduism—Harris.

Hindu Mythology—Wilkins.

Ethnography of the Punjáb—Ibbetson.

Gazetteer of the North-West Provinces.

Gazetteer of the Punjáb.

Gazetteer of the Central Provinces.

Gazetteer of Oudh.

Census Reports of 1881 and 1891.

Encyclopædia Britannica.

Encyclopædia of India—Balfour.

India—Strachey.

Indian Polity—Chesney.

The History of India—Talboys Wheeler.

A Student's Manual of the History of India—Meadows Taylor.

History of the Rise and Progress of the Bengal Army—Broome.

Historical Records of the Bengal Army—Cardew.

A short History of the Indian People—Hunter.

Asiatic Studies—Lyall.

The Races of the North-West Provinces of India—Elliott.

Bráhmanism and Hinduism—Monier Williams.

A Journey through the Kingdom of Oudh—Sleeman.

Akbar—Malleson.

Aurangzéb—Lane-Pool.

History of the Indian Mutiny—Kaye and Malleson.

History of the War in Afghánistán—Kaye.

Journal of the United Service Institution of India.

Treaties, Engagements, and Sanads—Aitchison.

The Annals of Rájasthán—Tod.

Essay on the languages, &c., of Nepál—Hodgson.

Reigions of India—Hopkins.

CONTENTS.

INDEX TO HAND-BOOK ON RAJPUTS.

CONTENTS.

CHAPTER I.

HISTORY AND ORIGIN.

Our earliest glimpse of ancient India discloses two races struggling for the soil. One was a fair-skinned, Sanskrit-speaking people of Aryan lineage, who entered the country from the North-West; the other a dark-complexioned race of lower type, the original inhabitants of the land, who were either driven by the Aryans into the hills, or reduced by them to servitude in the plains.

The races of ancient India.

The original home of the Aryan race was on the banks of the Oxus in Central Asia. From thence they migrated in two directions. One branch moved north-west towards Europe, the other south-east towards Persia and India. It is with the latter that we are here concerned.

The cradle of the Aryan races.

Crossing the Hindu Kush, the Aryans settled for some time in the valleys of Afghánistán; from thence they forced their way across the mountains into India, and gradually settled in the Punjáb about 2000 B. C.

We know very little of their manner of life. They roamed from one river valley to another with their cattle, making long halts in favourable situations, to raise the crops required for their food. They were constantly at war, not only with the aboriginal tribes, but also among themselves. At the head of each tribe was a chief or *Máhárája*, but each house-father was a warrior, husbandman, and priest, offering up sacrifices to the gods direct, without the intervention of a professional priesthood.

Early conditions of life among the Aryans.

The earliest records of the Aryans are contained in the *Védas*, a series of hymns composed in the Sanskrit language from the 15th to the 10th century B. C. by the *Rishis*, devout sages, devoted to religious meditation, whose utterances were supposed to be inspired. The early *Védas* must have been composed while the Aryan tribes were marching towards India; others after their arrival on the banks of the Indus. During this advance the race progressed from a loose confederacy of various tribes into several well-knit nations, and extended its settlements from the Himalayas in the

The Védas.

north to the Vindhyas in the south, and throughout the whole of the river systems of Upper India, as far to the east as the Sône.

It has been explained that each head of a family conducted his own religious rites, but in course of time many ceremonial observances were added to the primitive religion, necessitating the service of a special priesthood. It became the custom to call upon the *Rishis* to conduct the great sacrifices, and to chant the *Védic* hymns. The art of writing was at this time unknown, and hymns and sacrificial phrases had to be handed down by word of mouth, from father to son. It thus came about that certain families became the hereditary owners of the liturgies required at the great national festivals, and were called upon time after time to chant the tribal battle hymns, to invoke the divine aid, and to appease the divine wrath. These potent prayers were called *Brahmás*, and those who offered them were *Bráhmans*. By degrees the number of ministrants required for a great sacrifice increased. Besides the high priests who superintended the ceremonies, there were the celebrants who dressed the altars, slew the victims, and poured out libations to the gods, while others chanted the *Védic* hymns and repeated the phrases appropriate to particular rites. In this manner there arose a special priesthood—a class which was entrusted with the conduct of religious offices, while the rest of the community carried on their ordinary avocations of war, trade, and agriculture.

Origin of the Bráhmans or Aryan priests.

As the Aryan colonists spread east and south, subduing the aboriginal races, they were to a large extent relieved from the burden of agricultural labour through the compulsory employment of the conquered people. In this manner there grew up a class of warriors freed from the toil of husbandry, who attended the *Máhárája*, and were always ready for battle. These kinsmen and companions of the kings gradually formed themselves into a separate class, and were referred to as *Kshatriyas*, *i.e.*, 'those connected with the royal power,' and eventually as *Rájpúts*, or 'those of royal descent.'

Origin of the warrior class.

The incessant fighting which had formed the common lot of the Aryans on their march eastward from the Indus, gradually ceased as the aboriginal races were subdued. Members of the community who from family ties, or from personal inclination, preferred war to the peaceful monotony of village life, had to seek for adventure in the hills and forests of the unknown country to the south of the Vindhyas. Distant expeditions were only undertaken by those to whom war was a profession, while others, more peacefully inclined

Origin of the agricultural and trading classes.

stayed at home, devoting themselves to agriculture and the manufacturing arts.

Thus the Aryans, by a process of natural selection, gradually resolved themselves into three classes :—

The organisation into four classes.

1. The *Bráhman* or priestly caste* composed of the *Rishis,* their descendants, and disciples, to which was entrusted the expounding of the *Védas*, and the conduct of religious ceremonies.

2. The *Kshatriya, i.e., Rájpút* or governing and military caste, composed of the *Máhárájas* and their warrior kinsmen and companions, whose duty it was to rule, fight, administer justice, and protect the community in general.

3. The *Vaisiya* or trading and agricultural caste, which, assisted by the conquered aborigines, tilled the land, raised cattle, and manufactured the arms, implements, and household utensils, required by the Aryan commonwealths.

It must be remembered, however, that in the early days of the Aryan settlements the line of separation between the three classes was far from being sharply defined. The transfer of individuals and their families from one to the other was not an uncommon occurrence, and numerous instances are recorded of kings and warriors terminating their careers as *Rishis* or saintly ascetics. Moreover in very early times the *Máhárájas* often combined the offices of the priesthood with kingly power, a custom which in rare instances† has survived to the present day. In the same way it was not unusual for the more adventurous Vaisiyas to abandon agriculture, and join the ranks of the Kshatriyas.

In course of time these occupational distinctions developed into separate castes, and as intermarriage became first of all restricted, and afterwards prohibited, each caste devoted itself more strictly to its own hereditary employment. All, however, were recognized as belonging to the twice-born or Aryan race, all were permitted to attend the great national sacrifices, and all worshipped the same gods.

* The term 'caste' is derived from the Portuguese *casta*, 'a family;' but before the word came to be extensively used in European languages, it had for some time been identified with the Bráhmanic division of Hindu society into classes. The corresponding Sanskrit word is *Várna* 'colour.' The three Aryan *Várnas* or castes were of light complexion. *Bráhmans* were said to be white, *Kshatriyas* ruddy, and *Vaisiyas* yellow: on the other hand, the *Sudras* and *Dasyus* or aboriginals are described in the *Védas* as black.

† The Rána of Meywar can still perform the offices of High Priest when he attends the temple of the tutelary deity of his race, without the assistance of Bráhmans: and among the Rájpúts of the hills it is still not an uncommon thing for the Rája to promote a *Girth* or labourer to a *Ráthi* or cultivator, and similarly a *Ráthi* to a *Thakúr* or low-grade Rájpút.

4. Besides the three Aryan castes, but immeasurably beneath them, there was the servile or *Sudra* caste, composed of captured aborigines whose lives had been spared, and of the progeny of marriages between Aryans of different castes and Aryans and the women of the country, all of which, by the rigid exclusiveness of caste custom, came to be regarded as degraded.

It must not be supposed, however, that Bráhman supremacy was accepted without protest. Their claims to recognition as a distinct Levite class, of divine origin, and possessed of supernatural powers, were rejected by the Kshatriyas, who insisted, with perfect truth, that many of the *Rishis* who had composed the *Védas* were kings and warriors rather than priests, and that no authority for the pretensions of the Bráhmans could be found in the *Védic* legends. There are traditions of a great struggle having taken place between the Bráhmans and the Kshatriyas, in which the former were completely victorious. The details of this quarrel, however, are obscure, for the Bráhmans, as exclusive custodians of the sacred writings, took care to efface all reference to a struggle, which, from its very existence, cast a doubt on their pretensions to a divinely appointed origin. It may here be noticed that many of the Aryan tribes rejected the theory of Bráhminical supremacy. Thus the earlier settlements west of the Indus never adopted the principle of caste; those between the Indus and the Jumna accepted it, but in a modified form; it was chiefly in the tract watered by the Jumna and the Ganges, from Delhi on the west to Ajudhya and Benares on the east, that the Bráhmans consolidated their influence, and became a compact, learned, and influential body, the authors of Sanskrit literature, and the lawgivers, scientists, and philosophers of the whole of the Hindu world.

Resistance of the Kshatriyas to the pretensions of the Bráhmans.

The principle of caste not of universal acceptation.

By the 5th century B. C. the original simplicity of the *Védic* worship had been replaced by a philosophical creed, accompanied by an elaborate ritual. The early conception of a Supreme Being, made manifest through the physical forces of Nature, gave way to the mystic triad of Bráhma, Vishnu, and Siva, the Maker, Preserver and Destroyer, with a tendency to create new gods, to worship the elements in various personifications, and to embody the attributes of each member of the Hindu Trinity in numerous *avatars* or incarnations. The new religion puzzled the people without satisfying them, while the growing arrogance of the Bráhmans caused a universal desire for a return to more primitive beliefs.

The change from Védism to Bráhmanism.

At this juncture, Sakya Muni, a prince of the Kshatriya caste, began the great reformation which eventually developed into a new religion. Universal charity, liberty, and equality, with the total rejection of caste, formed the fundamental principles of the new doctrine, and the personal character of Buddha, the 'Enlightened,' as he was named by his disciples, at once attracted a large following.

The Buddhist reformation.

The growth of Buddhism was very rapid. By about 200 B. C. it had become the State religion in Hindustán. From thence it spread north into Nepal, and through Central Asia into China and Japan. At the same time Buddhist missionaries carried their faith into Ceylon, and from thence it was extended to Burma, Siam and Java. But though Bráhmanism was materially modified by Buddhism, it was never displaced. Even in the 6th century, Buddhism had commenced to decline, and before the Muhammadan faith had come fairly upon the scene, it had entirely disappeared from India. For more than a thousand years the two religions had existed side by side, and modern Hinduism is undoubtedly the product of both.

The vitality of Bráhmanism and the decline of Buddhism.

About 400 B. C. the Bráhmans, finding in Buddhism a religious movement which threatened their spiritual authority, designed a code which, besides maintaining their privileges, formed a definite authority on all points connected with Hindu law and ritual. This celebrated work, called the Code of Mánu, and known also as the *Dharma-Shástras*, is a compilation of the customary law current about the 5th century B. C. in the Aryan principalities on the banks of the Ganges and Jumna. The Bráhmans claimed for it a divine origin, and ascribed it to Mánu, the first Aryan man. In it the four-fold division of society is said to have been ordered by Bráhma, the Creator of the Universe. The Bráhmans are supposed to have emanated from his head, the Kshatriyas from his arms, the Vaisiyas from his thighs, and the Sudras from his feet. The code consists of a mass of precepts religious and secular, rules for the administration of justice, and special enactments with regard to purification and penance. It was written with a view to stemming the tide of Buddhist reform by stringent rules against the intermingling of castes by marriage, and by forbidding the higher castes under severe penalties from eating, drinking or holding social intercourse with any of those ranking beneath them.

The Dharma-Shástras or Institutes of Mánu.

The reaction in favour of Bráhmanism began to have effect about 200 B. C. By the 8th century the Bráhmans had completely re-established their spiritual

The Brahman revival.

authority. The simplicity of the *Védic* faith was transformed beyond recognition. No efforts were spared to materialise the Hindu religion. The gods were provided with wives. Caste was revived, no longer with the four-fold division of the code of Mánu, but with all the complicated occupational subdivisions which exist to the present day. In all these changes we trace the efforts of an astute priesthood to establish a popular religion. No section of the community was forgotten. The smouldering enmity of the Kshatriyas was appeased by attributing a celestial origin to the ancestors of their ruling families. The Solar and Lunar races of Ajudhya and Mathúra were flattered by the elevation of Ráma and Krishna, their respective heroes, to the dignity of *avutars,* or incarnations of the divine Vishnu. Aboriginal tribes were conciliated by the adoption of their tribal divinities. Their *totem** tree, and serpent worship, though utterly at variance with the spirit of the *Védas,* was affiliated to the orthodox beliefs, and their princes and warriors were accorded the status of Kshatriyas, as an inducement to accept the principle of caste. Buddhism, in spite of the antagonistic nature of its doctrines, was disposed of in a similar manner, and Buddha, whose whole life and teachings had been a protest against the formalism of the Bráhmans, was absorbed into the Hindu system, and, as an incarnation of Vishnu, was allotted a place in the pantheon of minor gods. Thus step by step, by diplomacy and adaptiveness, the Bráhmans consolidated their authority, and established a religion which, having the *Védic* faith of the Aryan race as its foundation, has absorbed and assimilated a portion of each of the religious systems which it successively displaced. Although the Bráhmans were successful in compelling the Kshatriyas in acknowledging their spiritual authority, they rarely aspired to temporal rule. They preferred to delegate the business of ruling as of fighting to the warrior race, reserving for themselves the more congenial offices of priests, ministers, and confidential advisers to their clients.

The early Rájpút kingdoms.

Prior to the Muhammadan conquests, the whole of Northern India was ruled by Rájpút princes. The capitals of the Solar race were at Ajudhya in Oudh, and at Kanouj on the Ganges, with tributary kingdoms at Mithila in Tirhut, and at Rhotas on the Sône. The capitals of the Lunar race seem to have varied. Indraprástha near Delhi was the principal seat of their power, but Dwarika (in Kattiawár), Hastinapúra (Hardwar), Mathúra (Muttra),

* "The ruder races of men are found divided into tribes, each of which is usually named after some animal, vegetable, or thing, which is an object of veneration or worship to the tribe. This animal, vegetable, or thing, is the *totem* or *god* of the tribe. From the tribe being commonly named after its *totem*, the word is also frequently employed to signify merely the tribal name."—Chamber's Encyclopædia.

Prág (Allahabad), Mahéswar (on the Nerbudda), and Rájgráha (Rájmahal) were their principal cities at different times.

Origin of the Solar and Lunar races.

The primary division of the Kshatriya order was two-fold, and consisted of the Solar and Lunar races. To these were afterwards affiliated the four Agnicula or fire-tribes. The legend of a Solar race at Ajudhya and Kanouj is apparently an outgrowth of the worship of the Sun. The so-called Lunar race had no real connection with the Moon, and the legend of the race is only associated with that planet as an antithesis or antagonism to the Sun. Even in Hindu legends the distinction appears as a mere dream of the genealogists, without any authentic origin. From a remote period, however, there was a traditional struggle for supremacy between the Rájpúts of the Ganges and the Jumna; and when the hordes of Islám poured through the Khaibar into India, the *Chauháns* of Delhi were at feud with the *Ráthors* of Kanouj. The ultimate success of the Muhammadans was in fact largely due to the dissensions and rivalries of the Hindu princes, who could rarely bring themselves to forget their private differences in so far as to combine against the invaders of their country.

The dissensions of the Rájpút princes.

Greek, Bactrian, and Scythian invasions 327 B.C. to 60 A.D.

In ancient days the Rájpút principalities were India's stoutest bulwarks against foreign invasion. Kshatriya armies fought not only Alexander and his victorious Greeks, but also the hordes of Scythians and Bactrians which poured into India up to the end of the 1st century.

Invasion of Sind by Arabs from Baghdad in 711.

About the same time as Indian Buddhism was being crushed by the Bráhmanic revival, Muhammad had founded a new faith in Arabia. In 711, or 79 years after his death, Hejaz, an officer of the Kaliph Omar, despatched an expedition under his nephew Kasim for the conquest of Sind. After capturing the temple-fortress of Dwarika, the Arabs laid siege to Bráhmanabad,* which after the death of her husband, was bravely defended by the Rája's widow. Scarcity of food drove the garrison to despair. The Ráni and her entire bodyguard of Rájpúts perished in a final sortie. The example of their heroism, however, was not without fruit, for about 40 years later the Rájpúts succeeded in expelling the Arabs.

The next Muhammadan invasions were those of Mahmúd of Ghazni, whose conquests extended from Persia to the Ganges. He is said to have led his armies into India no less than seventeen times.. In 1017, he sacked Kanouj, Meerut, Muttra, Benares, and Kalinjar, threw down the temples, and melted the gold and silver idols which they enshrined. Mahmúd

---

* The ruins of Bráhmanabad are about 44 miles north-east of Hyderabad.

was a fanatical Muslim, and having heard of the wealth and sanctity of the great Siva temple at Somnáth on the Kattiawár coast, determined to destroy it. Accompanied by 30,000 volunteers, he left Ghazni in 1024, and marched rapidly across the Sind desert to Somnáth. The holy city was bravely defended by Rája Bhim Déo and his *Solanki* Rájpúts, but superiority of numbers prevailed in the end, and the fortress was taken by storm, 5,000 of the garrison perishing in its defence. Mahmúd not only destroyed the great idol, but carried off the sandal wood gates of the temple to his home. The victory, however, was dearly bought. The Muhammadan army was lost in the desert of Sind. Thousands perished of heat and thirst in its sandy wastes, and only a remnant returned with their leader to Ghazni.

Invasion of Mahmud of Ghazni, 1017 and 1024.

The Ghaznivide dynasty was succeeded by that of the Afgháns of Ghor, which held India from 1186 to 1328. In 1191 Muhammad of Ghor was utterly defeated at Narrain,* on the banks of the Saraswáti, by Pirthiráj the *Chauhán* Rája of Delhi. The shame of this reverse rankled in the Afghán's mind. Returning two years later he crushed his foes in detail, overcoming Pirthiráj at Thanésar in 1193, and Jaichand, the *Ráthor* king of Kanouj, in the following year. So decisive was the defeat of the latter, that after he had perished in the Ganges, his son with a gallant band of followers cut his way through the Afghán hosts, and abandoning his ancient home, established a new kingdom in Marwar,† which survives to the present day.

The Rájpút victory at Thanésar in 1191.

The fall of Kanouj and emigration of the Rahtors to Marwar in 1194.

After the fall of Kanouj the resistless tide of Muhammadan invasion swept through the Punjáb, and the valleys of the Ganges and Jumna, carrying everything before it. All the Rájpút settlers in this vast tract became subjects of the Afghán kings, and numbers were forcibly converted to the religion of their conquerors. It was only in Rájpútána, Bundelkhund, and the Jummoo and Kangra Hills, that they preserved their religion and independence. There each prince ruled over his kinsfolk and vassals, all acknowledging the Rána of Chitór or Meywar as their suzerain or over-lord.

Subjection of the Rájpúts throughout the Punjáb plains and the valleys of the Ganges and Jumna.

During this period nearly the whole of India was subjected to Islám. "The early Muhammadan invaders inspired the Rájpúts with peculiar horror. The fanatical marauders overwhelmed the luxurious cities of

* Narrain is about seven miles from Karnal.

† The Rathor State of Marwar is also known as Jodhpore, from the name of its capital

Lahore, Delhi, and Kanouj, shouting for God and the Prophet, but caring for nought save women and plunder. Their war-cry spread terror far and wide. The Rájpút nobles and their retainers rode forth to take the field, or manned the walls of their fortresses. The multitude flocked to the temples, whilst Bráhmans performed their sacrifices and incantations, and implored the gods for succour. It was a war of iron and rapine against gold and beauty. The brown and hardy hosts of Central Asia scaled the walls, scimitar in hand, or burst open the gates in overwhelming numbers. The fair-complexioned Rájpúts fought with chivalry and desperation, but they fought in vain. A rush of mailed warriors, a clash of swords and spears, piles of dead and dying round the gateway, and the city was left at the mercy of soldiers who knew not how to pity or to spare. In a few moments licentious ruffians were penetrating the recesses of *zanánas*, and subjecting the inmates to insults from which humanity recoils. They filled the streets with blood, they threw down the temples, profaned the gods, and carried off young men and maidens to sell as slaves in the bazaars of Kábul and Ghazni."*

The cruelty of the Muhammadan invaders.

About 1303, Ala-ud-din Khilji† gathered up all his strength for the destruction of the Rájpút principalities. During his reign the two great Rájpút fortresses of Ranthambor and Chitór fell into the hands of the Musalmans. After a prolonged and heroic defence, the garrison of the latter preferred to die rather than surrender. The men rushed on the swords of the besiegers, while the Ráni and several thousand women performed the horrible rite of *johur*, by immolating themselves on the funeral pyre, in order to escape capture and pollution by their ruthless foes.

Capture of Chitor by Ala-ud-din Khilji, 1303.

In 1321, a successful revolt introduced the Tughlak dynasty, which lasted until 1398, when it was swept away by the Mughals under Timur or Tamerlane, who marched through India committing frightful atrocities. The Sayyads and Lodis succeeded the Tughlaks, and in 1526 Bábar invaded India, and after crushing the forces of the Delhi king at Pánipat, founded the Mughal Empire, which lasted, at any rate in name, until 1857.

The Mughals under Bábar conquer India, 1526.

While the power of the Lodi kings was on the wane, that of the Rájpút princes was increasing and had to a great extent become consolidated under Sanga Rána, the celebrated Rája of Chitór. So long as the Mughals were the foes of the Lodi kings, the Rájpúts regarded them as friends; but when Bábar assumed the imperial title, Rána Sanga summoned to his

* History of India,—*Talboys Wheeler.*

† *Khilji* is said to be the Túrki word for a 'swordsman.' These *Khiljis* or *Ghilzais* as they are now called, form one oi the largest of the tribes of Afghánistán.

aid all the bravest warriors of the Rájpút clans; and exciting their patriotism by stirring appeals, and references to the chivalrous deeds of their forefathers, obtained their immediate and enthusiastic support. All were convinced that once overthrown, the Muhammadan power would rise no more, and the Hindu faith would be restored. In 1526 the Rájpút coalition, consisting of the Rájas of Chitór, Malwa, Meywar and Ajmere, met Bábar and his Mughals at Futtehpur-Sikri. The Rájpúts fought with a valour and desperation that astonished even Bábar himself; but they sustained a crushing defeat and fled.

Bábar crushes the Rájpút coalition at Futtehpur-Sikri.

From 1530, the year of Bábar's death, to 1555, when the throne of Hindustán was reconquered by his son Humáyun, the Rájpúts were perpetually at strife with Shér Shah and the Afghán settlers in Bengal. In 1556 Humáyun died, and was succeeded by the famous Akbar, the wisest and most capable of the Mughal Emperors. The latter early realised that for his dynasty to keep its hold on India, it must depend largely on the loyalty of Hindus, whose confidence he sought, and won, by a broadminded policy of conciliation and religious tolerance. He was the first of the Muhammadan rulers of India who strove to bring the whole of the continent under the sway of one sceptre, by enlisting the sympathies of the various races included in his dominions. After a series of brilliant campaigns, Kábul, Kandahar, and the whole of India as far south as the Dekhan, was reduced to his authority. He then turned his attention to Rájpútána.

Akbar's conciliatory policy towards his Hindu subjects.

It was part of Akbar's policy to win over the Rájpút princes by confirming them in their possessions, which he allowed them to enjoy on condition of their becoming his feudatories. He further cemented his friendship with their chiefs by marrying the daughters of the Rájas of Jodhpore, Bikaneer, and Jeypore. Only one of the Rájpút princes proudly declined a matrimonial alliance with the Emperor—the haughty Udai Singh, Rána of Meywar, who, as the descendant of the Sun, regarded such a connection as a disgrace. Udai Singh's principal fortress was Chitór, which had indeed succumbed to Ala-ud-din Khilji in 1303, but had since been repaired, and was again regarded as impregnable.

Akbar's marriages to Rájpút princesses.

"The great stronghold of Chitór was garrisoned by 7,000 picked Rájpúts, while Udai Singh, with a force of equal strength, retired to the hills to await the issue of events. Akbar himself sat down before the fortress but though he pressed the siege vigorously, the Rájpúts defended themselves with equal constancy and courage. Never had Akbar met such warriors. As their pertinacity increased, so likewise did his pride and resolution. At length the breach was reported practicable, and orders were given for the assault. The operation was to be personally directed by the Emperor, from a lofty platform, which had been specially erected for the purpose. As Akbar sat there, matchlock in hand, he observed the gallant Rájpúts assembling in the breach, awaiting the onslaught of the Mughals. By the light of torches, he easily recognised the Rájpút general, and believing him to be within range, fired, and killed him on the spot. This fortunate shot, discharged when the parties were approaching one another, so discouraged the Rájpúts, that at the critical moment they made but a sorry defence."* They rallied indeed subsequently, but it was too late. When the day dawned, Chitór was in possession of Akbar. The brave garrison after immolating their women and children, retired to their temples, where, rejecting all offers of quarter, they perished to a man.

Capture of Chitór by Akbar.

The marriage of Akbar to the daughters of Rájpút princes secured the devotion of their families to his throne. Chief among his adherents were Bhagwán Dás, the Rája of Jeypore, and his famous nephew Mán Singh, one of the most brilliant warriors of his day. During the reign of Akbar and his immediate successors, the Rájpút soldiery, from bitter enemies, became the thews and sinews of the Mughal armies; and under their own leaders, carried the banners of the Emperors from Kashmir to the Dekhan, and from Kábul to Assam. They even fought their own brethren in the imperial cause. In 1576, Mán Singh of Jeypore attacked and defeated Pertap Singh, Rána of Meywar, who, like his obstinate father, Udai Singh, defied the authority of Akbar, from his fastnesses in the Aravulli Hills. As a reward, the Emperor bestowed the government of the Punjáb upon Mán Singh, and married his own son Selim to a lady of the Rájpút's family. Marriage indeed, was one of the most effectual means employed by Akbar, to weld together his disunited empire. The Rájpút princes felt that their relationship to the heir of the throne, and often to the throne itself, assured their position; and when they came to consider Akbar's toleration, his justice, generosity, and the order and good government he established, they must have recognised in him something more than an ordinary human being—something approaching to an incarnation of a deity—a fancy which he fostered by representing himself as the attribute of their favourite god, the divine Sun, which was the object of his daily worship.

Akbar's success in winning over the Rájpút soldiery.

Akbar founds a new religion.

* Akbar.—*Malleson.*

In 1579, Akbar's brother, the Governor of Kábul, revolted and invaded the Punjáb. His forces were opposed by those of Rája Todar Mal and Mán Singh of Jeypore. These generals manœuvred with great skill. Cautiously supporting their line of advance by a chain of fortified posts, they defeated the hill tribes near Jamrúd, forced the Khaibar Pass, and entered Kábul, of which Mán Singh was immediately appointed governor. It is interesting to note that no objection seems to have been made by the Rájpúts to cross the Indus or to serve in Afghánistán. Later on, Mán Singh was transferred to the government of Bengal, from which he conquered Orissa.

Rájpút troops reconquer Kábul for Akbar in 1580.

In 1644, the Emperor Shah Jahán despatched a large army for the conquest of Balkh, under Ali Mardán and Rája Jagat Singh, who brought with him 14,000 Rájpúts of his own clan. Despite the severe climate and stupendous mountain passes they traversed, these brave Indian warriors achieved splendid successes. The difficulty, however, was not so much how to take, as how to keep this distant region, separated from the rest of the empire by the snowy ranges of the Hindu Kúsh, inaccessible in winter, and exposed at all times to the attacks of the hardy hill tribes. When Aurangzéb, a son of Shah Jahán, reached Balkh, of which he had been appointed governor, he soon perceived the true character of the country and its defenders, and, like a wise general, counselled a retreat from a position which was obviously untenable. He made terms with the Usbeg chiefs and began his homeward march. The retreat over the mountains was attended with disaster. The hillmen hovered about the flanks of the retreating Rájpúts, cut off detached parties, and harassed the column at every step. The baggage fell over precipices, and the Hindu Kúsh was deep in snow. The army reached Kábul with a loss of 5,000 men, to say nothing of the horses, camels, and elephants, killed by cold and exposure."*

Shah Jahán employs his Rájpút feudatories in the conquest of Balkh, 1644.

In the struggle between the sons of Shah Jahán for their father's throne, the Rájpúts espoused the cause of Dára, the Emperor's eldest son. The latter despatched the Rája Jai Singh against his brother Shúja, Governor of Bengal, and the Máharája Jaswant Singh of Marwar against his youngest brother Murad-Baksh, Viceroy of Guzerát. Meanwhile, Aurangzéb, the hero of the expedition to Balkh, affecting the manners of a Muhammadan *fakir*, played a strictly subordinate part, and sympathised discreetly with his brother Murad

The Rájpúts espouse the cause of Dára and are defeated by Múrád Baksh and Aurangzéb on the Nerbudda.

* Aurangzeb.—*Lane-Pool.*

Baksh, whose forces he eventually joined. Dára's troops under Jaswant Singh met them on the banks of the Nerbudda. Dára's Mughals fled like traitors at the commencement of the battle, leaving the Rájpúts to fight it out alone. They struggled desperately against fearful odds until only 600 of the 8,000 remained. "The wounded remnant sadly returned with their Rája to his desert fastness in Marwar. There he was received with bitter scorn. His high-mettled wife shut the castle gates in his face, saying that a man so dishonoured should not enter her walls. I disown him as my husband; these eyes can never again behold him. If he could not vanquish, he should have died." This was the true Rájpút spirit, and the fact that, the princess eventually became reconciled to her husband only proves that though a daughter of the proud house of Chitór, she was after all, but a woman."*

The news of Jaswant Singh's defeat filled Dára with rage. He resolved to wipe out the disgrace by a victory the glory of which should be entirely his own. Hastily assembling a force of 100,000 horse, 20,000 foot, and 80 guns, he marched rapidly to the Chambal, and met the army of his brothers at Sámúgarh. The month was June, and the soldiers on both sides were fainting from the heat and the weight of their heavy armour. Both armies were marshalled in line of battle. The artillery was placed in front, the guns linked together by chains, so that the cavalry might not charge through the intervals. Immediately behind them was a line of camel-guns, worked on swivels from the animal's backs, and fired by the riders. Then came the infantry armed with matchlocks. The mass of the army was composed of cavalry—the Mughals being armed with scimitars, bows, and arrows, and the Rájpúts with a pike or short lance. The battle began with an artillery duel and the discharge of rockets and grenades, to stampede the elephants and horses; then the infantry came into action, while flights of arrows flew over their heads from the mounted archers in rear. Victory at first inclined towards Dára. The legs of Murad Baksh's elephant were tied with chains, and Rája Rám Singh, who surrounded him with his Rájpúts, hurled a spear at the prince, and tried to cut the girths of his howdah. The Mughal wounded as he was, shot the Rájpút dead.

The Rájpúts at the battle of Sámúgarh.

"The fallen Rájpúts in yellow garb, and stained with their war-paint of orange turmeric, were heaped about the elephants' feet, and made the ground yellow as a field of saffron. In another part of the field the *Ráthor* Rája Rúp Singh sprang from his horse, and having washed his hands of life, cut his way through the Mughals, and throwing himself beneath the elephant, strove to cut the girths of Aurangzéb's howdah, but was

* Aurangzéb.—*Lane-Pool.*

killed in his heroic attempt. The Rájpúts had been slain in heaps and many of their chiefs were dead, but the advantage was still on the side of Dára's forces, for Murad Baksh and Aurangzéb were perilously hemmed in by crowds of raving Rájpúts, maddened with *bhang*, and furious at the death of their leaders."* It needed hardly anything to turn the balance of fortune either way. At this crisis Dára committed a fatal mistake. Alarmed by a rocket which struck his howdah, he dismounted from his elephant, which up to then had been regarded as the standard of victory. It was as though the sun had vanished at midday. A blind panic seized his army, and every man fled for his life. In a brief moment the tide had turned. For a terrible quarter of an hour Aurangzéb had steadily maintained his seat on his sorely harassed elephant, and the reward of his valour was the imperial throne. 'Nothing succeeds his success.' The victory of Sámúgarh was the signal for all the world to come and tender their homage to Aurangzéb. The Rájpúts were quick to make their peace with the conqueror. Rája Jai Singh gave in his adhesion at once, and the Máhárája Jaswant Singh presently followed his example, and tendered his fealty to the rising power. The great battle of Sámúgarh has been described in detail, as it gives a vivid picture of the bearing of the Rájpúts in action, at the time when their martial qualities appear to have reached their zenith.

Aurangzéb was a stern puritan. Nothing weighed for an instant in his mind against his fealty to the principles of Islám. For religion's sake he persecuted the Hindus and destroyed their temples; from religious motives he waged unending wars in the Dekhan, not so much to enlarge his empire as to bring the lands of heretical Shiahs† within the dominion of orthodox Islám. Up to 1668 there were no religious persecutions and no religious disabilities, but on the death of Rája Jai Singh of Jeypore, and Rája Jaswant Singh of Marwar, the most powerful of the friendly Rájpút princes, the Emperor found himself free to carry out that repressive policy towards Hindus, which had long been his most cherished desire.

In 1677 Aurangzéb revived the *jaziah* or poll-tax on Hindus, and gave mortal offence to every prince in Rájpútána by his injudicious attempt to kidnap the sons of Rája Jaswant Singh on their return from

---

* Aurangzeb—*Lane-Pool.*

† Muhammadans are divided into several sects, the two chief being the *Sunnis* and *Shiahs*. Of these, the *Sunnis* may be looked on as representing the orthodox faith, and recognise Abu-Bakr as Muhammad's successor in preference to Ali, who married Fatima the Prophet's daughter. The *Shiahs* are followers of Ali, and declare that the essence of the Mussulman religion is a knowledge of the true *Imám* or leader, a point which the *Sunnis* consider unimportant.

Kábul, of which their father had been the governor. Aurangzéb's intention was no doubt to convert the young princes to Islám, but his projects were frustrated by the loyalty and pride of the Rájpúts, which forbade such ignominy to their hereditary chiefs. They repudiated the poll-tax, concealed the princes, and broke into open rebellion. The Emperor marched at once upon Rájpútána and found the leading states Oodeypore (Meywar) and Jodhpore (Marwar) united against him, and only Rája Ram Singh of Jeypore (Ambar) loyal to the empire.

Aurangzéb revives the poll-tax on Hindus and attempts to kidnap the young princes of Marwar.

The Rájpúts kept 25,000 horse in the field, mostly *Ráthors* of Jodhpore, and although frequently driven into the mountains, were never really subdued. At one time they seemed to be on the point of victory. The Emperor's three sons were ravaging the Rájpút country with the bulk of his forces, while he himself remained at Ajmere with hardly a thousand men. While there he learnt that his younger son Akbar had joined hands with the Rájpúts, had proclaimed himself Emperor, and was marching to capture his father at the head of a considerable army. Aurangzéb's presence of mind did not desert him in this crisis. He wrote a letter congratulating the rebel prince upon his success in *deceiving the Rájpúts and luring them to their destruction*, and contrived that this compromising epistle should be intercepted by one of the rebellious Rájas. The effect of this plot surpassed his brightest hopes. The Rájpúts melted away, and the repentant Mughals flocked back to the imperial standards.

The Rájpút rebellion.

The Rájpút insurrection, though checked, was still very far from being suppressed. The insults which had been offered to their chiefs and to their religion, and the ruthless severity of Aurangzéb's campaigns in their country, left a sore which nothing but time could heal. A race which had been the right hand of the Mughals was now hopelessly alienated, and never again served the throne without distrust. The war went on. The cities were in the hands of the Mughals, who ravaged the rich lands of Meywar; but the mountain defiles were thronged with implacable Rájpúts, who never lost an opportunity of dealing a blow at the invaders. At last, weary of the struggle, an honourable peace was concluded. The hated *jaziah* was not so much as named in the treaty, and Jaswant Singh's son, the young Rája of Jodhpore, was installed with honour in his father's principalities.

Even these concessions did not appease the indignant Rájpúts, and all Rájpútána, until the end of the reign, was in a state of perpetual revolt. But for his poll-tax, and his interference with their inborn sense of honour, Aurangzéb might have employed the Rájpúts in the conquest of the Dekhan, as his father and grand-father had employed them in Afghánistan and Central Asia. As it was, he alienated them for ever. No Rájpút would stir a finger to help the Mughal. The Dekhan had to be subdued without their aid, and in the religious persecutions which had caused their revolt, two new nations sprang into existence—the Mahrattas and the Sikhs, both of which were soon after destined to subdue their Muhammadan oppressors.

The loyalty of the Rájpúts alienated for ever by the religious persecution of Aurangzéb.

The break up of the Mughal Empire began in 1707, shortly after the death of Aurangzéb. Provincial governors and feudatory states asserted their independence, and in the general dismemberment of their dominions, the Delhi Emperors became mere puppets in the hands of a Mahratta confederacy. By 1772, the Mahrattas had occupied Delhi, and subdued the greater part of Northern India, including some portions of the Punjáb.

Decay of the Mughal Empire.

While the crumbling authority of the Emperors was being directed with barbarous cruelty against the Sikhs, the princes of Rájpútána were shaking off the Mughal yoke. By 1715 they were practically free, and had commenced to ravage the territories of their old oppressors, raiding to the very gates of Dehli.

The Rájpúts shake off the Mughal yoke, 1715.

Throughout the early part of the eighteenth century Rájpútána was desolated by civil wars. Taking advantage of these disputes, the Mahrattas established themselves at Ajmere, from which they levied tribute from all the Rájpút States and fostered disputes which furnished them with a pretext to scour the country for plunder. The lands were left uncultivated, trade languished, and through the weakening of the authority of their princess, the Rájpút nobles became insolent and unruly. To counteract the turbulence of their vassals, the Rájas began to entertain corps of foreign mercenaries consisting of Arabs, Sindis, Rohillas, and Hindustánis, who at a later period degenerated into Pindáris, or bands of independent marauders. "These hired companies were entirely composed of infantry, and were partially drilled and disciplined. They received their orders direct from the Rája or his officers of State, by whom they were entrusted with the performance of all important duties. They soon formed a com-

The Mahrattas establish themselves in Rájpútána.

The princes of Rájpútána raise corps of mercenaries as a check against the turbulence of their nobles.

plete barrier between the princes and their subjects, and became objects of jealousy and strife."

Meanwhile the growing power of the Játs and Mahrattas compelled the Rájpút chieftains to form a league against them, for the preservation of their political existence. In 1787 the Rájas of Marwar and Jeypore united their forces, and met the Mahrattas at Tonga, where a decisive action took place. Despising discipline, the Rájput horsemen charged through the battalions of De Boigne,* sabred his artillerymen, and forced Scindia to seek refuge in flight. The Mahrattas, however, were not long in repairing this loss. In 1791 De Boigne collected a powerful force and a numerous artillery, and met the Rájpúts at Pattan and Mairta, on the northern border of Jeypore. In these sanguinary actions Rájpút courage was heroically but fruitlessly displayed against European tactics and discipline; they were utterly defeated, and compelled to restore Ajmere to the Mahrattas, besides paying them an indemnity of 60 lakhs.

The Rájpúts defeat the Mahrattas at Tonga in 1787.

De Boigne defeats the Rájpúts at Pattan and Mairta, 1791.

From 1795 to 1805 the Mahrattas were at war with the British, by whom they were crushingly defeated; but from 1805 to 1815, while the latter were engaged in a struggle with Napoleon, Rájpútána was abandoned to the Mahrattas, and independent bands of foreign mercenaries, whose leaders founded principalities† and assumed the titles of Rája and Nawáb. Hosts of these marauders under the name of Pindáris settled in Málwa, whence they plundered the whole of Rájpútána and the adjoining British districts. In 1817, two British armies entered Málwa for the purpose of exterminating these freebooters. Many of them were slain; some perished in the jungles; while others surrendered and settled down as peaceful cultivators. In 1818 the Mahratta power was finally crushed, and peace was restored to India. The Rájpúts were delivered from their oppressors, and their princes became feudatories of the British whom they have served ever since with the same loyalty and good faith as

Rájpútána is overrun by bands of Pindáris until their dispersion in 1817.

The Rájpút princes acknowledge the British supremacy.

* The Comte de Boigne was a Savoyard and had served in the French, Russian, and Indian Armies. He was an able administrator, and raised an efficient and well-equipped army for his patron Scindia, which was composed of Afghåns, Rohillas, Hindustánis, and Mahrattas, commanded and drilled by Europeans.—Annals of Rájasthan—*Tod.*

† The principal Pindári leader was Amir Khan who at one time maintained 52 battalions of infantry, 150 guns, and a large force of Pathan cavalry. He afterwards came to terms with the British Government, which allowed him to retain the small principality of Tonk in Rájpútana with the title of Nawáb, on his disbanding his troops, and giving up his artillery.

characterised their relations with Akbar and Shah Jahán. The organization of Imperial Service Troops has now enabled the princes of Rájpútána to render to the suzerain power that military service which won such renown for their ancestors, and is so thoroughly in accord with the martial traditions of their race.

Imperial Service Troops.

Such, briefly, is the history of the Rájpút race. If much has been said regarding Rájpútána, and but little regarding the Punjáb and Hindustán, it must be remembered that it was only in Rájpútána and the Kangra Hills that the Rájpúts preserved their nationality and freedom.

Upper India, and more especially the Punjáb, has from time immemorial borne the first shock of each wave of invasion from the north. There the fanatical hordes of Patháns and Mughals generally succeeded in forcing their religion on the Hindu princes and warriors whose territories they conquered. For this reason the Rájpúts of the Punjáb nearly all accepted Islám, and those who preserved the faith of their fathers were either the inhabitants of remote districts, like the Jummoo and Kangra Hills, where natural obstacles separated them from the tracks of invaders, or of the southern and eastern portions of the province, where they were more or less protected by the powerful principalities of Rájpútána.

Reason for the preponderance of Musalmán Rájpúts in the Punjáb.

In Hindustán, after the capture of Kanouj and Benares by Muhammad Ghori in 1194, the centre of Rájpút influence was shifted from the banks of the Ganges to the borders of the Bikaneer desert. The remnants of the principal clans sought refuge in Rájpútána and the Doáb. A few humbled and dispirited, retained their former possessions by abject submission to their conquerors. Others, scorning to remain as servants where they had formerly been rulers, fled across the Ganges into Oudh, which was then an unknown country, covered with impenetrable forests and jungles. In course of time these scattered colonies developed into separate clans, and many strengthened their position by absorbing the aboriginal races which they had subdued. The history of these Rájpút colonies is dimly preserved in their tribal legends, which form a vague record of fights with aborigines, struggles among themselves, and occasional revolts against the Muhammadan Governors. In the 16th and 17th centuries the number of these clans was increased by the immigration of adventurers from Rájpútana, upon whom the Delhi Emperors had bestowed grants of land, in recognition of their military services. In course of time, though hating the Muhammadans as aliens in race and religion, the

Influence of the Muhammadan conquest on the Rájpúts of Hindustán.

Rájpút chiefs accepted the fact that employment under the Emperors was the source of all honours and rewards, and as a natural consequence we find that from about the 17th century bands of Purbiah* Rájpúts were largely employed as mercenaries in most of the Mughal armies. The nature of their service, however, was essentially different from that of their brethren of Rájpútána. The latter served the Mughals more as allies than as feudatories, each Rája leading his own contingent, over which he exercised supreme and unquestioned authority.

Difference between the military service rendered to the Mughals by the Rájpúts of Rájpútána and the Rájpúts of Hindustán.

The position of the Purbiah Rájpúts was one of greater dependence. The tribal organization was no doubt preserved, but the clans, besides being smaller and of minor political importance, were generally employed by one of the *Mansabdars*, or great Muhammadan nobles, their service being to them rather than to the Mughal Emperors. Intrigues at the Delhi Court caused constant changes in the *personnel* of provincial governments, and the Purbiah Rájpúts, unbound by any considerations but their own interests, naturally shifted their allegiance from one employer to another, each tribal chief acting according to his own inclination and judgment. The Rájpúts of Hindustán were thus accustomed to mercenary service long before the arrival of European settlers in India, and when the anarchy which ensued on the breaking up of the Mughal Empire compelled the latter to raise troops for the protection of their ports and factories, they were among the first to seek employment in their armies. At first these levies were unorganized, each man providing his own weapons and equipment. The idea of giving them discipline originated with the French, but other nations and the Native Princes were not slow to follow their example, and by the middle of the 18th century the Madras and Bombay settlements possessed a considerable force of well-trained *topasses*† and *sepoys*‡ armed, drilled, and equipped like Europeans.

After the re-capture of Calcutta in 1757 from Suraj-ud-Dowla, it was decided to form a similar force in Bengal, and early in that year Clive raised the 1st Regiment of Bengal Native Infantry, long known as the *Lál Paltun*,§ because it was the first native corps to be dressed in red.

Raising of native troops in Bengal.

---

* The Rájpúts of Rájpútána are sometimes called Dési Rájpúts to distinguish them from the eastern or Purbiah Rájpúts who, among themselves, are more often called **Chhatris** or Thákurs. In Rájpútána a *Thákur* is a Rájpút landholder or petty chieftain.

† *Topasses* were Portuguese half-castes and native Christians, enlisted by the East India Company, and so called because they wore *topis* or hats.

‡ *Sepoy* is a corruption of the Hindustáni word *sipahi*, 'a soldier.' In the French Army native soldiers are still called *spahis*, a term which is clearly of Indian origin.

§ The word *pultun* is a corruption of the French *peloton* 'a squad.'

Nearly all the warlike races of Northern India were represented in the new battalions, for owing to the Muhammadan conquest of Bengal the lower provinces were overrun by bands of military adventurers from Oudh, the Punjáb, and even from beyond the Indus. It was from men of this stamp that Clive selected his first recruits, and in the corps raised at this time near Calcutta were to be found Patháns, Rohillas, Játs, Rájpúts, and Bráhmans. The majority of the men, however, were Musalmans, but as most of our early campaigns were directed against Muhammadan princes, it was considered expedient to gradually replace them by Hindus. It thus came about that the ranks of the Bengal regiments were filled almost entirely by Rájpúts and Bráhmans from Behar, Oudh, and the Doáb, until our military service became practically the monopoly of these classes. The Rájpúts of these districts were for the most part mercenaries, willing to enter the service of any leader, in any cause, provided they were fairly treated and regularly paid. For this reason, service under the British colours was peculiarly attractive. The East India Company gave high pay and liberal pensions, their forces were almost invariably victorious; and though European discipline was stricter than that to which they had been previously accustomed, the Rájpúts were quick to recognize its value in the field, and the immense advantage which it conferred on the British armies over the unorganized rabbles of the native princes. Other reasons tended to encourage the enlistment of high caste Hindus. They were docile and quick to learn their drill, while their natural cleanliness, fine physique, and soldierly bearing, made them more popular with the majority of their officers than the truculent Muhammadans to whom pipeclay and discipline were abhorrent.

Constitution of the corps first raised in Bengal.

Causes which led to the enlistment of Rájpúts and other classes of high caste Hindus.

Rájpúts have served in our ranks from Plassey to the present day. They have taken part in almost every campaign undertaken by the Indian armies. Under Forde they defeated the French at Condore. Under Monro at Buxar they routed the forces of the Nawáb of Oudh. Under Lake they took part in the brilliant series of victories which destroyed the power of Mahrattas. The 2nd Battalion of the 15th Native Infantry,* the oldest of our Rájpút regiments, took part in every action of this campaign, and carries, to this day, an honorary standard bearing the words 'Lake and Victory' granted for distinguished service. An interesting anecdote may here be given to illustrate the *esprit de corps* and devotion of the Rájpút soldier. "At the first siege of Bhurtpur in 1805, this regiment behaved with cons-

* Now the 2nd (Queen's Own) Bengal Light Infantry.

picuous gallantry. Their colours had been planted on one of the bastions, and before the regiment was recalled, had been completely riddled with shot. On the occasion of new ones being presented, an order was given to burn the old ones; before the order could be accomplished, however, the sepoys tore the fragments into ribands. The circumstance was thought little of at the time, and was soon forgotten, but at the 2nd siege of Bhurtpur in 1824, the regiment was again employed, and for a second time after an interval of 20 years, ascended "its imminent and deadly breach." Just as the hour of danger arrived, a shred of the old colours, which had been carefully preserved as a sacred relic, was produced and tied round the new ones, and a solemn vow uttered by each sepoy that he would do his utmost to earn, when fighting round the new colours, as high a reputation as his predecessors, who had fallen in defending the old ones."*

The *esprit de corps* of these classes.

The troops selected for the conquest of Java in 1814 included a division of Bengal troops. "It was composed of volunteers from every regiment and was a remarkably fine body of men. Bengal sepoys are mostly Rájpúts, who next to Bráhmans, are of the highest caste of Hindus. To those therefore who are unacquainted with their religious prejudices, and the consequent hardships and privations they endure on boardship, it is surprising to see them come forward to make such sacrifices when not bound to do so by the conditions of their enlistment.† There cannot be a stronger proof of their attachment to the service."

Their readiness for foreign service.

Rájpúts took part in the Nepal campaign and in the victories and disasters of the first Afghán War, including the defence and relief of Jalálabad. Referring to their behaviour in the battle which took place in 1841, outside the ramparts of Kandahar, General Nott wrote as follows:—"Our troops carried the enemy's positions in gallant style: it was the finest thing I ever saw. These 8,000 Afgháns could not stand our 1,200 men for an hour; and yet the cry of all the Press is that our sepoys cannot cope with Patháns. I would at any time lead 1,000 Bengal sepoys against 5,000 Afgháns."

The gallantry in Afghánistan.

In the Sikh Wars, Rájpúts helped us to win the Punjáb. The bearing of the 33rd, 47th, and 59th Native Infantry‡ in the battle of Sobraon is thus described:—"Moving at a firm, steady pace, these regiments never fired a shot till they had passed the barriers opposed to them; they advanced rapidly

* Asiatic Register, 1839.

† Native troops were not enlisted for general service until 1856.

‡ Now the 4th, 7th and 8th Rajputs.

to the attack of the enemies' batteries, entered the fortified position after a severe struggle, and sweeping through the interior of the camp, drove the Sikhs in confusion before them."* After the battle of Chillianwalla, on the 13th January 1849, the 70th Native Infantry† was complimented by Lord Gough for its valour in recapturing the colours of the 56th Native Infantry which had fallen into the hands of the enemy. At Gujrat the regiment captured 3 Sikh standards, and again greatly distinguished itself.

Their bravery in the Sikh Wars.

In 1857 the great bulk of the Bengal Army, forgetful of the glorious traditions of a century of splendid service, forswore their allegiance, and broke into open revolt. It would here be out of place to discuss the political and other circumstances which led to the Mutiny, but mention must be made of the heroic devotion of the faithful few "who remained true to their colours at a time when the overthrow of the British dominion in India appeared to be almost inevitable."

The Mutiny.

The native troops of the gallant garrison which defended the Residency at Lucknow was composed of some Sikhs and the loyal remnants of the 13th, 48th, and 71st Native Infantry, whose conduct is thus referred to by Sir William Inglis:—" It is difficult to praise too highly the fidelity and gallantry of these men. They were exposed to a most galling fire of round shot and musketry which materially decreased their numbers. They were so near the enemy that conversation could be carried on between them; and every effort, persuasion, promise, and threat, was alternately resorted to, in vain, to seduce them from their allegiance. They vied with their European comrades in the work of the trenches, in the ardour of their courage, and in their resolution to defend to the last the spot of ground assigned to them."‡ If further proofs were wanted of their staunch and loyal conduct, it may be mentioned that "the casualties among the native soldiers of the Lucknow garrison amounted to more than their whole strength, owing to the number that were wounded more than once."§ On the raising of the siege, the gallant survivors of this faithful band were formed into a corps called the Regiment of Lucknow,‖ in which Hindustánis of all castes were represented, the Rájpúts, however, preponderating.

Gallantry and fidelity in defence of the Lucknow Residency.

* Historical Records of the Bengal Army.—*Cardew.*

† Now the 11th Bengal Infantry.

‡ History of the Indian Mutiny—*Kaye and Malleson.*

§ Lucknow and Oudh in the Mutiny.—*McLeod Innes.*

‖ Now the 16th Bengal Infantry.

During the Mutiny, the 70th Native Infantry* stationed at Barrackpur, volunteered for service against the revolted regiments. They received the thanks of the Governor-General for their loyalty, but were not sent at once against the enemy. The Calcutta Press of the time having hinted that the regiment had not volunteered in good faith, the men begged to be sent to China, and their offer was shortly afterwards accepted. Two other Bengal battalions, the 47th† and the 65th,† having followed the example of the 70th, the three corps were formed into an Indian Brigade and were employed at Hongkong, Canton, and other places, where they gained a high reputation for steadiness and exemplary conduct.

Loyal regiments volunteer for service in China.

In the Afghán War of 1878-80, the Hindustáni regiments were mostly employed on the lines of communication. Among them the 11th Bengal Infantry specially distinguished itself by the successful defence of Ali Khel against a large force of Musazai tribesmen. The soldier-like bearing of the regiment during this action, and the steadiness of all ranks under fire, was favourably noticed in despatches.‡

The 2nd Afghán War.

The Rájpúts who took part in the Egyptian Campaign of 1882, including the battle of Tel-el-Kebir, were mostly in the ranks of the 7th Bengal Infantry. "The regiment formed part of the Indian Contingent which advanced at dawn on the 13th September 1882, along the southern bank of the freshwater canal, and carried the enemy's batteries on that flank at the point of the bayonet. After the action the regiment was ordered to Zagazig, which was reached after a most arduous march. The battalion had been under arms for 17 hours and had covered 27 miles, besides taking part in a general action."‡

The Egyptian Campaign, 1882.

The last important campaign in which Rájpúts had an opportunity of showing their mettle, was the Burmese War of 1885. At Minhla while the 2nd Bengal Infantry turned the enemy's right flank, the 11th Bengal Infantry gallantly broke through a thorny screen, tore over the entrenchments and breastwork of carts and bamboos which concealed the enemy, and dislodged them from the village of Yima. The column then advanced against the Minhla fort, which was carried with the greatest gallantry. The thanks

Burma, 1885.

---

* Now the 11th Rájpúts.

† Now the 7th Rájpúts and 10th Játs.

‡ Historical Records of the Bengal Army.—*Cardew.*

of Major-General Prendergast, C. B., V. C., were communicated to both regiments in the following words :—"Convey to the officers and men of the 2nd and 11th Bengal Infantry my great satisfaction at their gallant conduct in the action fought to-day. The brilliant leading of the officers and the dashing onslaught of the men prevailed against the undisciplined bravery of the Burmans, who broke and fled, leaving six guns as trophies to the victors. The 11th Bengal Infantry bore the brunt of the contest."*

Under the present organization of the Hindustáni infantry into class regiments, a great impetus has been given to *esprit de race*. To each regiment is now entrusted the military reputation of the class which it represents, and in this we have a moral factor which cannot fail to be a powerful incentive to efficiency. To no class are these observations more applicable than the Rájpúts. Soldiers by tradition, and taught by their religion to regard the profession of arms as their legitimate occupation, they form a military caste which should hold its own, and bear favourable comparison with the most warlike of the races now serving under our colours.

General observations.

* Historical Records of the Bengal Army.—*Cardew.*

CHAPTER II.

CLASSIFICATION AND GEOGRAPHICAL DISTRIBUTION.

As has already been noticed in Chapter I, the Kshatriyas or Rájpúts were primarily divided into two great nations—the *Surya* or Solar race of Ajudhya, and the *Yádu* or Lunar race of Delhi and Hastinapur. The mythical ancestor of the former was Ráma, and from his two eldest sons, Láva and Kúsh, are descended the reigning families of Meywar, Jeypore, Marwar, and Bikaneer. The founder of the *Yádu* race was Krishna, and from him are sprung the rulers of Jeysalmere and many of the petty principalities of Kutch and Kattiawar. The four *Agnicular** or fire tribes which were absorbed into the Kshatriya order about the 8th century, are generally considered to have been "Scythian invaders who sided with the Bráhmans in their struggles against the Bactrians and Buddhists, and whose warlike merits, timely aid, and subsequent conformity to Hinduism, secured their recognition as Rájpúts, and got them enrolled as 'fire-born,' in contradistinction to those who claimed the sun and moon as their ancestors."†

Primary division of the Rájpúts into Solar, Lunar, and Agnicular tribes.

The triple division of Solar, Lunar, and Agnicular Rájpúts was subsequently changed by secessions and subdivisions, into numerous clans and septs, of which thirty-six were called "royal," and singled out for special distinction on account of their power and numbers. Of these many no longer exist, and in the following list their names are shown in italics, in order to distinguish them from those whose representatives are still to be found.

The thirty-six Royal Races.

Surya or Solar race.	Chalúk or Solanki.	Gohil.	Séngarh.
Sóm or Lunar race.	Parihára.	Jaitwar or Kamari.	Sakarwar.
Gáhlot or Grahilot.	Chawúra.	Silar.	Bais.
Yádu, Indu, Jádu or Jadon.	Tak or Takshak.	*Sarwaiya.*	*Dahia.*
Tuár or Tónwar.	Jit, Gét, or Ját.	*Dabi.*	Johya.
Ráthor.	*Hán or Hún.*	Gaur.	Mohil.
Kachwáha.	Katti.	Dor or Doda.	Nikumpa.
Pramára or Pónwar.	Balla.	Gaharwál.	*Rájpáli.*
Chauhán.	Jhalla.	Bargújar.	*Dahima.*

* Derived from *agni* 'fire' and *kula* 'a race.'

† Cyclopædia of India—*Balfour.*

"Scattered over Northern India are numerous clans of Rájpúts more or less connected with the royal races which from intermarriage with them and with one another, and also by reason of local association, have established for themselves the position of separate tribes bearing their own distinctive names. Such as can trace their Rájpút lineage and are of undoubted purity of descent are recognized as belonging to the great Kshatriya brotherhood, and frequently intermarry with the ancient houses;"* on the other hand certain clans of Oudh and the North-West Provinces which are probably connected with aboriginal races are looked down on by the blue-blooded Rájpúts of Rájasthán, who regard them as spurious, and thus practically disown them.

The Rajpúts of Oudh and the North-West Provinces.

"The natural feeling of a Hindu is to yield feudal obedience and in return to receive protection from his natural lord or leader, and the latter, according to Aryan usage, must be a Rájpút. In ancient India every man was necessarily a soldier, and every soldier was according to the *Védas* a Kshatriya. Such a thing as a Bráhman or Ahir king was an utter anomaly, and if by chance or by force any low-caste man succeeded in rising to power, a fabulous Rájpút origin was at once devised for him, and his descendants admitted into the soldier brotherhood. Several foreign elements were thus united to form the Chhatri caste, and the profession of arms, with its absorbing passions, welded them into one race."†

Mixed origin of the Kshatriyas.

The Rájpúts of Oudh and the eastern portion of the North-West Provinces may be divided into three classes—

(1) Clans such as the *Bisén, Gaharwár,* and *Chandél* whose settlements date from the prehistoric period, when a Solar dynasty ruled over Ajudhya.

(2) Those descended from clans which after their defeat by the Musalmans under the Ghoris in Upper India, fled into the *terra incognita* across the Ganges, where hidden by forests and jungles, they sought refuge from the vengeance of their conquerors. These settlements were all made from about 1200 to 1450, and are represented by the *Chauháns, Dikhits, Raikhwárs, Janwárs* and *Gautams.*

Origin of the Eastern or Hindustani Rájpúts.

* Gazetteer of Oudh.

† Hindu Tribes and Castes.—*Sherring.*

(3) Those descended from bands of adventurers or single leaders who as time went on entered the service of the Delhi Emperors and acquired tracts of country either by direct grants from their rulers, or by the sword. These colonies, which are comparatively recent, were mostly established from 1415 to 1700, and are represented by the *Séngars, Gáhlots, Gaurs,* and *Parihars.**

Reasons for their mixed origin.

When the fall of Kanouj in 1194 shifted the centre of Rájpút influence from the banks of the Ganges to Rájpútána, the scattered Rájpúts who remained, and the colonists who afterwards joined them, frequently contracted irregular alliances with the women of non-Aryan races in their midst. They thus lost the purity of their race, and only retained their status as Kshatriyas by the connivance and good will of the Bráhmans, who thereby obtained an influence and a hold on them, which survives to the present day.

The Bràhmans bestow Kshatriya rank on the aboriginal chieftains who accept Hinduism.

The attraction of numerous aboriginal chiefs into the fold of Hinduism by the subtlety and adaptiveness of the Bráhmans, led to a further admixture of the Rájpút races. "The Bráhmans found the natives illiterate and without faith, but fierce and proud. They saw that the barbarians had vacant minds ready to receive their doctrines, but spirits not apt to stoop to degradation, and they acted accordingly. To the earliest and most distinguished of their converts they communicated, in defiance of their creed, the lofty rank and honours of the Kshatriya; while to the rank and file of their followers suitable positions were allotted in the innumerable subdivisions of the Sudra."† Clans of this lineage can generally be traced by their names, which are often identical with those of hunting and pastoral races such as the *Barwár, Khangar, Gújar, Chamár-Gaur, Domwar, Nágbansi,* and *Baheliya.*

The ranks of the Kshatriyas were also recruited from another source. Bráhmans, like their Rájpút neighbours, occasionally condescended to ally themselves with the women of low-caste tribes. In theory the progeny of such malalliances were outcasts, but in practice

* Ethnographical Handbook for the North-West Provinces and Oudh.—*Crooke.*

† Essays on the Languages, etc., of Nepal.—*Brian Hodgson.*

the Bráhman father, in utter defiance of Hindu usage, often bestowed upon his bastard offspring, the rank of the second order of Hinduism. Thus from the illegitimate progeny of Bráhmans sprang several of the Rájpút tribes of Oudh such as the *Kanhpuria*, *Bandhalgoti*, and *Chaupat Khamb.*

The ranks of the Rájpúts recruited by bastard Bráhmans.

The two processes above described were repeated in Nepal in the 12th century, and are still going on, as in the case of the *Khasiyas* of the hills, and the Singrauli Rája of Mirzapur, who within the present generation has developed from an aboriginal *Kharwár* into a *Bénbans* Rájpút. Sleeman,* writing in 1842, states that "*Pásis* became Rájpúts by giving their daughters to *Ponwárs* and other Rájpút clans, when by robbery and murder they had acquired wealth and landed property. These *Pásis*† call themselves *Ráwats* and are considered to be Rájpúts since they have acquired landed possessions by the ruin of the old proprietors."

As has already been noticed, the term Rájpút is more a social than an ethnic one, and the Rájpúts are really descended from a number of tribes of various stock and origin, some Aryan, some Scythian, and some aboriginal, which on accepting the supremacy of the Bráhmans were accorded the second place in the hierarchy of Hindu rank. They are moreover often derived from congeries of various races which, from being collected under the leadership of a Chhatri warrior, were granted a tribal name, and in course of time borrowed the pedigree of their founder, as a convenient explanation of their lineage.

The constitution of the Rájpút race.

Taking the Rájpúts as a whole, those of the west rank higher than those of the east. Their well known proverb "*Púrab ki béti aur pachhim ka béta,*" indicates the common custom among them of marrying their daughters to members of western clans ranking higher than themselves. Thus the Oudh Rájpúts look down on the Thákurs of Behar, and acknowledge the Mainpuri *Chauháns*, *Bhadauriyas*, and *Ráthors* as their superiors; while these in their turn look up to their brethren in Rájpútána as ranking above them in the social scale.

Rank among Rájpúts.

* "A Journey through the Kingdom of Oudh."

† *Pásis* are a tribe of agriculturists, toddy makers, watchmen, and thieves. They were at one time robbers by profession, and were formerly *Thugs* and poisoners as well. Previous to the annexation of Oudh the great Rájpút landlords maintained large gangs of *Pásis* to fight the revenue authorities and plunder their neighbours. They were all armed with bows and arrows, and gave considerable trouble in the Mutiny.

It will be seen from the two maps at the end of this volume that the Rájpút recruiting ground extends from the Himalayas in the north to the Vindhyas and Nerbudda in the south; and from Guzerat, Bikaneer and the Sutlej on the west, to the Sône and Behar on the east. This vast tract may be conveniently divided into two areas separated by the Jumna and the Chambal rivers—

Geographical distribution.

Area I is occupied by the *Dési* or Western Rájpúts and includes portions of the Punjáb, the whole of Rájpútána, Guzerat, Kattiawar and Kutch.*

Area II is occupied by the *Purbiah* or Eastern Rájpúts, and includes the whole of Hindustán, *i.e.*, the North-West Provinces, Oudh, Behar, and the Gwalior and Rewah States.

Many Rájpút tribes are found in both of these areas, but some are peculiar to one or the other. In the following pages will be found a short account of each of the principal clans, which for convenience of reference have been described in alphabetical order. Map 1 indicates the geographical distribution of the Western Rájpúts inhabiting Area I: Map 2 that of the Eastern Rájpúts included in Area II. An index number is allotted to each clan by which its location may easily be traced.

As explained in Chapter IV, the establishment of messes among certain classes of Rájpúts, depends almost entirely upon the social relations of the septs to which they belong. Members of clans which habitually intermarry, will also, as a general rule, eat at the same *chauka* or cooking place; for this reason it has been considered advisable to include a table of marriages in the account given of each clan.

AHBAN.

Shown in map as 1.

The name of this clan is derived from the Sanskrit *ahi* a snake. The clan claims to be the oldest in Oudh, and to be descended from two brothers of the *Chawura* clan called Gopi and Sopi, who came from Anhalwarra Pattan, on a pilgrimage to Gya, early in the first century.

Traditional origin.

* Guzerat, Kattiawar and Kutch are however not included in the coloured portion on the map although belonging to this area, they furnish no recruits for the army.

The *Chawuras* of Shaurastra or Guzerat belonged neither to the Solar nor Lunar race, and it is consequently supposed that they must have been Scythians. They must have been established in India at a very remote period, for we find that the *Gáhlóts* intermarried with them while they were rulers of Balabhi. Their capital was at Deobander, near Somnath on the coast of Kattiawar. It is probable that the Oudh colony founded in the 1st century by Sopi and Gopi, was reinforced by refugees from Anhalwarra Pattan on the destruction of that city in 1298 by Alá-ud-din Khilji. The two *Ahban* brothers settled at Gopamau and Bhurwára in the Kheri district, and were powerful land-owners during the reigns of Humayun and Akbar. A branch of the family was converted to Islám towards the end of the 15th century, by a Muhammadan saint called Kála Pahár. *Ahbans* are noted for their willingness to deceive, and the ease with which they are deceived themselves. The cunning, treachery, and sluggishness of the clan is proverbial. In the unsettled times which preceded the British dominion, they were famed for their ill luck, which arose from the fact that they always hesitated about taking sides in civil wars till the contest was almost decided, and then invariably took the wrong one. At the battle of Buxar in 1764, the *Ahban* Rája Mán Singh having delayed to join his sovereign till it was too late, presumed to oppose the march of the victorious English by his raw levies. At the first charge his men fled, the Rája tumbled off his horse, and was bayonetted by a British soldier. At the annexation of Oudh, Rája Lone Singh *Ahban* was treated with marked generosity, which was repaid by the blackest ingratitude. He was tried after the Mutiny for selling the British fugitives from Shahjahanpur to the rebel Government for Rs. 8,000, and was sentenced to transportation for life, and forfeiture of his estates.

History.

The *Ahban* clan is peculiar to Oudh. It has a male population of 3,000, found chiefly in the Hardoi and Kheri districts.

Geographical distribution.

The *Ahbans* have a tribal divinity called *Addnu* who is supposed to have assisted the brothers Gopi and Sopi. The Muhammadan *Ahbans* dine on the same floor as their Hindu brethren, but a line is drawn to separate the former from the latter.

Religion.

The *Ahbans* are divided into two septs—

Triba divisions.	Ahbans proper.	Kunwar Ahbans.

The *Ahbans* intermarry with the following clans—

Give their daughters to	Take wives from
Rathor.	Gaharwar.
Kachwáha.	Chandel.
Chauhán.	Raikwar.
Ponwar.	Janwár.
Katheriya.	Gaur.
Gautam.	Sombansi.
Báchal.	Dhákre.
Chamar-Gaur.	Nikumbh.
Sakarwar.	
Sombansi.	
Dhákre.	
Nikumbh.	

AMETHIYA.

Shown in Map as 2.

The title of this clan is derived from the name of a village in the Lucknow district called Améthi. They are generally supposed to be a sept of the *Chamar-Gaurs* (q. v.), a tradition which they preserve by the worship of the *ránpi* or curriers scraper. The clan is supposed to have been originally settled at Kalinjar in Bundelkhund, whence they emigrated into Oudh, under Raipál Singh, about the time of Tamerlane's invasion. His descendants say that he was sent by the Delhi Emperor to suppress a rebellion in Oudh, and that he defeated and slew Balbhadra Sén, and a number of his *Bisén* followers. Raipál Singh who was wounded in the shoulder by a musket ball, was recompensed by a * *khilat* and the title of Rája of Améthi. Towards the end of the 12th century three *Améthiya* brothers, named Dingur Sáh, Rám Singh, and Lohang, led their clan from Améthi to Jugdíspur, and drove out the Musalmáns from their villages. The clan is divided into two branches—the *Améthiyas* of Kumhráwán in Rai Bareli, and the *Améthiyas* of Unsári in Bara-

Traditional origin and history.

* A *khilat* is a dress of honour.

Banki. The latter, though the junior of the two, seems to have always been the most important. The heads of the clan are the Rájas of Kumhráwán and Unsári.

Geographical distribution.

Améthiyas are found in the Gorakhpur, Rai Bareli, and Bara-Banki districts of Oudh and the North-West Provinces, and have a male population of 5,000.

Religion.

The principal deity of the *Améthiyas* is Durga. They are of the *Bharaddwáj* gotra.

Améthiyas contract marriages with Rájpúts of the following clans :—

Give their daughters to	Take wives from
Tilókchand Bais.	Bhalé Sultán.
Chauhán.	Kalhans.
Bhadauriya.	Janwár.
Kachwáha.	Kánhpuriya
Jádón.	Gautam.
	Bándhalgoti.
	Sómbansi.
	Súrajbansi.

BACHHAL.

Shown in map as 3.

The title of this clan is said to be derived from *báchhna* 'to distribute.' The *Báchhals* are said to be of the *Chandrabansi* or Lunar race, and claim descent from a mythical personage called Rája Véna. Their earliest settlements were in Rohilkhund, where they were the dominant race until 1174, when the Muhammadans and *Katheriya* Rájpúts invaded their territories, and drove them into the jungles. It has been suggested that the founder of the clan was Rája Bairat of Barkhar in the Kheri district, who is said to have entertained the five *Pandávas** during their exile from Hastinapur. The principal incident of their sojourn was the passion conceived by Kichaka, the brother-in-law of the Rája, for Drapaudi

Traditional origin and history.

* The feuds of the *Pandávas* and *Kaurávas*, scions of a Rájpút race inhabiting the neighbourhood of Delhi, are described in the *Mahabharata*.

the beautiful wife of the *Pandáva* brothers. After being insulted by Kichaka, Drapaudi appealed for protection to Bhim, the strongest of her five husbands. The latter had a tremendous fight with the former, and after defeating him, pounded his body into pieces and kneaded it into a ball, in order that it might be thought that the deed was the work of a demon. It is curious to note that the Pharoahs of Egypt were contemporaries of this Rája Bairat. The *Báchhals* of these early times were an enterprizing race, and constructed several canals, of which traces can be found to the present day. When the Muhammadans assisted by the treacherous *Katheriyas* had driven the *Báchhals* across the Deoha river in Pillibhit, the latter made a successful stand, and managed to retain a small territory between that river and the forests of the *Tarai*. In the last great fight with their enemies, the twelve principal *Báchhal* Ránas were slain, but one of their wives, who was pregnant, escaped, and from her son was descended Chhábi Singh, a celebrated robber chief, who established himself at Nagohi, in the Shahjahanpur district, about the time of Akbar. An attack on the escort of a lady of the Emperor's household attracted the notice of that monarch, and caused him to issue orders for Chhábi Singh's apprehension. The Rájpút, however, succeeded in conciliating the Mughal, and was given a *jághir* of the whole of the lands he occupied. In the reign of Sháh Jahán, a *Báchhal* chief was employed by the Emperor in quelling an insurrection in Mánikpur. He defeated the rebels, and returning rapidly to Delhi, entered the presence with his clothes covered with blood. The courtiers were shocked at the Rájpút's want of manners, but the Emperor, taking no notice of the matter, good humouredly addressed him as *Chhipi Khan*, "the gore-besprinkled chieftain," a title which he afterwards adopted. Chhipi Khan appears to have rebelled soon afterwards, for in the reign of Alamgir his fort at Kamp in the Kheri district was besieged by a contingent of Rájpútána *Chauháns* who formed part of the Imperial army. The *Báchhals* held out gallantly for 18 months, but at the end of that time the Mughals ran a mine into the interior of the fort, by which they entered it at night, and put the entire garrison to the sword. During the 18th century the *Báchhals* lost all their former prestige, and degenerated into robbers and dacoits. The *Báchhals* of Azamgarh are of aboriginal origin and themselves admit that their ancestor was a *Ráj-Bhar*. In the Muttra district, the *Sissodiyas* of *Gaurua* or impure descent are usually called *Báchhal*, from the Bachhban at Sehi where their *Gúrú* always resides. They say they emigrated from Chitór 700 or 800 years ago, but it is more probable that their move took place after Allá-ud-din's famous siege in 1303.

Báchhals are found chiefly in the Bulandshahr, Muttra, Moradabad, Shahjahanpur, Sitapur, and Kheri districts of Oudh and the North-West Provinces. The clan has a male population of 11,000.

Geographical distribution.

Báchhals contract marriages with Rájpúts of the following clans :—

District	Give their daughters to	Take wives from
Shahjahánpur.	Chauhán.	Janwár.
	Ráthor.	Janghárá.
	Bhadauriya.	Katheriya.
	Katiyar.	Ponwár.
	Kachwáha.	
Sitapur and Kheri.	Chauhán.	Gaur.
	Ráthor.	Nikumbh.
	Bhadauriya.	Janwár.
	Kachwáha.	Ponwár.
Bulandshah[r].	Bhátti.	Bargala.
	Bargújar.	Bhalé Sultán.
	Chandarbansi.	Jais.
	Gáhlót.	Jaiswár.
	Chauhán.	Jarauliya.
	Ponwár.	Bais.
	Kachwáha.	Gaur.
	Chhonkar.	
	Bais.	
	Gaur.	

BACHHGÓTI OR RÁJKUMAR.

Shown in map as 4.

The title of this clan is derived from *Vatsa* or *Batsa,* the name of the *Rishi* who founded the *gotra* to which the tribe belongs. They claim descent from some Mainpuri *Chauháns* who fled from Delhi about 1200, under a leader named Bariár Singh, in order to escape from the vengeance of Muhammad Ghori. The fugitives settled in the Sultanpur district of Oudh, and as their clan had been specially singled out for extirpation by the Musalmans, they changed their name to *Bachhgoti* in order to better escape recognition. Another story is that Rána Sangat, great nephew of Pirthiráj *Chauhán*, aspired to the hand of a young bride and the only condition on which she would agree to marry him was that in the event of a son being born, he should succeed to the family title. The Rána accepted this proviso, and in due time the young Ráni bore him a son, which so discomfited his 22 sons by former marriages, that they abandoned their home, and dispersed all over the country to seek their fortunes. One of these sons was Bariár Singh who according to another tradition is said to have joined Muhammad Ghori at Mainpuri, and served him as an officer in his campaign against the Bhars, receiving the conquered country as a reward for his exertions. It is probable that Bariár Singh entered the service of the *Bilkhariya* Rája Rám Déo, and after marrying his daughter, possessed himself of his estates. Bariár Singh left three sons—Asal Singh, Gajráj Singh, Ghátam Déo, and Ráj Sáh. The Rája of Kurwar, the head of the Hindu *Bachhgotis*, and the Diwán of Hassanpur-Bandhúa, the chief of the Muhammadan branch, are both descendants of Ráj Sáh. Early in the 17th century the offspring of Bariár Singh and his retainers, finding themselves cramped for space on the right bank of the Gúmti, crossed over into Fyzabad, and established six colonies in that district. These Fyzabad *Rájkumars* were notoriously turbulent, and gave great trouble to the Muhammadan authorities. Besides despoiling their neighbours, they were often at feud with one another, and several sanguinary actions took place between different septs of the tribe. Towards the early part of the century the headship of the clan devolved upon the Thákúráin Dariáo Kunwar, the widow of Rája Mádho Singh, a lady of extraordinary ability, who not only held her own for 25 years, but after the fashion of the Oudh landholders of that time, added greatly to her estates and possessions. She was succeeded by her husband's nephew Rústam Sáh, who rendered the British Government excellent service in the Mutiny, and gave shelter and safe convoy to Benares to a party of the Sultánpur fugitives, for which he was rewarded by the title of Rája. The *Bachhgotis* proper generally wear caps to distinguish them from their *Rájkumar* and *Rájwár* brethren who as a rule wear turbans.

Traditional origin and history.

Rájkumárs **and** ***Bachhgotis*** are found chiefly in the Jaunpur, Sultanpur, Allahabad, Fyzabad and Partabgarh districts of Oudh and the North-

Geographical distribution.

West Provinces. The *Bachhgotis* have a male population of 19,000, and the *Rájkumárs* of about 13,000.

Religion. The favourite deity of the *Bachhgotis* is the goddess Dúrga.

The principal septs of the clan are as follows :—

Tribal divisions.

Bachhgoti proper.	Rájwár.
Rájkumár.	

Bachhgotis contract marriages with Rájpúts of the following clans :—

Give their daughters to	Take wives from
Súrajbansi.	Gargbansi.
Sómbansi.	Raghubansi.
Sirnét.	Kath Bais.
Kalhans.	Bhalé Súltán.
Kánhpúriya.	Súrwár.
Tilókchandi Bais.	Raikwár.
Bandhalgóti.	Pálwár.
	Nikumbh.
	Dirgbansi.
	Chaupat Khambh.
	Tésahiya.
	Bilkháriya (Dikhit).

BAGHÉL.

Shown in map as 5.

The name of this clan is derived from the Sanskrit *Vyaghra,* 'a tiger,' which was probably the tribal totem. Tod traces their title and descent from Bágh Ráo, or Vyaghra Déva, son of Rai Jai Singh, one of the *Solanki* or *Chalukya* rulers of Anhalwára Pattan in Rájpútána. It is said that *Baghéls* claim descent from a tiger, and protect it whenever they can.

Traditional origin.

The *Baghêls* emigrated from Pálgarh in Guzerat about 1300 years ago, and settled in the upper valleys of the Sône, and Tons, under Vyaghra Déva. This district is now called Baghelkhund, and includes the Rewah State, where they are numerous and powerful.

Settlements in the North-West Provinces.

During the reign of Jai Chand, Rája of Kanouj, a *Baghél* colony from Madhogarh settled under Bhairu Partáb in the Farrukhabad district. The small *Baghél* communities in Banda and Allahabad are probably offshoots from Rewah.

Geographical distribution.

True *Baghéls* are not found in Rájpútána, although their kinsmen the *Solankis* are fairly numerous. Their principal settlements are in the Rewah State, where they furnish the reigning family, and in the Farrukhabad and Allahabad districts of the North-West Provinces. Their total male population amounts to about 5,000.

Religion.

The favourite *Baghél* divinity is Ram Chandra.

Tribal divisions.

The clan is divided into two *gotras*—the *Bharaddwaj* and the *Kaysap*.

Bhághéls intermarry with the following clans:—

In Rewah.		In North-West Provinces.	
Give daughters to	Take wives from	Give daughters to	Take wives from
Sisodiya.	Sisodiya.	Jádón.	Jàdón.
Chandel.	Chandel.	Chauhán.	Ráthor..
Gaharwar.	Gaharwar.	Kchwáhá.	Kachwáha.
Kachwáha.	Kachwáha.	Tonwar.	Tonwar.
Parihar.	Parihar.		
Chauhán.	Chauhán.		
Hára.	Hára.		
Bhadauriya.	Bhadauriya.		
Ráthor.	Ráthor.		
Dikhit.	Dikhit.		

Bais.

Shown in map as 6.

The name of this clan is derived from the Sanskrit *Vaisiya,* 'an occupier of the soil.' It ranks as one of the 36 royal races, but is probably only a sub-division of the *Suryavansi.* The *Bais* claim descent from their tribal hero Saliváhana, the mythical son of a snake, who about 55 A.D. conquered the celebrated Rája Vikrámajit of Ujjain. The tribal symbol is the cobra, and it has been suggested that this snake totemism indicates an intermixture with aborigines; it may, however, with almost equal probability, indicate a *Takshak* or Scythian origin.

Traditional origin.

The original home of the *Bais* was at Mangi Pattan in the Dekhan, but towards the middle of the 13th century the immediate ancestors of the clan emigrated from thence into Oudh. The story of their adventures is very romantic. About 1250 the *Gautam* Rája of Argal refused to pay tribute to the King of Delhi, and utterly defeated the troops sent against him by the Muhammadan Governor of Oudh. Soon after this victory, his Ráni, without his knowledge, and with only a very small escort, went secretly to bathe in the Ganges at Buxar. The Governor of Oudh hearing of this, sent men to the *ghát* to capture her. Her escort was dispersed, and she was on the point of being carried off, when lifting the curtains of her litter, she cried out: "Is there no Kshatriya who will rescue me from the barbarian and save my honour?" Abhai Chand and Nirbhai Chand, two *Bais* Rájpúts from Mangi Pattan, heard her, came to her rescue, beat off her assailants, and guarded her litter till she arrived in safety at Argal. Nirbhai Chand died of his wounds, but Abhai Chand recovered, and the Rája, in gratitude for his gallant conduct, though he was of a clan inferior to his own, gave him his daughter in marriage, and bestowed on her as a dowry all the *Gautam* lands to the north of the Ganges. He also conferred on his son-in-law the title of Ráo which is still the highest dignity among the *Bais.* Abhai Chand fixed his home at Dúṇdhiya Khera on the Ganges, and the title and estates descended in an unbroken line through seven generations to Tilok Chand, the great *Bais* hero, from whom the senior branch take their name, to distinguish themfrom minor septs of the same tribe. To this day the marriage of a *Bais* with a *Gautam* is considered peculiarly lucky. Tilok Chand who lived about 1400 extended the *Bais* dominion all over the neighbouring country, and it is

History.

from his victories that the limits of *Baiswára* became definitely fixed. The *Tilokchandi* is probably the only sept of the *Bais* clan which can claim to be of pure descent. As the *Bais* Ráos extended their authority, numbers of military adventurers joined their service, and in course of time came to be regarded as genuine members of the tribe. It is related that Tilok Chand, in addition to his two legitimate wives, had no less than 300 concubines, and a family described as innumerable. Feeling themselves disgraced by their husband's conduct, the legitimate Ránis deserted him. This gave rise to the distinction of *Bhitariya* and *Bahariya*—the latter being the children of pure Rájpút blood, while the former were the offspring of low caste concubines. The most important distinction among the *Bais* is that between the *Tilokchandi* and the *Kath-Bais*. The *Tilokchandi* are rarely met with outside *Baiswára* and regard all other *Bais* as *Kath Bais* or impure. The *Bais* of Mirzapur are a spurious sept. The *Bais* of Kohilkhund emigrated into that district from *Baiswára* about the time of Akbar. The *Bais* of the Mainpuri district emigrated from Dúndhiya Khera in the 15th century.

The Bais clan has a male population of 147,000. It is practically unknown in Rájpútána, but is scattered throughout the Farukhabad, Mainpuri, Budaun, Cawnpore, Fatehpore, Banda, Hamirpur, Allahabad, Benares, Mirzapur, Jaunpur, Gazipur, Ballia, Gorakhpur, Basti, 'Azamgarh, Lucknow, Unao, Rai Bareli, Sitapur, Hardoi, Fyzabad, Gonda, Bahraich, Partabgarh, and Barabanki districts of Oudh and the North-West Provinces.

Geographical distribution.

The Bais worship Débi. The tribal *totem* or symbol is the cobra. They perpetuate the tradition of a serpent origin, and assert that no snake has or ever can destroy one of the clan; for the same reason no *Bais* will even kill a cobra.

Religion.

The *Bais* clan is divided into 360 sub-divisions, of which the most important are noted below:—

Ráo.	Branches of the Tilokchandi sept.	Tilsari.
Rája		Chak Bais.
Sainbaisi.		Nánwag.
Naihastha.		Bhanwag.
Chotbhaiya.		Bach.
Gudaraha.		Parsariya.
Madhour.		Bijhoniya.
		Bhetkariya.
Kath-Bais.		Gargbansi.

The *Bais* intermarry with the following clans :—

Give their daughters to	Take wives from
Chauhán.	Améthiya.
Ráthor.	Bisén.
Bhadauriya.	Báchhgoti.
Kachwáha	Bándhalgoti.
Baghél.	Chandél.
Katiyar.	Dikhit.
Tonwar.	Raghubansi.
Parihar,	Gahlot.
Sengar.	Gautam.
Dikhit.	Kalhans.
Gaharwar.	Khichar.
	Raikwar.
	Kanhpuriya.
	Janwar.
	Karchuliya.

The *Bais* being a very scattered tribe, comprising many septs differing in social grade, their marriages with other clans vary greatly. The *Tilokchandi Bais* are the only ones who can marry into superior clans like *Chauháns* and *Kachwáhas*; the other septs generally marry into third grade clans, and if they aspire to more illustrious alliances, have to pay very dearly for the privilege.

Tribal peculiarities.

The *Tilokchandi Bais* have some curious customs. None of the *Sainbaisi* branch will ride mares. The reason given is; that their famous ancestor Rája Mitúrjit, when on a visit to Delhi, was insulted by the Rájas of Jeypore and Marwar, and challenged them to fight. Mitúrjit appeared on the field on a mare, which ran away with him. Stopping her with great trouble, he pronounced a curse on her, and on anyone of his race who would thenceforth ride a mare. Mitúrjit then dismounted, and returning to the field on foot, wounded both his antagonists. After this exploit he was taken into high favour at the Delhi court, and led his *Bais* contingent in an expedition to Kábul. *Bais* females can never wear cotton clothes of any colour but white, and above the feet and ankles their ornaments must be made of gold. The *Bais* pride themselves on being the most enterprising, the wealthiest, the best housed, and the best dressed people in Oudh.

BANDHALGOTI.

Shown in map as 7.

Traditional origin.

The clan takes its name from Pandhu, one of its ancestors, and claims descent from Suda Rai, a scion of the reigning family of Jeypore who came to Ajudhya on a pilgrimage about 900 years ago, and settled in the Sultanpur district. This would make them a branch of the Solar race.

History.

On his way to Ajudhya, Súda Rai passed through Améthi, which was then held by a Bhár Rája. Having performed his devotions at the shrine of Débi, he fell asleep, and dreamt that the goddess appeared before him and promised that he and his descendants should become the lords of the territory in which he was a temporary sojourner. Prepared to further to the utmost the fulfilment of this vision, he determined to abide in his future domain, and relinquishing his uncompleted pilgrimage, entered the service of the Bhár Rája. His innate worth soon manifested itself in many ways, and secured his elevation to the post of minister. Soon after, his Bhár master, as a crowning act of favour, offered him his daughter in marriage; but a *Súrajbans* Rájpút though he might condescend to serve an aboriginal barbarian, might not sully his lineage by a misalliance, and Súdá Rai contemptuously declined the honour. The Bhár chief, in offended pride, at once dismissed him, and Suda Rai returned to his home in Marwar. But his interest in the promised land had been awakened; he collected a picked band of followers, and marched to the conquest of Améthi. The Bhars were defeated with great slaughter, and the *Súrajbans* occupied their territory. The descendants of Súda Rai ruled over Améthi for 6 generations, when the line threatened to become extinct. Through the intercessions, however, of a Hindu saint, the Rája at last obtained an heir, who was called Bandhu. It is from him that the clan derives its name. The clan increased in power and numbers, but we know very little of its history until 1743, when Rája Gurdatt Singh, the head of the tribe at that period, distinguished himself by his defiance of the Nawáb Safdar Jang, who besieged and captured his fort of Raipur. In the Mutiny, the *Bandhalgoti* Rája, Madho Singh of Améthi, distinguished himself by the protection and kindness he afforded to some fugitives from Sultanpur, who were endeavouring to make their way to Allahabad; nevertheless he afterwards warmly espoused the rebel cause, nor did he tender his submission until his fort was surrounded by a British force under Sir Colin Campbell. It is stated by some authorities that the descent from Súda Rai is a pure invention and that the clan is really descended from a Bráhman called Chuchu Pánde by a woman of the Dóm or Dhakár caste. In proof of this assertion it is said that the *Bandhalgotis* still make offerings to the *báṅka*, or bamboo splitter, made use of by their maternal ancestors. This is, however, explained away by the elision of the final *a*, which transforms the *banka* of the Dhakár bamboo-cutter, into the *bánk* or poniard of the Rájpút. Moreover, this explanation strengthens the claim of the clan to a western origin, for the poniard, the professed object of their reverence, is the symbol of Márwar, the very state from which Suda Rai is represented to have come. The heads of the clan are the Rája of Améthi, and the Talúkdar of Sháhgarh in the Sultanpur district.

Geographical distribution.

The *Bandhalgoti* clan is not represented in either Rájpútána or the Punjáb. In Oudh it has a male population of 6,000, and is practically confined to the district of Sultanpur.

Religion.

The *Bandhalgotis* worship Dúrga and Indra.

The *Bandhalgotis* are divided into the following septs :—

Bikram Sháhi.	Sultán Sháhi.

Tribal divisions.

The *Bikram Sháhi* rank highest of the two.

Bandhalgotis intermarry with the following clans :—

Give their daughters to	Take wives from
Surajbansi.	Bachhgoti.
Sombansi.	Rajkumar.
Kalhans.	Rajwar.
Kausik.	Bisén.
Gaharwar.	Dikhit.
Kanhpuriya.	Raghubansi.
Tilokchandi Bais.	Bhalé Sultán.
Sirnet.	Gargbansi.
Bisén.	Kath-Bais.
Gahlot.	Bilkhariya.

BANAPHAR.

Shown in map as 8.

A small tribe of the *Jádubansi* or Lunar race formerly established at Mahoba in Bundelkhund. They were either vassals or allies of the *Chandéls*, and fought for them against the *Chauháns*, in the *Chauhán-Chandél* war. In the final battle, which resulted in the defeat of the latter, the *Banáphar* heroes Alhal and Udal covered themselves with glory, but failed to save their allies from destruction. After this catastrophe the clan dispersed, and is now very much scattered and reduced in circumstances.

Traditional origin and history.

Banáphars are found chiefly in the Hamirpur, Banda, Jalaun, Benares, and Ghazipur districts of the North-West Provinces. They have a male population of 2,900.

Geographical distribution.

The favourite deity of the clan is the goddess Debi. *Banáphars* belong to the *Kassyap gotra.*

Religion.

Banáphars contract marriages with Rájpúts of the following clans :—

Give their daughters to	Take wives from
Gautam.	Bais.
Dikhit.	Raghubansi.
Bais.	Sómbansi.
Chandél.	Gautam.
Gáharwar.	Surwar.
Raghúbansi.	Gaur.
Sómbansi.	Nándwak.
Monas.	
Bachhgoti.	
Baghel.	
Sirnet.	
Ráwat.	

BARÉSARI OR BARÉSIR.

Shown in map as 9.

Traditional origin, history and distribution.

This clan is a sept of the *Jádóns* (*q. v.*) They are of local importance in Agra, where they have a population of 2,000 males. The Thákur of Dhimsari is the head of the tribe. During the Mutiny the *Barésaris* greatly distinguished themselves by their efforts to protect life and property, and maintain order. The clan is losing status through marrying with *Gaurúa* or widow-marrying Rájpúts.

Barésaris contract marriages with members of the following clans :—

Give their daughters to	Take wives from
Indauliya.	Indauliya.
Chauhán.	Chauhán.
Kachwáha.	Kachwáha.
Sikarwar.	Gaurúa.

BARGALA.

Shown in map as 10.

Traditional origin and history.

This clan is a spurious branch of the *Jadubansi* or Lunar race. It is ranked as *Gaurúa* or impure, because it permits *karao* or widow marriage. *Bargalas* claim descent from two brothers named Drigpál and Bhatpál who are said to have been emigrants from Indore in Malwa, and to have held important commands in the royal forces at Delhi in the attack on Pirthiráj. They are an ill-conducted tribe, and lost most of their villages for rebellion in 1857. As a general rule enlistments from this clan are undesirable.

Geographical distribution.

Bargalas are found chiefly in the Gurgaon and Bulandshahr districts of the Panjáb and the North-West Provinces. They have a male population of 5,400.

Bargalas contract marriages with members of the following clans :—

Give their daughters to	Take wives from
Bhalésultán.	Jais.
Báchhal	Jaiswar.
Jaiswar.	Jarauliya.
	Gaurúa.

BARGÚJAR.

Shown in map as 11.

Traditional origin.

The name of this clan is derived from the Hindi *bara* 'great,' and *gújar*, the title of a well known tribe of herdsmen, with which it is probably connected. It is one of the 36 royal races, and, like the *Gahlot*, claims descent from Láva, the eldest son of Ráma of Ajudhya.

History.

Very little is known of the traditions of this clan. They were expelled from Rájpútána by the *Kachwáhas*, which accounts for their very small numbers in the west. They are said to have fought with distinction in the wars of Pirthiráj, the *Chauhán* Rája of Delhi, but their subsequent history has been lost, as the majority of the clan have either become Muhammadans, or have been dispersed throughout the North-West Provinces.

Bargújar settlements in Oudh and the North-West Provinces.

After their expulsion from Jeypore by the *Kachwáhas*, the *Bargújars* settled at Anúpshahr in the Bulandshahr district, where they intermarried with the aboriginal Dórs, and expelled the Mewátis and Bhárs. The Aligarh branch trace their descent from a *Súrajbans* Rája called Rajdéo who built the fort of Rajor in Jeypore. His great grandson married a daughter of Pirthiráj, the *Chauhán* Rája of Delhi, and the emigration of the *Bargújars* dates from the time of their son Partáb Singh, who was sent by his grandfather to conquer Kumaun. On his way, when passing through the Bulandshahr district, he exterminated the Mewátis by a stratagem suggested by a Kahár woman. As a reward, he was given a large territory by the Dór Rája of Koel, which was supplemented by a further grant from Pirthiráj after the successful termination of the conquest of Kumaun. A number of *Bargújars* were converted to Islám in the time of Ala-ud-din Khilji, but they still retain many of their Hindu customs.

Geographical distribution.

The *Bargújar* population of Rájpútána only numbers about 2,200 males. They are found chiefly in Jeypore and Ulwar and in the Gurgaon and Hissar districts of the Punjáb. The *Bargújars* of the North-West Provinces have a male population of 17,000. They have settlements in the Bulandshahr, Aligarh, Etah, Budaun, and Moradabad districts.

Religion.

The *Bargujars*, being of the Solar race, worship Ráma; but in the North-West Provinces the tribal divinity is a figure representing a *Kaharin*, or female bearer, which they paint on their doors and worship, in memory of the woman who by her timely advice gave their ancestor, Partab Singh, his first footing in the province. The *Bargújars* of Rájpútána have no sub-divisions, but in the North-West Provinces, whether Musalmans or Hindus, they are divided into the following septs which adopted their Muhammadan appellations in the reign of Jahangir.

Tribal divisions.

Lál Khán.	Bikram Kháni.
Ahmad Kháni.	Kamál Kháni.

Bai Máni.

Bargujars intermarry with the following clans:—

In Rájpútána.		In the North-West Provinces.	
Give their daughters to	Take wives from	Give their daughters to	Take wives from
Gahlot. Ráthor. Tonwar. Kachwáha. Chauhán. Gaur.	Ponwar. Tonwar. Chauhán. Gaur.	Gahlot. Bhatti. Chauhán. Pundir. Ponwar. Tonwar. Janghára. Katheriya. Katiyar. Bais. Ráthor. Parihar. Sakarwar. Solanki. Jádón.	Bachal. Bhal. Jais. Jaiswar. Jarauliya. Chhonkar. Bangar. Barésari. Dhakre. Indauliya.

BARHELIYA.

Shown in map as 12.

The name of this tribe is derived from Bahralla, a village in the Bara Banki district of Oudh, to which they emigrated, probably in the 17th century, from either Dehli or Mungi Pattan in the Dekhan. The *Barhéliyas* claim to be of *Súrajbansi* origin, but are really an offshoot of the *Bais*; the connexion, however, is now denied, as they have found it convenient to intermarry with the latter. The head of the clan is the Rája of Súrajpur in Bara Banki.

Geographical distribution.

The clan is practically confined to the Bara Banki district of Oudh and has a male population of nearly 2,000.

Religion.

The favourite tribal deity is the goddess Débi. Like the *Bais*, *Barhéliyas* venerate snakes and will on no account destroy them.

Barhéliyas contract marriages with members of the following clans:—

Give their daughters to	Take wives from
Améthiya.	Chauhán.
Bais.	Bisén.
Chauhán.	Kath-Bais.
Kánhpuriya.	Janwár.
Ponwar.	

BARWAR, BIRWAR, BERWAR.

Shown in map as 13.

Two explanations are given by this clan as to the derivation of the tribal name. According to one account they are *Tonwars*, who emigrated from Bernagar near Delhi, under a leader named Garakdéo, about the beginning of the 15th century. According to another legend *Barwar* is connected with *Bara* 'a pulse cake' and *Khanda* 'broken', because at a feast given by another clan, their ancestors were treacherously slaughtered on the calling out of the words "*bara khanda chaláo*,"* "pass round the broken pulse cakes," which had

* *Khanda* also means a sword, the true significance of the sentence was thus entirely different.

previously been agreed upon as a signal. To this day, at marriage and other festivals, *Barwars* will neither take broken *bara* cakes from their hosts, nor offer them to their guests.

Traditional origin and history.

The *Barwars* of Fyzabad describe themselves as of *Tilokchandi Bais* origin, and like the latter claim Mangi Pattan in the Dekhan as the home of their ancestors, who, according to their account, settled in Oudh about 300 years ago, under two brothers named Bariar Singh and Chahu Singh. The former is said to be the ancestor of the *Barwars* proper, and the latter of their sept the *Chahus*. The sacred place of the clan is Rám Ghát on the Gogra, which was selected by their chief Dilási Singh, in consequence of their being excluded from Ajudhya by the enmity of the *Súrajbans* Thákúrs. There is a Bhúinhár branch of the *Barwars*, and though the Bhúinhar and Kshatriya sections ignore one another, their neighbours regard them as of the same stock.

Barwars are found chiefly in the Ballia, Basti, Azamgarh, and Fyzabad districts of Oudh and the North-West Provinces. They have a male population of 9,500.

Barwars have a special tribal deity called Kariya Dorta whose effigy is worshipped at a village called Chitawan in Fyzabad. They belong to the *Kassyap* and *Bharaddwaj gotras*.

The clan is divided into the following septs :—

Tribal divisions.	Barwar proper.	Chahus.

Barwars contract marriages with members of the following clans :—

Give their daughters to	Take wives from
Gargbansi.	Palwar.
Raghúbansi.	Kinwar.
Palwár.	Kath-Bais.
Janwar.	Hayobans.
Bhalé Súltán.	Ujjaini.
Kath-Bais.	Nikumbh.
Hayobans.	Donwar.
Ujjaini.	Sengar.
Kinwar.	
Bisén.	
Raghúbansi.	

BHADAURIYA.

Shown in map as 14.

This famous and loyal clan derives its title from the village of Bhadáwar in Gwalior, which was the capital of their tribal territory The founder of the clan was probably Manika Rai, a *Chauhán* o Ajmere, who established himself with his followers on the banks of the Chambal towards the close of the 7th century. About 1246 this *Chauhán* colony was all but exterminated by some foe unspecified. The sole survivor was a pregnant Ráni of Rája Ráut Sál. Flying across the Jumna, she gave birth to a boy named Rajju, who, about 1259, when only 12 years old, appeared before the Emperor Nasir-ud-din at Dehli, and obtained leave to eject some Méo marauders from Panáhat in the Agra district. His efforts proved successful, and he was rewarded by the grant of the Bhádáwar principality.

In the reign of Akbar (1556-1605) the *Bhadauriya* Rája was given the title of *Mahendra*, which is still borne by the head of the clan. Some years later his son became a *Mansabdar* of 1,000, and fought with his contingent in Guzerat. In the reigns of Jahangir and Shah Jahan (1605-58) two *Bhadauriya* Rájas served with their clansmen in Afghánistan, and became great favourites of the Mughal Emperors, who enriched them at the expense of the *Chauháns*. In the reign of Aurangzéb, Rája Maha Singh of Bhadáwar served with distinction against the Búndélas and Yusufzais, and his son was made Governor of *Chitór* in Rájpútána. About the time of the Mughal decline, the clan became extremely powerful; but about 1748 they were attacked by Mahrattas and Játs, who annexed a great part of their territories. Shortly after, the *Bhadauriya* Rája resumed possession of his lands, and made friends with the Mahratta court of Gwalior. The Rája, however, incurred the wrath of Scindia for giving assistance to his friend the Rána of Gohad, and the clan remained in poor circumstances until the Mahratta war of 1803, when the *Bhadauriyas* declared for the British, and sent a contingent to assist in the capture of Gwalior. To punish their loyalty to the British during Monson's disastrous retreat, Holkar detached a force of 20,000 men to ravage the *Bhadauriya* country, but the clansmen held their own until a British force came to their assistance. In 1808, much of the territory conquered during the first Mahratta war was restored to Scindia, who promptly cancelled the rent-free grant which had been given to the *Bhadáwar* Rájas by the British. On consideration of the loyalty of the family, and to compensate for these losses, it was decided to grant the Rájas Rs. 24,000 per annum, an allowance which is continued to this day. The seat of the Rája is now at Nandgáon in the Agra district. Although the rise of the *Bhadáwar* Rájas only dates from the 16th century, their achievements and illustrious marriages have raised them greatly in the estimation of the neighbouring Rájpút princes, and they take precedence of the *Chauhán* Rájas of Pertapnér and Maìnpuri.

Geographical distribution.

The *Bhadauriyas* of Oudh and the North-West Provinces number 16,000 males, and they are numerous in the Gwalior State. They are found chiefly in the Agra, Etawah, and Cawnpore districts.

The *Bhadauriyas* have six sub-divisions—

Athbaiya.	Tasseli.
Kulhaiya.	Chandarseniya.
Mainu.	Raut.

Tribal sub-divisions.

The *Raut* sub-division ranks highest. The *Tasseli* and *Maìnu* have a little Méo blood in their veins. The *Bhadauriyas* are undoubtedly of *Chauhán* origin, but since the two clans began to find intermarriage convenient, this relationship has been denied, as marriage within the clan is prohibited among pure blooded Rájpúts.

Bhadauriyas intermarry with the following clans:—

Give their daughters to	Take wives from
Chauhán.	Chauhán.
Ráthor.	Ráthor.
	Kachwáha.
	Chandél.
	Sirnet.
	Ponwar.
	Tonwar.
	Gautam.
	Raghubansi.
	Gahlot.
	Gáharwar.
	Dikhit.

The *Bhadauriyas* love their country along the banks of the Chambal and take more readily to service in the Gwalior Army than in ours. There are nevertheless a good many in the ranks of our regiments, and efforts should be made to enlist more, for they are renowned for their valour, and are less troubled by caste prejudices than many of the Rájpúts of Oudh and the North-West Provinces.

Tribal characteristics.

BHALÉ SÚLTÁN.

Shown in map as 15.

The name of this clan is derived from *Bhala*, 'a javelin,' and *Súltán* 'a lord,' the title of "lord of the lance" having bestowed upon one of the ancestors of the clan by Shahab-ud-din Ghori. The *Bhalé Súltáns* of Bulandshahr are a debased branch of the *Solankis* probably connected with the Rájas of Bhal in Guzerat. Their ancestor, Sarang Déo, took service under Pirthiráj *Chauhán*, and was killed in the attack on Kanouj. As a reward, his descendants received lands in Bulandshahr, which were added to by Shahab-ud-din Ghori for the assistance rendered him by their leader, Hamir Singh, upon whom he bestowed the title above described.

Traditional origin and history.

The *Bhale Súltáns* of Oudh give a totally different account of their origin. They say they are descended from Rai Dudhrich, a cadet of the great *Tilokchandi Bais* family, who turned Muhammadan. It is stated by some that they are sprung from Rai Barihár, a *Bais* Rájpút, whose descendants expelled the aboriginal Bhárs, while others deny their Rájpút ancestry and say that they are simply *Báris* (torch bearers) who were ennobled for their bravery by Raja *Tilok Chand.* It is probable that they are one of the mixed Rájpút tribes.

Bhale Súltáns are unknown in Rájpútána and the Punjáb. In Oudh and the North-West Provinces they have a male population of 9,000 and are found chiefly in the Sultanpur and Bulandshahr districts.

Geographical distribution.

The Bulandshahr *Bhale Súltáns* worship Rám Chandra and Vishnu; those of Oudh Débi. The latter regard sugarcane fields, tiled houses, and pucca wells, as unlucky, and never have them in or about their villages.

Religion.

The *Bhale Súltáns* intermarry with the following clans :—

In Bulandshahr.		In Oudh.	
Give their daughters to	**Take wives from**	**Give their daughters to**	**Take wives from**
Bargújar.	Bargújar.	Kalhans.	Raghubansi.
Jarauliya.	Jaiswar.	Kanhpuriya.	Gargbansi
Bais.	Bais.	Amethiya.	Chandauri.
Kachwaha.	Kachwáha.	Band halgot.	Bisén.
Chauhán.	Bargala.		Raikwar.
Tonwar.	Jais.		
Pundir.			
Gaur.			
Chandarbansi.			

BHÁTTI.

Shown in map as 16.

Their traditional origin.

The name of this clan is derived from the Sanskrit *bhatta*, 'a d.' It is really a sept of the *Jádus*, but is of far greater importance than the parent stock, and therefore needs a separate description. The *Bhátti* is the largest and most widely distributed Rájpút tribe in the Punjáb. Its members are the modern representatives of Krishna, and the heads of the Lunar race. At a very early period the *Bháttis* were driven from India across the Indus, but they afterwards returned and settled in the Punjáb. The *Bhátti* kingdom extended from the Salt Range to Kashmir, their capital being at Gaznipur near Rawal Pindi. About the 2nd century B.C. they were driven across the Jhelum by Indo-Scythian invaders, who followed them up, and dispersed them south of the Sutlej. The *Bháttis*, however, retained their hold on Kashmir until 1339. The clan have a tradition that they crossed the Indus about 700 years ago under a chief called Bhátti, who had two sons—Dusal and Jaisal. Dusal founded Bhattiána, *i. e.*, Sirsa and Hissar, and Jaisal, Jaisalmere. Though deprived of their principalities in the Punjáb, they left numerous settlements in that province, some of which may be traced by the names of certain places such as Bhattinda and Bhátnér. Most of the Rájpúts of the Punjáb plains are of *Bhátti* origin. The *Ráthors* emigrated from Kanouj to Bikaneer in 1194, and treacherously possessed themselves of a portion of the *Bhátti* territory.

Bhátti settlements in Oudh and the North-Western Provinces.

The *Bháttis* of the North-West Provinces claim to be *Jádóns* who returned from beyond the Indus in the 7th or 8th century. A considerable number were forcibly converted to Islám by Alá-ud-din Khilji in the 14th century. The Bulandshahr colony claim to have settled there, under the protection of Pirthiráj, after expelling the aboriginal Méos.

Geographical distribution.

In Rájpútána, the *Bháttis* are found in Meywar, Marwar, Jaisalmeer and Bikanir, and number 31,000 males. In the North-West Provinces *Bhátti* settlements are found in Bulandshahr, Etah, and Bareilly, with a male population of 5,000.

The principal septs of the clan are as follows :—

In Rájpútána	In Oudh and the North-West Provinces.
Kelan. Khiánh. Jaisalmeria. Púgalliya. Maldót. Arjanót.	Bhátti. Jaiswar.

The Muhammadan *Bháttis* of Hariána and the Doáb are called *Ránghars*.

The *Bháttis* intermarry with the following clans :—

RÁJPÚTÁNA.		OUDH AND THE NORTH-WEST PROVINCES.	
Give their daughters to	Take wives from	Give their daughters to	Take wives from
Gahlót. Parihar. Ráthor.	Ráthór. Pariha. Gáhlót.	Ráthor. Parihar. Gahlót. Pundir. Chauhán. Tonwar. Kachwáha.	Bargújar. Dhákre. Jarauliya. Jaiswar. Bais. Gaur. Janghára. Katheriya. Chandarbansi. Bhalesultan. Chhonkar.

The *Bháttis* are clean and fair complexioned, and though rather short, are sturdy and well set up. They will not eat pig. Being of the Lunar race their favourite god is Krishna, and they consequently belong to the *Vaishnáva* sect. The tribal divinity is Karniji.

BHIRGHUBANSI.

Shown in map as 17.

This clan claims descent from a Rájpút adventurer named Narautam Rai, who accepted service as a *baid* or family physician to the Seori Rája of Bhataur in the Benares district, on his return from a pilgrimage to Gaya. By fair means or foul Narautam Rai succeeded his master, and like a great many other Rájpút heroes married the daughter of Rája Banár, a mythical ruler of Benares. Two sons, Bhao Rai and Bhantu Rai, were the result of this union, and their descendants are now the principal representatives of the clan.

Traditional origin and history.

Bhirghubansis are almost entirely confined to the Benares district of the North-West Provinces. They have a male population of 5,000.

Geographical distribution.

The tribal divinity is the goddess Débi. The clan belongs to the *Savaran gotra*. The *Bhirghubansis* are divided into the following septs:—

Religion.

Tribal divisions. | Bhirghubansi proper. | Badhauliya.

Bhirghubansis contract marriages with members of most of the clans belonging to the Benares district.

Marriages.

BISÉN.

Shown in map as 18.

The name of this clan is derived from the Sanskrit *visva* 'entire' and *séna* an 'army'. They claim descent from a Hindu adventurer called Mayúra Bhatta, and through him from a famous *Rishi* called Jamadagni.

Traditional origin.

At a remote age, Mayúra Bhatta left Benares with a few followers to wrest a kingdom from the aboriginal tribes. He settled at first in the Azamgarh district, and then, crossing the Gogra, obtained a victory over several Bhar chiefs, by which he greatly increased his territories. He is said to have had three sons by wives of different caste—one by a Rájpútni, another by a Bhúinharin, and a third by a Bráhmani. This fact, if true, shows that Mayúra Bhatta lived at a time when the laws of caste were either ignored or unknown. Certain

History.

classes of *Biséns* claim to be the descendants of emigrants from Tikári near Delhi. The clan is much divided, which leads us to infer that the title of *Bisén* was assumed by a congerie of various tribes. The head of the clan is the Rája of Majhauli in Gorakhpur.

The *Bisén* clan is not represented in Rájpútána. In Oudh and the North-West Provinces it has a male population of 51,000, and is found chiefly in the Allahabad, Benares, Mirzapur, Jaunpur, Ghazipur, Ballia, Gorakhpur, Básti, Azamgarh, Fyzábad, Gonda and Bahraich districts.

Geographical distribution.

The *Bisén* are divided into two houses—the *Biséns* of Majhauli, and the *Biséns* of Deorhi, and are further separated into the five following *gotras* :—

Tribal divisions.

Parasar.	Sandil.	Batas.
Bharraddwaj.	Atri.	

The *Biséns* intermarry with the following clans :—

Biséns of Majhauli.		Biséns of Deorhi.	
Give their daughters to	Take wives from	Give their daughters to	Take wives from
Chauhán.	Surajbansi.	Bais.	Chandél.
Bhadauriya.	Sirnet.	Bhale-Sultán.	Kanhpuriya.
Ráthor.	Kausik.		Kath Bais.
Parihar.	Bandhalgoti.		Chauhán.
Gaharwar.	Sombansi.		
	Bachhgot.		
	Kanhpuriya.		

BÚNDELAS.

Shown in map as 19.

A Rájpút tribe, generally considered to be of spurious descent. Popular tradition ascribes the origin of the name *Búndela* to Rája Pancham, a descendant of the *Gaharwar* Rájas of Benares and Kantit in Mirzapur, who being expelled from his kingdom by his brother, retired to the shrine of Bindáchal, and became a votary of Bhawáni. While residing there, he resolved to offer himself up as a sacrifice to that deity, and in pursuance of his vow, had already inflicted a wound on his person, when suddenly Bhawáni appeared and restrained him. In reward for his devotion she promised him that his kingdom should be restored, and directed that in commemoration of the drop of blood (*búnd*) which flowed from his wound, his descendants should be called *Búndelas*. Needless to say, this story is completely apocryphal, and was fabricated merely to conceal an ignoble parentage. It is probable that the founder of the clan was Hardéo, an illegitimate son of one of the *Gaharwar* Rájas of Kantit. Accompanied by a slave girl he took up his residence near Orchha, where the Khangar Rája of Karár asked for his daughter in marriage. Hardéo consented on condition that he should come with all his brethren and feast with him. The Khangars accepted the invitation, and were all treacherously poisoned. The *Gaharwars* then took possession of their country, and the name of *Búndela* or *Bandéla* was given to the offspring of Hardéo and his concubine, as they were the sons of a *bandi* or slave girl. The *Búndelas* are universally regarded as spurious Rájpúts, from which it may be inferred that the clan originated in a congerie of various adventurers who flocked into Bundelkhund about the 14th century, after the *Chandéls* had been humiliated by the *Chauháns*, and they in their turn had been forced to yield to the Musalmans.

Traditional origin.

The *Búndelas* first settled at Kalinjar, Kalpi, and Mahoni. In the 14th century their Rája Malkhan founded Orcha. From his time the *Búndelas* became the most powerful of the tribes to the west of the Jumna, and gave their name to the tract now known as Bundelkhund. Most of the leading *Búndela* families claim descent from the 12 sons of Rudr Partáp, the son of Rája Malkhan. By 1608 the *Búndelas* had become very numerous, and were divided into 3 kingdoms—Orcha, Chanderi, and Mahoba. In that year, Bir Singh Déo, the Rája of Orcha, incurred the wrath of Akbar by waylaying and murdering Abu Fazl, the favourite minister of the Emperor, when he was passing through Bundelkhund on his way from the Dekhan to Delhi. It is said that the murder was committed at the instigation of Selim, afterwards known as Jahangir; at any rate Bir Singh Déo rose to great favour at court on Jahangir's accession to the throne. Soon after the accession of Shah Jahán in 1627, the *Búndelas* of Orcha revolted, but were defeated by the Muhammadans, who confiscated their territory. Meanwhile Champat Rai of Mahoba frustrated all the efforts of the Mughals to reduce him to submission. Although three large armies were sent against him, he held out in the rugged country bordering on the Betwa, where by the celerity of his movements he defied the attempts of the Musalman leaders to capture him. Wearied of the struggle, the Mughals at last withdrew. When the principal portion of their troops had retired, Champat Rai rapidly assembled his adherents, and began to make reprisals by driving in the imperial outposts, attacking convoys, and harassing their minor garrisons by night attacks, until at length, emboldened by these successes, he met the Mughals in the open field, and totally routed them near Orcha. After various fruitless expeditions, a peace was concluded about 1640, by which the Delhi court acknowledged the independence of the Orcha State. In the struggle between the sons of Shah Jahán for their father's throne, the *Búndelas* of Orcha espoused the cause of Dára, while those of Mahoba, under Champat Rai, took service under Aurangzéb, and fought for him at the battle of Sámugarh (1658). Chhatarsál, the son of Champat Rai, induced the Hindu princes of Málwa and Bundelkhund to unite in a league to resist the proselytising efforts of Aurangzéb. In this he was partly successful. With consummate skill he avoided a general action but wasted the country held by his enemies, cut off the convoys from the Dekhan, and by ambuscades and an intimate knowledge of the country, managed to cut off or elude the imperial troops. After a series of victories Chhatarsál possessed himself of the fortress of Garhakota near Saugor, and the whole of the country to the east and south of the Chambal as far as Rewah. In 1707, he was confirmed in these possessions by the Emperor Bahadur Shah. Seven years later, Muhammad Khan, the Pathán Governor of Farrukhabad, made a raid into Bundelkhund, defeated the *Búndelas*, and forced Chhatarsál to call in the Mahrattas to his assistance. The latter restored him to his possessions, and in gratitude Chhatarsál bestowed upon them Kalpi, Saugor, Jhansi, and Garhakóta, on the express condition that his heirs and successors should be maintained in possession of the rest. The descendants of Chhatarsál still hold the independent principalities of Charkhari, Ajaigarh, Bijáwar, Panna, and Orcha. The State of Chhatarpur was also formerly ruled by *Búndelas*, but the present dynasty is descended from a *Ponwar* adventurer who dispossessed his master early in the present century. *Búndelas* are not found in Rájpútána. In the North-West Provinces they have a male population of 4,800, chiefly located in the Jhansi and Lalitpur districts. They form the principal portion of the inhabitants of the small native states included in the Bundelkhund Ageny.

Geographical distribution.

Búndélas worship Krisnna, but are inclined to *Shákta* worship as they reverence Dúrga.

Religion.

Marriages.

Búndelas intermarry with *Dhanderes* and *Ponwars*. The *Ponwars* rank a shade higher in caste than the *Búndelas*, and the chief of the latter are consequently anxious to take their daughters in marriage.

Tribal peculiarities.

The *Búndelas* have always been a turbulent and troublesome race, averse to labour, and ever ready to quarrel with each other or their rulers, if they happen to think themselves aggrieved. Speaking of their petty Rájas before the Mutiny, Sleeman states "there is hardly a single chief of the Hindu military class in Bundelkhund who does not keep a gang of robbers of some kind or other, and consider it a valuable and legitimate source of revenue."* In 1857 the *Búndelas* plundered the country and roamed about in organized gangs, and the recent revival of dacoity in Bundelkhund shows that they have not altogether abandoned their old pursuits.

CHANDÉL.

Shown in map as 20.

Traditional origin.

The name of this clan is a corruption of the Sanskrit *chandra*, 'the moon.' The tribal legend is that their ancestor Chandra Bráhm was the son of Chandra the Moon God, by Hemaváti, the daughter of Hémráj the Bráhman *parohit* of the *Gaharwar* Rája of Benares. The legend was no doubt invented to conceal some impurity of origin.†

History.

Chandra Bráhm was a distinguished warrior. He took Benares, and founded the two great fortresses of Mahoba and Kalinjar in Bundelkhund, which were the principal cities of the *Chandél* dynasty which ruled over Bundelkhund up to the beginning of the 12th century. It had been predicted that the *Chandél* sovereigns would lose their property as soon as they abandoned the title of *Bráhm*. In 1184, Parmál Déo, the reigning Rája, discarded this affix, and was defeated and deposed by Prithiráj, the *Chauhán* king of Delhi. The *Chauhán-Chandél* war is a favourite theme for the poems of Hindu bards. A series of battles took place which lasted 18 days, in which the celebrated *Banáphar* heroes, Alhal and Udal, performed prodigies of valour for their *Chandel* overlords but without success. The *Chandél* army numbering 110,000 men was completely destroyed. After the capture of Mahoba the *Chandéls* repaired to Kalinjar, which was taken from them early in the 13th century by Kutub-ud-din Aibeg. After these defeats the

---

* A Journey through the kingdom of Oudh.

† This is confirmed by the fact that the term *Chandél* is generally held to mean 'an outcast.'

remnants of the *Chandél* clan were scattered, and a portion fled into Oudh. A band of *Chandél* refugees settled at Kanouj, whence they migrated to Shiurajpur, in the Cawnpore district, at the bidding of one of the early Muhammadan Emperors. The Unao settlement was formed by colonists from Chanderi in the Dekhan in the reign of Alamgir. Up to the time of the Mutiny, the head of the clan was the Rája of Shiurajpur. The Mirzapore *Chandéls* are closely connected with aboriginal Seoris; the Oudh branch with aboriginal Bhárs.

Geographical distribution.

The *Chandéls* are not found in Rájpútána. In Oudh and the North-West Provinces they number 38,000 males, and have settlements in the Shahjahanpur, Cawnpore, Benares, Mirzapur, Jaunpur, Ballia, Gorakhpur, Azámgarh, Unao, and Hardoi districts.

Religion.

The special divinities of the *Chandél* are Mahadeo and Débi. The former is worshipped by the men, and the latter by the women of the clan.

The *Chandél* intermarry with the following clans:—

Give their daughters to		Take wives from	
Baghél.	Bhadauriya.	Parihar.	Báchhal.
Chauhán.	Janghára.	Gaharwar.	Gaur.
Ahban.	Gaur.	Raikwar.	Sakarwar.
Bachhal.	Katheriya.	Janwar.	Nikumbh.
Chamar-Gaur.	Gáhlot.	Dhakré.	Katiyar.
Sakarwar.	Bais.	Bais.	Ujjaini.
Dhakré.	Bisen.	Sengar.	Gahlot.
Sómbansi.	Bachhgoti.	Katheriya.	Ponwar.
Ponwar.	Bandhalgoti.	Kausik.	Dirgbans.
	Kanhpuriya.	Donwar.	Khichar.
	Sirnet.		

CHANDRABANSI.

Shown in map as 21.

Traditional origin and history.

The title of this clan is derived from the Sanskrit *chandra*, 'the moon.' Like the appellation *Sómbansi*, it has come to represent a distinct tribe

The clan is small and unimportant, and of no historical interest.

The *Chandrabansi* are only found in the Bulandshahr and Aligarh districts of the North-West Provinces. They have a male population of 3,000.

Geographical distribution.

Religion.

Many *Chandrabansis* are *Vaishnávas*, but like most Rájpúts reverence Káli, Débi, or Dúrga.

The *Chandrabansi* intermarry with the following clans:—

Give their daughters to	Take wives from
Gaur. Báchhal. Bhalé Sultán. Gahlot. Chauhán. Bargújar. Pundir. Tonwar. Kachwáha.	Gaur. Báchhal. Bhalé Sultan.

CHAUHÁN.

Shown in map as 22.

The derivation of the title of this clan is doubtful. Some authorities suggest that it comes from the Sanskrit *chaturbáha* 'four-armed'; Tod states that it is a corruption of *chaturanga*, 'quadriform' because Anhal, the founder of the race, was so shaped. It is stated by the spurious *Chauháns* of Bijnor that their tribal name is derived from *chau* 'four' and *hán* 'loss' because when crossing the Indus in 1580 as part of Rája Mán Singh's army for the recovery of Kábul, they lost the four requisites of Hindu communion—religion (*dharm*), ceremonies (*riti*), piety (*diya*) and duties (*karma*). The *Chauháns* are one of the agnicular or fire tribes, and a detailed account of their origin will be found on page 111, under the heading of *Ponwar*.

Traditional origin.

The *Chauháns* of Delhi were the hereditary foes of the *Ráthors* of Kanouj. The last of the *Chauhán* Máhárájas of Delhi was Pirthiráj, who was defeated, and either killed or carried off to Ghazni as a captive in 1193, by Muhammad Shahab-ud-din Ghori. The ruling families of Kotah, Boondi, and Sirohi belong to this clan. The *Háras* of Boondi (a *Chauhán* sept) were originally vassals of Meywar but became independent in the time of Akbar, to whom they tendered their tribal allegiance. The *Háras* greatly distinguished themselves in the Mughal cause, but unlike the *Kachwáhas* of Jeypore always served in India, as they had stipulated in their treaty with Akbar that they should never be required to cross the Indus. In the reign of Jahangir, Rao Ratan of Boondee alone remained faithful to the Emperor at a time when all the other Rájpút princes had joined in the rebellion of his son Khurm. With his two sons Madho and Heri, Rao Ratan gained a complete victory over the insurgents at Burhanpur. As a reward, the Emperor bestowed the principality of Kotah upon Heri, the younger son, which thenceforth became independent.

History.

On the death of Aurangzéb, a contest took place between his sons Shah Alum and Azim for the throne. Their armies met near Dholpur. In the sanguinary battle which ensued, the *Háras* of Kotah sided with Prince Azim, while the *Háras* of Boondee remained faithful to the cause of Shah Alum. The latter triumphed, and as a reward bestowed the title of *Rao Rája* on the princes of Boondee. The rivalry which commenced between the two *Hára* principalities at Dholpur led to constant feuds between the two states, which lasted throughout the 18th century. In 1804 when the ill-fated army of Monson traversed Central India to attack the Mahrattas under Holkar, the Kotah State, trusting to the invincibility of the British arms, co-operated with men and supplies; but when Monson in his retreat demanded admission to the Kotah fort, he met with a decided refusal. The Regent offered to cover the British retreat with the Kotah troops, and to furnish the army with provisions, but he utterly declined to allow a panic-stricken force to enter within his walls. This was interpreted by Monson as an act of treachery, but a greater wrong was never inflicted, for besides supplying him with money and supplies, the Kotah troops fought manfully against the Mahrattas, without thought of the consequences which their action might bring upon themselves.

Chauhán settlements in Oudh and the North-West Provinces.

In Oudh and the North-West Provinces, the clan is very scattered. The Mainpuri *Chauháns* are supposed to have settled there in the 12th century under the leadership of Déo Bráhm, a descendant of Pirthiráj, the last of the *Chauhán* kings of Delhi. The Oudh *Chauháns* claim origin from Mainpuri, but have lost rank through inferior marriages. The Unao *Chauháns* are often called *Kushmao Chauháns* to distinguish them from their brethren of the Doáb, and their country is locally known as *Chauhána*. The *Chauháns* of Bijnor, Moradabad, and Gorakhpur are admittedly of doubtful origin. The Bareilly *Chauháns* claim to have emigrated into the district in 1550, after expelling the Bhils. The principal *Chauhán* families in the North-West Provinces are those of Mainpuri, Rajor, Partapnér, and Cháknagar, all of which claim descent from Pirthiráj who according to the Muhammadan historians was killed in action, but according to *Chauhán* tradition died in captivity at Ghazni. As a proof of the vitality of this legend, it may be mentioned that at the capture of Ghazni in 1842, many *Chauhán* sepoys sought out and professed to find the *Chhatri* or monument of their great ancestor within the fort.

The *Chauháns* of Rájpútána number 42,000 males and are found in Meywar, Dungarpur, Marwar, Sirohee, Bikaneer, Jeypore, Ulwar, Boondee, Kotah, and in the Gurgaon and Rohtak districts of the Punjáb. In the North-West Provinces their male population amounts to 220,000. They are found in the Saharanpur, Muzaffarnagar, Meerut, Bulandshahr, Aligarh, Muttra, Agra, Farukhabad, Mainpuri, Etawah, Etah, Bareilly, Bijnor, Moradabad, Shahjahanpur, Cawnpore, Gorakhpur, Azamgarh, Lucknow, Unao, Rai Bareli, Sitapur, Hardoi, Kheri, Fyzabad, Gonda, Bahraich, Sultanpur, Partabgarh and Bara Banki districts.

Geographical distribution.

Religion.

The favourite *Chauhán* deity is Mahadeo. In Rájpútána, the tribal divinities are Góga, Sakambari-Mata, and Ásápurna.

Chauháns are divided into the following principal septs which in the North-West Provinces are called *als*. Each *al* professes to be descended from one of the 23 sons of Rajá Lákhansi.

In Rájpútána.		In Oudh and the North-West Provinces.		
Purbiya.	Mori.	Bijai.	Kamodari.	Golbál.
Tak.	Dhúndhoti.	Hára.	Kanji.	Gal.
Bhadauriya.	Hára.	Khíchi.	Deoraya.	Barha.
Sonigirra.	Khichi.	Bhadauriya.	Kopla.	Chaleya.
Nirbhan.	Deora.	Siyáhiya.	Náhariya.	Dhandera.
Golwál.		Khera.	Avel.	
Chitha.		Puya.	Shiunagara.	
Bagore.		Deora.	Báli.	
Sanchora.		Bhahu.	Banáphar.	

The *Khichi, Narbán, Nikumbh, Thún, Bhadauriya, Bachhgoti, Rájkumár, Hára, Bilkhariya, Chirariya* and *Bandhalgoti* are generally considered to be sub-divisions of the *Chauháns.* Tod enumerates 24 *sákhas* of *Chauháns* in Rájpútána, but many have been degraded and are now Baniyas, while others have become Muhammadans. The *Kaimkháni, Ladkháni, Karárkháni, Nimkháni,* and *Ámkháni* Musalmáns were *Chauháns,* who abandoned Hinduism to save their lands from confiscation.

The *Chauháns* intermarry with the following clans:—

In Rájpútána.		In Oudh and the North-West Provinces.	
Give their daughters to	**Take wives from**	**Give their daughters to**	**Take wives from**
Kachwáha	Ponwars, and all the clans to which they give their daughters.	Kachwáha ...	Kachwáha.
Ráthor		Bhadauriya ...	Bhadauriya.
Tónwar		Ráthor ...	Ráthor.
Bargújar		Chauháns of Oudh: Bisén ...	Chamar-Gaur.
Gaur		Bandhalgoti ...	Tilókchandi Bais.
Jádu		Bhalé Sultán ...	Katiyar.
Gahlot		Bais ..	Jadon.
Sisodiya		Raikwar ...	Parihar.
Jhalla		Gaur ...	Chauháns of Oudh: Kath Bais.
		Surajbans ...	Ahban.
		Kalhans ...	Palwar.
		Barheliya	Raotar.

Chaupat Khambh.

Shown in map as 23.

This clan furnishes an instance of the fact that the barriers which separate Hindu castes, were at one time not so rigid as their traditions would have us believe. The *Chaupat-Khambh* are now Rájpúts and as such intermarry with genuine Chhatri clans; but they and their neighbours affirm that their ancestors were Bráhmans who came from beyond the Gogra, and settled in the Jaunpur district. They relate that their leaders were two brothers and that one of them, Baldéo, having married a daughter of Rájà Jaichand of Kanouj, the other brother set up a pillar (*khambh*) to denote that the family was degenerate. The history of the pillar is probably an invention to account for the name which may simply mean 'lost caste.' The mention of Rája Jai Chand in connection with one of the founders of their race, though probably a fiction fabricated for the raising of their dignity, shows how recent must be their appearance as Rájpúts.

History.

Geographical distribution.

Chaupat Khambhs are found only in the Jaunpur district. They have a male population of 1,200.

Religion.

The favourite divinity of the clan is Mahádéo. They are of the *Kassyap gotra.*

Chaupat Khambhs contract marriages with members of the following clans:—

Give their daughters to	Take wives from
Raghúbansi. Chandél. Gautam. Dirgbansi.	Bais. Gáhlót.

DHÁKARA, DHÁKRA, OR DHÁKRE.

Shown in map as 24.

The derivation of the title of this clan is unknown. They claim *Surajbansi* origin, a pretension not generally admitted. Some are said to be emigrants from the banks of the Nerbudda, but the main body of the clan emigrated from Ajmere in the 16th century, and settled in the Agra and Etawah districts of the North-West Provinces, where they acquired an evil reputation for thuggi and dacoity. They seem to have maintained their power by a close alliance with the *Bhadauriyas.* The clan gave a good deal of trouble in the Mutiny.

History and traditional origin.

Geographical distribution.

The *Dhákre* clan is only found in the Agra District and is unknown either in the Punjáb or Rájpútána. It has a male population of 6,500.

The *Dhákre* intermarry with the following clans :—

Give their daughters to	Take wives from
Gaur. Chandél. Ahban. Janwar. Ponwar. Kachwáha. Gaharwar. Nikumbh.	Gaur. Chandél. Ahban. Janwar. Kath-Bais.

DHEKAHA.

Shown in map as 25.

History.

This clan, like the *Ujjaini*, claims to be of *Ponwar* origin, and say that their ancestors emigrated from Delhi in the time of Raja Bhoj.

Geographical distribution.

The *Dhekaha* are found chiefly in the Sháhabad or Bhojpur district of Behar. Their exact numbers are not stated in the Census Report, but their male population is believed to amount to about 2,000.

Religion.

The favourite deity of the clan is the goddess Dévi, whom they propitiate at births and marriages by the sacrifice of a he-goat.

Dhekahas contract marriages with members of the following clans :—

Give their daughters to	Take wives from
Donwar. Lautamiya. Tilaunta. Gáhlót.	Lautamiya. Surwar.

DIKHIT.

Shown in map as 26.

Traditional origin.

The title of this clan is from the Sanskrit *Díkshita* 'initiated', a title bestowed upon one of their ancestors by Rája Vikramajit of Ujjain about 50 B. C. They claim to be *Surajbansis* of Ajudhya.

The founder of this clan was Rája Dúrg Bháo who emigrated at a remote period from Ajudhya to Guzerat, where his descendants took the title of *Dúrgbansis.* Twenty-four generations later, Kalian Sáh, *Dúrgbans* received from Rája Vikrámajit of Ujjain the title of *Díkshita*,* which thenceforth became the name of his clan. The *Díkits* remained in Guzerat for several centuries, but in the 11th century they entered the service of the *Ráthor* monarchs of Kanouj who gave them land in Banda. The *Díkhits* shared in the ruin of the *Ráthors* when their capital Kanouj was taken by Shahab-ud-din Ghori in 1194, and the clan was then broken up. The eldest branch retained the family estate at Samoni in Banda, where they are found to the present day. The Rája's second son Udaibhan, founded the Oudh colony called *Díkhitána*; the third son crossed the Gogra and the Rapti and settled at Bansi in Gorakhpur; the fourth migrated east and founded the town of Bilkhar in Partabgarh. The *Díkhit* dominions in Oudh were at one time very extensive, and the clan held a high position among Rájpúts. In 1556, Hému the Hindu general of the Pathán Muhammad Shah Adily, King of Bengal, opposed the Mughals, under Akbar, at Pánipat near Delhi. It was the first time for years that a Hindu has been seen at the head of affairs, and as a natural result, a vast number of Rájpúts flocked to his standard. This gave to the campaign something of the nature of a religious war, the consequence being that, after Akbar's victory, a fear of forcible conversion to Islám spread over the whole country. This fear was probably the immediate cause which prevented the *Díkhit* chief from tendering his submission to the Mughals. Shortly afterwards, a Muhammadan army invested his fort, and forced him to decisive action. Clad in armour, and dressed in saffron robes to indicate that they meant to win or die, the Rájpúts charged the Mughal infantry and scattered them. Victory seemed certain, but at this juncture the imperial cavalry charged the Rájpúts before the latter had time to reform, and killed nearly all their leaders. The *Díkhits* never recovered from this defeat, and from that time began the decadence of the clan. In the Mutiny their Rája Daya Shankar Singh remained loyal to the British Government and gave valuable assistance to the Civil authorities. The *Dúrgbansis* of Jalaun are a branch of the *Díkhits* of Bilkhar, who entered the district about 400 years ago, and drove out the Bhárs at the request of the Oudh Government.

History.

The *Díkhit* clan is not represented in Rájpútána and the Punjáb In Oudh and the North-West Provinces it has a male population of 33,000, and is found in the Fatehpur, Banda Hamirpur, Ghazipur, Gorakhpur, Azamgarh, Jalaun, Unao, and Rai Bareli districts.

Geographical distribution.

---

* *i.e.* 'initiated'

The *Díkhits* intermarry with the following clans :—

	Give their daughters to	Take wives from
Rewa and Bundelkhand.	Baghél.	Baghél.
	Parihar.	Parihar.
	Gaharwar.	Gaharwar.
Dóab.	Parihar.	Baghél.
	Chauhán.	Khfchar.
	Bhadauriya.	Sombans.
	Kachwáha.	Ponwar.
	Hára.	Bisén.
	Jdon.	
Oudh.	Chauhán.	Bisén
	Bhadauriya.	Gautam.
	Kachwáha.	Chauhán.
	Sengar.	Gahlot.
	Ráthor	Gaharwar.
	Sombansi	Raikwar.
		Janwár.
		Ponwar.
		Sombansi.
		Raghubansi.
		Amethiya.
		Kath-Bais.

Dirgbansi, Drigbansi, or Dúrgbansi.

Shown in map as 27.

This clan is really a sub-division of the *Díkhits.* It claims descent from the *Surajbans* kings of Ajudhya. At a remote period a cadet of the family name Dúrg Bhao is said to have emigrated to Guzerat, where his descendants took the title of *Dúrgbansi, i. e.,* children of Dúrg. Several generations later, one of their chieftains named Kalyán Sáh, received the title of *Díkhit* (*q. v.*), which thenceforth became the tribal name. About 550 years ago, a number of *Díkhit* adventurers entered the service of Muhammad Tughlak and settled in Oudh. About a century later their descendants were invited by the Muhammadan authorities to expel the Bhárs from Jaunpur. Their efforts were completely successful, and shortly afterwards this section of the clan reverted to its old name of *Dúrgbansi,* in honour of one of Dúrg Sahai, one of their principal leaders. It is stated that the title of Rája was conferred on Harku Rai, their elected chief, by the Emperor Akbar, in recognition of the valour displayed by the clan at a great tournament held at Allahabad. In the 18th century the *Drigbansis* were deprived of their possessions by Balwant Singh, Rája of Benares, but regained them in the annexation of the district by the British. Litigation and extravagance led to the loss of most of their ancestral domains, and by the time of the Mutiny the *Dirgbansí* Rája was in very reduced circumstances. From his antecedents, poverty, and relationship to the famous rebel Koer Singh, he might well have been tempted to rebellion; but on the contrary he behaved with conspicuous loyalty, and was rewarded with considerable estates and a title.

Traditional origin and history.

Dirgbansis are found chiefly in the Jaunpur District of the North-West Provinces. They have a male population of 7,600.

Geographical distribution.

The clan is addicted to *Shákta* worship and pays special reverence to Dúrga. Like the *Dikhits* the *Dirgbansis* belong to the *Kassyap gotra.*

Religion.

Dirgbansis contract marriages with members of the following clans :—

Give their daughters to	Take wives from
Sómbansi.	Bisén....
Rájkumar.	Nikumbh.
Gaharwar.	Kath-Bais.
Raghúbans,	Chuapat Khambh.
Nikumbh.	Gargbansi.
Bisén.	Chandél.
Surajbansi.	Donwar.
Sirnét.	

DORS.

Shown in map as 28.

The *Dors* give a curious account of the derivation of their tribal name. They state that one of their kings offered his head to some local goddess, and was thus called *Dund*, which was afterwards corrupted into *Dor*. They claim kinship with the *Ponwars*, and their name is certainly found in the genealogical tables of that tribe.

Traditional origin.

The *Dors* are supposed to have emigrated from the middle to the upper Doáb, early in the 10th century. They appear to have held a large tract of country between the Jumna and the Ganges, long anterior to the Muhammadan invasions. Hardatta, a *Dor* chieftain, who founded Meerut and built Hapur, preserved possession of his family domain at Baran by becoming a convert to Islám, and paying a large ransom to Mahmúd of Ghazni. About the beginning of the 12th century, the power of the *Dors* began to wane. They were attacked by Méos and Játs, who at last became such a source of trouble to the *Dor* Rája, that he was glad to call in others to aid him in restoring order. A large band of *Bargújars* were on their way from Alwar to aid Pirthiraj in his war with the Mahoba *Chandéls*. To Rája Partap Singh, the leader of the party, was entrusted the duty of subduing the Méos, and after a long and determined struggle he succeeded in driving them out. As a reward the *Dor* Rája gave him his daughter in marriage, with a dowry of 150 villages. The *Bargújars* remained nominal feudatories of the *Dors* until 1193, when the latter were again attacked by the Musal máns under Kutub-ud-din Aibeg, who captured Meerut and Baran. Chandra Sén who was the *Dor* Rája at this time, repelled the attacks of the enemy with great vigour, until betrayed by his kinsman Ajaipál, and a confidential Bráhman retainer. Chandra Sén perished in the assault of his fort, but not before he had killed with an arrow Khwája Lál Ali, the leader of the Muhammadan troops. The power of the *Dors* rapidly declined after this, and the clan has now but little influence and no land.

History.

The Rájpútána *Dors* are found in small number in Meywar and Dungarpur. In the North-West Provinces they are chiefly settled in the Meerut, Aligarh, Bulandshahr, Moradabad and Banda districts. Their total male population is about 1,000. A few *Dors* are also scattered throughout the Saugor district of the Central Provinces.

Geographical distribution.

Dors contract marriages with Rájpúts of the following clans :—

Give their daughters to	Take wives from
Gahlot.	Chamar-Gaur.
Tonwar.	Janghára.
Chauhán.	Gautam.
Bargújar.	Katheriya.
Chauhán.	Chauhán.
Sómwál.	Sómwál.
Pundir..	Pundir.
Jhotiyána.	Jhotiyána.

DÓNWAR OR DÓMWAR.

Shown in map as 29.

This clan is of doubtful origin, and it is probable that it is in some way connected with the aboriginal *Dóms* as the tribal title seems to indicate. Even in the 12th century their status as Rájpúts was doubtful (*vide* account of the *Sirnet* clan on page 125), and they are now of little consideration among their Kshatriya brethren. There is a Bhúinhár branch of the tribe, and both acknowledge descent from a common ancestor. The *Dónwar* Rájpúts claim Dón Darauli in the Sáran district as the ancient seat of their race, and say they are descended from Mayúra Bhatta, the mythical progenitor of the *Biséns* of Majhaulí; the latter, however, disclaim all connection with them. The *Dónwars* at one time ruled over a considerable portion of Tirhút. They are of dark complexion with non-Aryan features, which seems to confirm the suspicion of their aboriginal origin. If men of this clan are considered suitable for enlistment, care should be taken to ascertain that they are Rájpúts and not Bhúinhars. They are sometimes known as *Rainiya,* from the village of Raini in Azamgarh.

History.

Dónwars are found chiefly in the Ghazipur, Ballia, Azamgarh, and Gorakhpur districts of the North-West Provinces. Their male population is not stated in the last Census Report.

Geographical distribution.

Religion.

Dónwars are of the *Batas* and *Kassyap gotras.* Their favourite deity is the goddess Dúrga.

Dónwars contract marriages with Rájpúts of the following clans:—

Give their daughters to	Take wives from
Pónwar.	Kath-Bais.
Chandél.	Dhekhaha,
Pálwar.	Kákan.
Gahlot.	Nandwak.
Nikumbh.	Udmattia.
Drigbansi.	
Kákan.	
Nandwak.	
Udmattia.	

GAHALWÁR OR GAHARWÁR.

Shown in map as 30.

The name of this clan is connected with the Sanskrit *gah* meaning 'a dweller in a cave or deep jungle.' It is probable that they are of the same stock as the *Ráthors,* the latter having adopted Bráhmanism at a time when the *Gaharwars* stil adhered to Buddhism.

Traditional origin.

The early history of this clan is very obscure. They claim to be descended from Rája Jai Chand of Kanouj, but this must be a myth as the *Gaharwars* furnished Kanouj with a dynasty previous to its being occupied by *Ráthors.* It is probable that they became incorporated with the latter and were dispersed on the conquest of Kanouj by Muhammad Shahab-ud-din Ghori in 1194. The *Gaharwars* of Cawnpore even now derive their name from *ghar báhar,* because they were turned out of house and home after the fall of Kanouj. In Farukhabad there is a large and important colony founded in the 12th century by two brothers called Mán and Mahésh. In Gorakhpur they claim to have come from Benares, which is highly probable, as the kingdom of Kanouj extended as far as

History.

that city. The head of the clan is the *Gaharwar* Rája of Kantit in Mirzapur. The Ghazipur branch claim to be descended from a cadet of this family who was given land in the district by one of the Delhi Emperors.

Geographical distribution.

The *Gaharwar* clan is peculiar to Oudh and the North-West Provinces and is unknown in Rájpútána and the Punjáb. It has a male population of 28,000 and is found chiefly in the Farukhabad, Etah, Cawnpore, Allahabad, Mirzapur, Ghazipur, and Hardoi districts.

Religion.

The favourite *Gaharwar* deity is Dúrga.

The *Gaharwars* intermarry with the following clans:—

Give their daughters to		Take wives from	
In Oudh.	Gaur.	In Oudh.	Dhakré.
	Bais.		Janwár.
	Chandél.	In the Doáb.	Nikumbh.
	Sombansi.		Chandél.
	Dikhit.		Raikwar.
In the Doáb.	Chauhán.		Gaur.
	Ráthor.	Eastern districts.	Harihobans.
	Bhadauriya.		Banáphar.
	Kachwáha.		Kath Bais.
Eastern districts.	Raghubansi.		Sakarwar,
	Nikumbh.		
	Chandé.		
	Kausik.		

GAHLOT OR SISODIYA.

Shown in map as 31.

This clan belongs to the Solar race. Its name is derived by some from *guha* 'a cave,' because one of the wives of the Rána of Meywar, escaping from the sack of Balabhi in 524, took refuge among some Bráhmans, and was delivered of a son in a cave. The boy was called *Goha* or 'cave-born' by his protectors, and his descendants bear the title of *Gohilot*

Their traditional origin.

Grahilot, or *Gahlot*. Others derive the name of the clan from *gahla* 'a slave girl,' in allusion to their real descent.

History.

The *Sisodiyas* or *Gahlots* claim descent from Ráma, king of Ajudhya. The clan emigrated from Oudh in the 2nd century, and established itself in Guzerat in 319. A *Sisodiya* dynasty founded Balabhi in Kattiawar, and ruled over India and Ceylon for upwards of a thousand years. After being driven out of Kattiawar by Scythian invaders from the west, the clan settled at Ahár near the modern Oodeypore, from which they derive their title of *Aháriya*. In the 12th century the ruling family was represented by two brothers, one of whom settled at Dungarpur where his descendants still call themselves *Aháriyas*, and the other at Sisodha, which gave a name to the principal section of the clan. The *Gahlóts* have a very curious tradition that the Ránas of Oodeypore are of Persian descent. They state that Pratáb Chand *Gahlót*, the conqueror of Chitór, was married to a granddaughter of the famous Persian monarch Nausherwán, whose wife was Marian, daughter of Maurice the Greek Emperor of Byzantium. The *Sisodiyas* in ancient times were distinguished for their unyielding hostility towards Islám. Their celebrated chieftain Rána Sangar commanded the Rájpút army which was defeated by the Mughals under Bábar at Futtehpur Sikri, and by their haughty refusals to allow daughters of their house to marry the Mughal princes, they repeatedly incurred the wrath of the Delhi Emperors.

Gahlót settlements in Oudh and the North-West Provinces.

Gahlót settlers established themselves in Etawah about 1325, where they were assigned large grants of land by the Emperor Muhammad Tughlak. In 1189 a *Gahlót* adventurer called Govind Rao assisted Prithiráj, the *Chauhán* Rája of Delhi, against Jai Chand, the *Ráthor* Rája of Kanouj. For his services he received a grant of several villages in Farukhabad and Cawnpore, whence the clan spread itself all over Oudh and the North-West Provinces, expelling the aboriginal Bhars and Koris.

Geographical distribution.

The *Gahlót* and *Sisodiya* are numerous in Rájpútána, where they have a male population of 41,000. The Mahárána of Oodeypore or Meywar is the head of the clan, and ranks highest among the Rájpút princes. In Oudh and the North-West Provinces the *Gahlót* only number about 2,000 males, and occupy a comparatively humble position owing to their poverty, which has compelled them to seek wives from inferior clans. In Rájpútána the *Gahlót* and *Sisodiya* are found chiefly in Meywar; in Oudh and the North-West Provinces their settlements are scattered through the Mozaffarnagar, Meerut, Aligarh, Muttra, Agra, Etah, and Cawnpore districts.

The principal septs of the clan are as follows :—

Gahlót.	Kailwa.	Boránna.
Sisodiya.	Mohar.	Gohil.
Ahára.	Túberkiya.	Ranáwat.
Manguliya.	Chandráwat.	Sakhtawat.

Tribal divisions.

Both in Rájpútána and the North-West Provinces the chief tribal divinity is Mahádéo. The *Gahlót* belongs to the *Kassyap gotra*, and intermarry with the following clans :—

Rájpútána.		Oudh and North-West Provinces.	
Give their daughters to	Take wives from	Give their daughters to	Take wives from
Kachwáha.	Kachwáha.	Chauhán.	Báchal.
Jádu.	Jádu.	Kachwáha.	Dhakré.
Chauhán.	Bhátti.	Pundir.	Bais.
Ráthor.	Chauhán.	Solanki.	Baresari.
Ponwar.	Ráthor.	Ráthor.	Bhalé Sultán.
Bhátti.	Gaur.	Ponwar.	Chhokar.
	Bargújar.	Bargújar.	Indauliya.
	Ponwar.	Katheriya.	Jais.
	Tonwar.	Parihar.	Gaurahar.
	Bhátti.	Sakarwar.	Ráwat.
		Chandél.	Puraj.
		Bais.	Uriya.
		Ujjaini.	Dikhit.
		Raghubansi.	Parihar.
		Nikumbh.	Chandel
		Kansik.	Sengar.
		Gautam.	Chauhan.
			Donwar.
			Gautam.
			Kákan.
			Karchuliya.
			Banáphar.
			Raghubansi.
			Barheliya.

Garg or Gargbansi.

Shown in map as 32.

Traditional origin and history.

The title of this clan is derived from Garg, the name of a famous Hindu *Rishi* whom they claim as their ancestor. The latter is supposed to have been summoned from Kanouj by Rája Dasráth, the father of Ráma, to aid him in the performance of the *Aswaméda** or horse sacrifice. The *Gargbansis* are now of little importance, and take a low place among Rájpúts. There is a Bhúinhar branch which is admittedly of the same stock. The *Garg* Chhatris are generally regarded as inferior *Bais*, and should seldom be enlisted.

Geographical distribution.

The *Garg* clan is only found in Oudh and the North-West Provinces. It has a male population of 5,000, and is scattered throughout the Azamgarh, Fyzabad, and Sultanpur districts.

The *Garg* intermarry with the following clans:—

Give their daughters to	Take wives from
Kalhans.	Barwar.
Súrajbans.	Raikhwar.
Bisén.	Kausik.
Gautam.	Kath-Bais.
Bandhalgoti.	Palwar.
Bhalé Sultán.	
Sirnet.	
Kanhpuriya.	
Sombans.	
Gahlot.	
Bachhgot.	

Gaur.

Shown in map as 33.

Traditional origin.

This clan is supposed to take its tribal name from *Gauda*, one of the ancient names of the western portion of Bengal, which was ruled over by a dynasty of this race.

* See page 141.

Little is known of the history of the clan. They are believed to have held Ajmere previous to its conquest by the *Chauháns*. They served with distinction in the wars of Pirthiráj, and one of their leaders founded the small *Gaur* state of Sapur in Rájpútána which after surviving seven centuries of Mughal domination, was annexed in 1809 by the Mahrattas under Scindia.

History.

The *Gaur* clan is very numerous in the North-West Provinces. The Farukhabad settlement was founded about the 12th century, by emigrants from Katehar in the Shahjahanpur district, led by two brothers, Sarhé and Barhé. The Etawah branch state that they came from Rupur, in Rájpútána, as early as 650, expelled the Méos, and prospered exceedingly until the beginning of the 12th century, when they were crushingly defeated by the great *Banáphar* heroes Alhál and Udal. The Cawnpore colony claim descent from Rája Prithivi Déo, who came from Garh Gajni to the court of Jai Chand, the *Ráthor* king of Kanouj, whose daughter he married receiving land in the Kalpi and Manikpur districts as her dowry. In one of his raids on the Méos, Prithivi Déo saw and became enamoured of the daughter of Méo Rája, and carried her off and married her. The Méos dissembling their wrath, invited the *Gaurs* to a feast, and at a preconcerted signal murdered all their guests except the two Ránis who escaped. The *Méo* Ráni took refuge with a Bráhman, and the *Ráthorin* with a Chamár; hence the two great sub-divisions of *Báhman-Gaur and Chamar-Gaur*. The latter asserts its superiority over the former as being of pure Rájpút blood by both parents. It is, however, probable that the story was fabricated to conceal a connection with the low caste Chamárs. The third sub-division of the clan is the *Bhát-Gaur*, but the story of their origin is unknown. The *Améthiyas* of Oudh are a branch of the *Chamar-Gaur* and cherish the memory of their traditional origin by worshipping the *ránpi* or currier's scraper. The *Gaurahar* of Budaun, Aligarh, and Etah are also of *Chamar-Gaur* origin but have lost status by inferior marriages.

Gaur settlements in Oudh and the North-West Provinces.

The *Gaur* of Rájpútána only number 3,500 males and are found chiefly in Meywar and Jeypore. In Oudh and the North-West Provinces the *Gaur* have a male population of 39,000 and are scattered through the Farukhabad, Etawah, Etah, Budaun, Shahjahanpur, Moradabad, Cawnpore, Hamirpur, Unao, Sitapur, and Hardoi districts.

Geographical distribution.

The principal septs of the *Gaur* are as follows :—

In Rájpútána.		In Oudh and the North-West Provinces.	
Untahir ...	This is on the authority of Tod. It is probable that many of these septs are now extinct.	Chamar-Gaur ...	It is probable that the four first named are connected with Chamars, Bráhmans, and Bháts, and the fifth with Ahirs.
Silhala ...		Báhman-Gaur ...	
Tur ...		Bhát-Gaur ...	
Dusena ...		Améthiya ...	
Budaun ...		Gaurahar ...	

The *Gaur* intermarry with the following clans :—

In Rájpútána.		In Oudh and the North-West Provinces.	
Give their daughters to	Take wives from	Give their daughters to	Take wives from
Gahlot.	Kachwáha.	Ponwar.	Dikhit.
Rathors.	Ponwar.	Baghél.	Janwár.
Tonwar.	Bargújar.	Bais.	Chandél.
Kachwáha.	Tonwar.	Chandél.	Kath-Bais.
Bargújar.	Chauhán.	Raikwar.	Gaharwar.
Chauhán.		Katiyar.	Dhakré.
		Sombansi.	Raikwar.
		Nikumbh.	Ahban.
		Dhakre.	

In Oudh and the North-West Provinces the *Báhman-Gaur* and *Bhát-Gaur* can contract alliances with the same clans as the *Chamar-Gaur*, but have to pay heavily for the privilege.

GAUTAM.

Shown in map as 34.

This clan belongs to the Lunar race but is not one of the 36 royal tribes. Their history goes back to the times when the restrictions of caste were little regarded, for although admittedly Kshatriyas, the

Gautams claim a Bráhman called Siringhi as their ancestor, one of whose descendants married a daughter of the *Gaharwar* Rája of Kanouj and received as her dowry all the country from Allahabad to Hardwar. From this event the clan ceased to be Bráhmans and became Kshatriyas, the head of the family taking the title of Rája of Argal, a village in the Fatehpur district.

Traditional origin.

In the 11th century the *Gautam* Rájas ruled over a considerable tract of country on both banks of the Ganges. In 1183 they generously bestowed several villages on Pármal, the *Chandél* Rája of Mahoba, after his defeat by Pirthiráj *Chauhán*. About 1250 the *Gautam* Rájas of Argal refused to pay tribute to the Muhammadan kings of Dehli, and their Governor in Oudh tried to seize the *Gautam* Ráni while bathing in the Ganges at Buxar. An account of how she was rescued by two *Bais* adventurers will be found in the history of that clan. It is said that the Rája promised his son-in-law as a dowry all the villages whose names the bride could pronounce without stopping to take breath. She had already named 1,440, when the Rája's son, seeing his heritage slipping away from him, seized her by the throat, and prevented further utterance. The 1,440 villages referred to, all on the left bank of the Ganges, constituted what was afterwards known as *Baiswára*. In 1194 the *Gautams* were overwhelmed, along with their *Ráthor* allies, by the Musalmans under Muhammad Ghori. The clan gradually recovered its power, but in the reign of Humáyun they participated in the revolt of Sher Shah, which brought upon them the vengeance of the Emperor. Branches of the clan settled in Gorakhpur, Unao, and Ghazipur about 500 years ago. In Azamgarh they have mostly become Muhammadans. The head of the clan is the Rája of Argal in Fatehpur.

Geographical distribution.

The *Gautam* clan is not known in Rájpútána. In Oudh and the North-West Provinces it has a male population of 41,000 found chiefly in the Budaun, Cawnpore, Fatehpur, Banda, Hamirpur, Benares, Mirzapur, Jaunpur, Ghazipur, Ballia, Gorakhpur, Basti, Azamgarh, Unao, and Sitapur districts.

Religion.

The *Gautams* reverence Mahádéo. Their tribal divinity, however, is Dúrga, who is represented by a sword, which is worshipped with prayers and offerings. During the month sacred to the goddess, all *Gautams* abstain from shaving, the headmen of the clan live on milk and fruits, and all sleep on the bare ground.

The *Gautams* are divided into the four following branches :—

Tribal divisions	Rája.	Rána.
	Ráo.	Ráwat.

Gautams intermarry with the following clans :—

In the Doáb.		In Oudh.	
Give daughters to	Take wives from	Give daughters to	Take wives from
Bhadauriya.	Dikhit.	Tilokchandi Bais.	Janwar.
Chauhán.	Chandél.	Chauhán.	Raikhwar.
Kachwáha.	Kath-Bais.	Bhadauriya.	Dikhit.
Gahlot.	Khichar.	Améthiya.	Dirgbans.
Ráthor.	Panwar.	Ráthor.	Kath-Bais.
Jádon.	Bisén.	Súrajbansi.	Chandél.
Parihar.		Kalhans.	Gaharwar.
Bais.		Sirnet.	Palwar.
			Ráj-Kumar.
			Ahban.

Gaurάva.

Shown in map as 35.

Gaurάva, Gauraiya, and *Gaurua* are general terms applied to all Rájpúts who have lost rank by the practice of *karao* or widow marriage. They should therefore hardly be regarded as a clan, but rather as a collection of Rájpúts of fallen grade.

History and origin

Gaurávas are found in the Agra, Muttra, Bulandshahr, and Delhi districts. They generally describe themselves as belonging to the clans from which their ancestors were originally expelled. For this reason it is almost impossible to state their numbers.

Gaurávas are divided into the following septs :—

Tarkar.	Bhal.	Náre.
Jasáwat.	Bargala.	Uriya.
Jais.	Indauliya.	Mahadwar.
Jaiswar.	Báchhal.	Bangar.
		Porch.

Gaurávas marry among themselves. A few clans of pure Rájpúts occasionally take wives from *Gaurâva* septs. Towards Delhi they are said to be particularly quarrelsome, but sturdy in build and clannish in disposition.

Marriages.

HARIOBANS, HAYOBANS, HAIHA, OR HAIHAYA.

Shown in map as 36.

This clan belongs to the Lunar race, and though small in numbers, takes high rank among the Rájpúts of the eastern districts of the North-West Provinces.

The fabled ancestor of the clan was a mythical personage called Sahásra Arjún, who, though at one time possessed of a thousand arms, is said to have lost all but two in various encounters with Paráshu Ráma, the champion of oppressed Bráhmans. Eighteen centuries ago, the *Hayobans* clan was extremely powerful, and held all the eastern parts of what is now known as the Central Provinces. There they founded the cities of Mahéshwati, Raipur, and Ratanpur, and furnished the latter with a dynasty which ruled over Chhatisgarh for 32 generations and only became extinct towards the end of the century, after having previously been deposed by the Mahrattas.

The *Hayobans* of the North-West Provinces claim descent from a band of emigrants, who left Ratanpur about 1,000 years ago under the leadership of Chandra Got, and settled on the banks of the Gogra at Mánjhi in Sáran, whence they undertook a number of successful expeditions against the aboriginal Cherús. Two hundred years later their descendants moved to Behea in Sháhabad, where they remained for five centuries. In 1528, the head of the clan, Rája Bhopat Déo, or one of his sons, violated a Bráhman woman named Mahéni, who belonged to the household of their *Parohit* or family priest. Mahéni is said to have burnt herself to death, and when dying to have imprecated the most fearful curses on the *Hayobans* race. Soon after this the clan left Behea, crossed the Gogra, and settled near Haldi in Ballia. It is from this place that the *Hayobans* Rájas derive their title. The place of Mahéni's death is still pointed out under a *pipal* tree near the railway at Behea.

History and traditional origin.

The swarthy complexions and non-Aryan features of the *Hayobans* Rájpúts have led many authorities to suppose that they are really aboriginal *Tamils*; but it is very improbable that they would be permitted to retain the high place they hold among Chhatris were there any doubts as to the purity of their origin.

In the North-West Provinces, the *Hayobans* are found chiefly in Ballia: they are also scattered in small numbers throughout the Shahabad district of Behar. They number about 1,500 males.

Geographical distribution.

The *Hayobans* intermarry with the following clans:—

Give their daughters to	Take wives from
Ujjainis (Ponwars).	Ujjainis (Ponwars).
Gaharwar.	Lautamiya.
Sakarwar.	Kakan.

INDAULIYA OR INDAURIYA.

Shown in map as 37.

This clan is believed to be a degenerate offshoot of the *Tonwars*, and claims to have emigrated into the Agra district from Indore.

History.

The clan is practically confined to the neighbourhood of Agra and has a male population of nearly 3,000.

Geographical distribution.

Indauliyas intermarry with the following clans:—

Give their daughters to	Take wives from
Baresari.	Baresari.
Bargújar.	Bargújar.
Chauhán.	Chauhan.
Kachwáha.	Kachhwaha.

JÁDU, JÁDON, AND JÁDUBANSI.

Shown in map as 38.

A famous clan belonging to the Lunar race. It claims descent from Yádu, son of Yayáti, fifth in descent from Krishna, the tribal hero. Tod describes the *Yádu* as "the most illustrious tribe in Ind."*

Traditional origin.

* Annals of Rájasthán.

From the legends of the clan it would appear that the first of the *Jádu* settlements were at Indraprástha and Dwarika. After the death of Krishna the *Jádus* were driven out of India, founded Ghazni in Afghánistán, and ruled over the whole of that country and portions of Central Asia, as far north as Samarkand. The pressure of Græco-Bactrian and Muhammadan invasions forced them back into the Punjáb, and at a later period they were driven across the Sutlej into the Bikaneer desert, where they established themselves at Jeysalmeer. In the Punjáb the *Jádus* are known as *Bháttis*, but comparatively few are Hindus, the majority having accepted Islám, shortly after the early Muhammadan conquests. A large number of the Musalmáns of eastern Rájpútána are of *Jádu* descent, and are known locally as *Khanzádas* or *Méos*.

History.

In Oudh and the North-West Provinces where the *Jádons* have numerous settlements, the clan is divided. One branch calls itself *Jádubansi*, to distinguish it from the *Jádons* of the Doáb, who have lost status through practising *karao* or widow-marriage, and through violating Rajpút custom by marrying into their own clan. The latter state that while Arjuna was escorting the ladies of Krishna's family from Hastinapur to Dwarika, a number of them fell into the hands of the *Bhils*. They were recovered some months later, but owing to doubts as to the paternity of their children, the latter were regarded as inferior, and it is from them that the endogamous *Jádons* are descended.

Jádon and Jádubansi settlements in Oudh and the N.-W. Provinces.

Inferior *Jádons* are often called *Bágri*, which is used as a term of reproach. The *Jádons* of Bulandshahr are known as *Chhokazáda* or descendants of a slave girl. The *Baresari*, a *Jádon* sub-division found in the Agra district, say that they were given that title, which corresponds to *Bahádur*, by the Emperor Akbar, for their services at the siege of Chitór. The *Jasáwat*, another *Jádon* sub-division of the Agra district, describe themselves as emigrants from Jeysalmeer and Jeypore. The head of the *Jádon* clan in the North-West Provinces is the Awa Rája of Jalesar in Etah.

The *Jádons*, *Jádus* and *Jadubansis* number 9,000 males in Rájpútána, and are found chiefly in Jeysalmeer, Jeypore, Bhurtpur, and Kerowlee, where they furnish the ruling family. In Oudh and the North-West Provinces they have a male population of 35,000, of which 26,000 are *Jádons*, and 19,000 *Jádubansi*. They are found in the Bulandshahr, Muttra, Agra, Etah, and Aligarh districts.

Geographical distribution.

The principal septs of the clan are as follows :—

In Rájpútána.	In Oudh and the North-West Provinces.
Jádus (of Kerowlee).	Chhokar.
Jarécha (of Kutch-Bhúj).	Baresari.
Mudécha.	Bargala.
Bitman.	Jaiswár.
Soha.	Jasáwat.
Sumécha (now Musalmans of Sind).	Porch.
	Uriya.
	Nara.

The *Jádons* of Rájpútána and of the North-West Provinces both worship Krishna, and are consequently of the *Vaishnáva* sect. *Jádons* who are not endogamous and who do not practice widow marriage rank high in the social scale, but those who have adopted these customs are held in low estimation, and are in fact hardly recognized as Rájpúts by tribes of purer lineage. *Jádons* intermarry with the following clan :—

Marriages.

Rájpútána.		Oudh and the N.-W. Provinces.	
Give daughters to	Take wives from	Give their daughters to	Take wives from
Gahlot.	Solanki.	Tonwar.	Same.
Ráthor.	Baghél.	Chauhán.	
Kachwáha.	Ráthor.	Ponwar.	
Jhalla.	Gahlot.	Bargújar.	
Chauhán.		Parihar.	
		Gahlot.	
		Ráthor.	
		Ka hwáha.	
		Chauhán.	

JHALLA.

Shown in map as 39.

The history of this clan is very obscure. According to Tod, it must have emigrated into Rájpútána from Northern India at the invitation of the *Sissodiya* Ránas of Meywar. They furnish the ruling family of the petty State of Jhallawar, and owe their present high status as Rájpúts to the valour and heroism of their ancestors. "A splendid act of self-devotion of the *Jhalla* chief when Rána Partab of Meywar was oppressed with the whole weight of Akbar's power, obtained, with the gratitude of this Prince, the highest honours he could confer—his daughter in marriage, and a seat on his right hand."*

Traditional origin and history.

The *Jhalla* clan is found only in Rájpútána, and is most numerous in Meywar and Jhallawar. It has a male population of 2,900.

G ographical distribution.

Religion.

Jhallas are *Vaishnávas* and worship Krishna.

The clan is dvided into the following septs :—

Tribal divisions.

Jhalla proper.	Makhwána.

Jhallas contract marriages with Rájpúts of the following clans :—

Give their daughters to	Take wives from
Jádu.	Jádu.
Ráthor.	Ráthor.
Kachwáha.	

JANGHÁRA.

Shown in map as 40.

The designation of this clan is said to be derived from the Persian *Jang*, 'a battle,' and the Hindi *hára* 'defeated,' because the tribe under Prithiráj *Chauhán* was defeated by Shaháb-ud-din Ghori in 1193. This explanation, however, is denied by most of the clan, who say that their tribal name is a corruption of *jang* 'war,' and *ahára*, a local word indicating hunger, meaning "the men who hunger for war."

Traditional origin.

* Annals of Rájasthán.

The *Jangháras* were originally a sept of the *Tomars*, from whom they parted in disgust on the latter being conquered by *Chauháns*. They claim to have entered Rohilkhund under the chieftainship of one Dhápu Dhám whose love of fighting must have been proverbial to judge from the following couplet which is still sung by women of the clan :—

History.

" Below is earth, above is Rám,
Between the two fights Dhápu Dám."

The settlement in Rohilkhund probably took place about the 15th century. The traditions of the clan, however, point to an earlier occupation. The *Jangháras* of Bareilly state that they ejected the Gwálas in 1388, and the Ahirs in 1405. The *Katehriya* Rájpúts are said to have been expelled from Rohilkhund by this clan. The *Jangháras* have always been turbulent and warlike; they should furnish the army with some excellent recruits.

Geographical distribution.

Janghára are found in the Bareilly, Budaun, and Shahjahanpur districts of the North-West Provinces. They have a male population of over 10,000.

The clan is divided into two principal septs :—

Bhúr Jangháras. | Tarai Jangháras.

Tribal divisions.

The *Bhúr* sept ranks higher than the *Tarai*. The ancestors of the latter are stated to have lost grade through alliances with women of their own clan. This sept now practises *karao* or widow marriage, and has consequently fallen in status.

Jangháras contract marriages with Rájpúts of the following clans :—

Give their daughters to	Take wives from
Pundir.	Pundir.
Katheriya.	Katheriya.
Chauhán.	Bargala.
Katiyar.	Bais.
Gáhlot.	Bhalé Sultán.
Tonwar.	Jais.
Bargújar.	Jaiswár.
Bhátti.	Jarauliya.

Janwár.

Shown in map as 41.

The derivation of the title of this clan is very doubtful. It is possibly connected with *jánwar* 'an animal,' in allusion to a curious tradition that one of their earliest Rájas while hunting saw a wolf pick up a child and carry it off to his den. The Rá ja pursued it, and after having followed up the winding passages of the cavern for some time, came suddenly upon an open space, where he saw a venerable *fakir** sitting with the infant on his knees. Recognizing that the wolf was nothing less than a *jogi*† who had assumed that form, the Rája prostrated himself before him in silent reverence. In return for his religious conduct, the holy man blessed him and his offspring, and promised that no wolf should ever prey on a *Janwárs* child. The blessing is said to have retained its full efficacy to the present day.

Traditional origin and history.

The *Janwárs* claim as their ancestors, two *Chauhàn* Rájpúts named Súraj and Dásu, who emigrated into Oudh either from Balabgarh near Delhi, or from the banks of the Nerbudda, soon after the fall of Kanouj in 1194.

Dásu settled in a tract of country between Hardoi and Unao whence his descendants established themselves all over the latter district. The *Janwárs* of Unao were ever a bloodthirsty and unscrupulous race, and added largely to their possessions by the forcible retention of their neighbours' property. Jása Singh, the head of this portion of the clan, was a notorious character in the Mutiny. On the breaking out of disturbances he was the first to turn against us ; he seized the Fatehgarh fugitives and sent them in as prisoners to the Nána at Cawnpore, and his followers were prominent among those who opposed General Havelock's force at Unao. There Jása Singh was mortally wounded. One of his sons was afterwards hanged, and the whole of his estates were confiscated. The family is now extinct.

The descendants of Suraj, the joint founder of the clan, went further north, crossed the Gogra, and settled in Bahraich and Gonda towards the middle of the 14th century. One of the most famous mem-

---

* The term *fakir* is applied generally "to all ascetic and mendicant orders both Hindu and Muhammadan. Professed ascetics are called *Sádhus* if Hindus, and *Pirs* if Muhammadans. They live on alms, and have generally in their hands the custody of petty shrines, the menial service of village temples and mosques, and the guardianship of village cemeteries. They usually let their hair grow long, and many smear themselves with dust and ashes.—Ethnographical Handbook—*Crooke*.

† *Jogis* are Hindu devotees "who among other tenets maintain the practicability of acquiring even in life command over elementary matter by certain ascetic practices."

bers of this branch was Bariar Sáh, who in 1374 was a *risaldár* in the service of the Emperor Firoz Tughlak, and one of the leading pioneers of the Rájpút colonization of Oudh. Early in the reign of Jahángir (1605—1627) one of his descendants, named Balrám Dás, founded the town of Balrámpur. The *Janwár* Rájas of Balrámpur were always noted for the success with which they resisted the exactions of the Lucknow court. When the Mutiny broke out, the *Janwár* Rája alone of all the chieftains of the Gonda district never wavered in his allegiance to the British, and showed his loyalty by sending a powerful escort of his own followers, to protect the civil officers at Secrora who were at the mercy of the mutinous sepoys. On their arrival at Bahrámpur, he removed them to his fort at Pathánkót, and sent them thence under a guard to Gorakhpur. This loyal behaviour exposed him to the attacks of the rebels, but he proved too strong for them, and in the trans-Gogra campaign which terminated the Mutiny, Rája Dirgbijai Singh joined the British force with his tribal levy, and assisted in the final defeat and dispersion of the mutineers on the Nepál border.

Geographical distribution.

The *Janwár* clan is only found in Oudh and the North-West Provinces. It has a male population of 12,000, and is settled chiefly in the Lucknow Unao, Sitapur, Hardoi, and Gonda districts.

Religion.

The chief object of worship with the *Janwárs* is Bhawáni. Their sacred place of devotion is Débi Páttan in the Gonda district.

Janwárs intermarry with the following clans :—

Give their daughters to	Take wives from
Bais.	Raghubansi.
Dikhit.	Gargbansi.
Kanhpuriya.	Chandel.
ChamarGaur.	Gaur.
Surajbans.	Chauhán.
Kalhans.	Raikwar.
Sirnet.	Palwar.
Chandauriya.	Biwar.
Ponwar.	
Jadon.	

KACHWÁHA.

Shown in map as 42.

The name of this clan is derived from the Sanskrit *káchchapa* 'relating to a tortoise' which animal was probably the tribal god or totem. Their enemies the *Ráthors* used to taunt them by insinuating that their name of *Kachwáha* was derived from *kusa*, 'grass' because their swords would cut no deeper than one of its blades. The *Kachwáhas* claim descent from Kúsha, son of Ráma, King of Ajudhya, who is said to have first settled at Rohtas on the Sône, whence his descendants emigrated to Narwar in Western Bundelkhund.

Traditional origin.

In the 2nd century the *Kachwáha* princes of Narwar adopted the affix of *Pál*, which appears to have been the ordinary title of a Rájpút in early times; eight centuries later they changed this epithet for *Singh*. In 967, Sora Singh, Rája of Narwar, expelled his son Dhola Rai, who, after ejecting the *Minas* and *Bargújars*, founded the principality of Dhundur or Ambar, now known as Jeypore, which became the State capital in 1728. A *Kachwáha* dynasty ruled over Narwar and Gwalior up to 1129, when Rája Téjpál left Gwalior to marry a daughter of the Rája of Deora, and was so charmed by her society that he never returned. He was succeeded by his *Parihár* nephew Páramal, and is generally described in *Kachwáha* annals as "the bridegroom prince," in allusion to the romantic circumstance which caused him to abandon his throne. After an interval of several centuries the *Kachwáha* princes of Dhundur or Ambar reobtained possession of Narwar, through the marriage of their daughters to the Muhammadan Emperors. They owed their greatness, as others their decline, to the rise of the Mughal power. Rája Báharmal of Ambar was the first Rájpút chief who paid homage to Islám. His son Bhagwándás was an intimate friend of the Emperor Akbar, and his name is execrated among Rájpúts for having sullied the purity of the race by bestowing his daughter in marriage on a Musalmán. She married Selim, Akbar's eldest son, who succeeded his father on the imperial throne under the title of Jahángir. Bhagwándás was succeeded by his famous nephew Mán Singh, one of the most brilliant characters of Akbar's court, who with his *Kachwáha* clansmen subjugated Assam and Orissa, and quelled a formidable insurrection in Kábul. The Ulwar State which is ruled over by a *Kachwáha* dynasty, is composed of petty principalities which till the middle of the last century owed allegiance to Jeypore and Bhurtpur. Its independence only dates

History.

from 1803, when it was recognized by Lord Lake for services rendered in the Mahratta War.

Kachwáha settlements in the North-West Provinces.

Adventurers from the *Kachwáha* kingdom of Gwalior emigrated to Jalaun, where they settled in the Madhugarh tahsil, which was formerly known as *Kachwáhagarh*. In 1656 the Jalaun settlement established colonies in Etawah. The *Kachwáhas* of Bulandshahr state that their ancestors migrated from Narwar to Ambar and thence to the Doáb. The Rája of Rampur in Jalaun is the head of the clan in the North-West Provinces. The *Kachwáhas* of Muzaffarnagar call themselves *Jhotiyána* and are connected with the *Kachwáhas* of the Doáb.

Geographical distribution.

In Rájpútána the *Kachwáhas* number 68,000 males. They are found in Ulwar, Jeypore, and the two districts of the latter known as Shaikhawatti and Tonwarwatti.* In the North-West Provinces their male population amounts to 31,000. They are found chiefly in the Muzaffarnagar, Meerut, Muttra, Agra, Etawah, Cawnpore and Jalaun districts. The latter furnished some of the finest soldiers of the old native army.

Religion.

Kachwáhas are of the *Gautam* gotra and worship Rám Chandra. In Rájpútána their favourite deities are Jamwahi Mata, Dúrga, and Jinmata; Krishna and Hanuman are also worshipped under the local names of Gopinathji and Balaji respectively. The tortoise is an object of veneration to the clan and was probably the tribal totem.

The *Kachwáha* clan is divided into the 12 following *kotris* of 'chambers,' each of which claims descent from one of the 12 sons of Prithivi, who was Rája of Jeypore about 1600, during the reign of Sikandar Lodi.

Chatarbhojot.	Khangarot.	Khumbawát.
Kalyanot.	Sultanot.	Khambani.
Nathawat.	Pachaenot.	Sheobaranpota.
Balbhadarot.	Gogawat.	Banbirpota.

The *Kachwáhás* of a portion of Jeypore are known as *Shaikháwats* and their country as Shaikhawatti. They were ruled formerly by a confederacy of petty chieftains related to the Rájas of Jeypore, whom they acknowledged as their suzerains. They give the following curious account of the origin of their name. At the commencement of the fifteenth century, their chieftain Mokulsinghji, who was childless, was accosted one day by a Musalmán *fakir* called Shaikh Burhan, who

* Also called Torawatti.

demanded alms. The Rájpút courteously granted his request, and watched him with astonishment, as he drew a copious flow of milk from a female buffalo, whose udders were known to be exhausted. After witnessing this occurrence, the old chief, satisfied that the *fakir* was a worker of miracles, prayed that through his intercessions he might no longer remain childless. In due time his prayer was granted, and his wife bore him a son who was called Shaikhaji, in accordance with the *fakir's* injunctions. It was further ordained by the *Pir** that the child and his descendants should wear Muhammadan clothing, abstain from pork, and only eat the flesh of animals *halláled* in the orthodox fashion by a Musalmán. Four centuries have passed since the occurrence of this incident, but the *Shaikháwats* still reverence the memory of Shaikh Burhan, and obey the majority of his precepts. During the early part of the century Jeypore and Shaikhawatti suffered from the exactions of Mahrattas and Pindáris. The country was given up to rapine and bloodshed, and the inhabitants raided without scruple into the adjoining British districts. In 1834 it became necessary to despatch an expedition or the restoration of order, and the *Shaikhawatti* chiefs were called upon to "raise a corps of their own marauders, with which to keep the peace."† Two years later, this corps, which was led by British officers, was transformed into a brigade of all arms, and after rendering excellent service in Rájpútána, greatly distinguished itself in the Sutlej campaign, and behaved with conspicuous loyalty in the Mutiny. In 1861 the Shaikhawatti battalion was numbered the 13th, and became one of the regular regiments of the Bengal Army. After an interval of some years, the corps has returned to its old recruiting grounds, and is now chiefly composed of the sturdy Rájpúts of Shaikhawatti, Jeypore, and Ulwar.

The Shaikháwat Kachwáhas.

Kachwáhas intermarry with the following clans:—

In Rájpútána.		In Oudh and the North-West Provinces.	
Give their daughters to	Take wives from	Give their daughters to	Take wives from
			Ahban.
Ráthor.	Ponwar.	Tonwar.	Chauhán.
Gaur		Hára.	Ráthor.
Chauhán.	Solanki.	Bhadauriya.	Chamar-Gaur.
Hára		Jádon.	Parihar.
Sisodiya.	Jhalla.	Sisodiya.	Gautam.
Jádus.			Chandel.
Tonwa.	Bargújar.		Bais.
			Dikh

* A *Pir* is a Mahammadan Saint.

† Historical Records of the Bengal Army—*Cardew*.

Although the *Kachwáhas* under Mán Singh performed prodigies of valour in the service of the Mughals, they did not enjoy as high a reputation for courage as the *Háras* and *Ráthors.* "This may be attributed partly to their having succumbed to the enervating vices of the neighbouring court of Delhi, and still more to the degradations which they suffered at the hands of the Mahrattas, to which they were more exposed than their western brethren."*

KÁKAN.

Shown in map as 43.

Very little is known regarding the history of this clan. The only information they can give as to their origin is that they belong to the *Súrajbans* stock, and are descended from a Rájpút adventurer named Ratan Rai, who emigrated into the Ghazipur district from Fyzabad, sometime in the 16th century, and expelled the aboriginal Bhars. The *Kákan* of Azamgarh fix their original home at a place called Kapri Kedár, somewhere in the west, and say that they overcome the Suiris.

Traditional origin and history.

Kákans are found chiefly in the Ghazipur, Ballia, and Azamgarh districts of the North-West Provinces. They have a male population of about 6,000.

Geographical distribution.

The favourite deity of the *Kákans* is the goddess Durga. They are of the *Bhárgú gotrá.*

Religion.

Kakans contract marriages with Rájpúts of the following clans :—

Give their daughters to	Take wives from
Bais. Raghúbansi. Palwár. Gautam. Nándwak. Ujjaini. Hayobans. Bisén.	Birwar. Donwar. Singhél. Séngar. Karchúliya. Narauni. Udmattia. Bais.

KALHANS.

Shown in map as 44.

The traditional explanation of the name of this clan is that one of their Rájas used to pet a *kálá hans,* or 'black swan;' but it is more likely that the *kála hans* was the tribal totem. The legendary ancestor of the clan was one

Traditional origin.

* Annals of Rájasthán—*Tod.*

Saháj Sáh, who sometime in the 14th century took service under Malik Ain-ud-din, the Muhammadan Governor of Oudh, and was given estates in the Gonda district as a reward.

At this time Gonda was ruled by an aboriginal Dóm Rája called Ugrasén, who had the temerity to ask for the hand of Sáhaj Sáh's daughter in marriage. The Rájpút dissembled his rage at the indignity offered him, and pretended to comply; but when the Dóm came with his followers to claim the bride, plied them with liquor until they were insensible, and then murdered them. After this the Dóm kingdom was taken possession of by the *Kalhans* who also established *Bisén* and *Bandhalgoti* settlements in their territories, which were then very thinly populated.

History.

The *Kalhans* dynasty ruled in Gonda until the 16th century, when, after a career of unbridled oppression, Rája Uchal Narayan Singh brought destruction upon his family by outraging the daughter of a Bráhman called Ratan Pánde. Unable to obtain any reparation, the Bráhman sat at the ravisher's door for 21 days, refusing food of any kind, until death put an end to his sufferings. His wife died at the same time from grief. Before his spirit fled, he pronounced a curse of utter extinction on the family of his oppressor, modifying it only in favour of the family of the younger Ráni, who had shown him some kindness, and to whom he promised that her descendants, the present Rájas of Babhnipair, should succeed to a small *ráj*. The Bráhman's curse was fulfilled; a few months later one of the branches of the Sarju changed its course, overthrew the Rája's fortress, carried away everything in indiscriminate ruin, and left not a member of his household alive except the junior Ráni, who shortly afterwards gave birth to a son. After this the *Kalhans* country was divided among a number of clans, and the Rája ceased to have any political power.

Geographical distribution.

The *Kalhans* clan is not found in Rájpútána or the Punjáb. In Oudh and the North-West Provinces it has a male population of 12,000, and is found chiefly in the Basti, Gonda, and Bahraich districts.

Religion.

The *Kalhans* worship Dúrga or Débí. The tribal deity is Ratan Pánde, the Bráhman whom their ancestor oppressed. At marriages and deaths his spirit is propitiated by the sacrifice of a he-goat.

The *Kalhans* intermarry with the following clans :—

Give their daughters to	Take wives from
Sirnet. Súrajbans. Gautam. Chauhán. Améthiya. Tilokchandi Bais.	Sirnet. Súrajbans. Gautam. Rajkumar. Bachhgoti. Bisén. Sombansi. Bhalé Sultan. Janwar. Gargbansi.

KANHPURIYA.

Shown in map as 45.

The name of this clan is derived from Kanhpur, a village on the road from Salón to Partabgarh in Oudh. The clan claims descent from Kanh, the Kshatriya son of a Bráhman saint called Sachh, who married a daughter of the great *Gaharwar* Rája Manik Chand.

Traditional origin.

The *Kanhpuriyas* belong to the same wave of Hindu emigration as the *Bais*, and probably settled in Oudh about the 13th century, where they are now very numerous and powerful. Kanh, as his mother's heir, succeed to the throne of Manik Chand ; but having married a girl of the *Bais* clan, he abandoned Manikpur to her relations, and founded the village of Kanhpur, which is now the principal seat of the tribe. Sáhas and Ráhas, the sons of Kanh, increased their father's possessions by driving out the Bhárs, whose kings, the brother Tilohi and Biloki, they killed in battle. The head of the clan is the Rája of Tiloki, a village named after one of these Bhár heroes. During the reigns of the early Mughal Emperors the *Kanhpuriyas* were engaged in constant petty warfare against their neighbours the *Sombansis, Biséns, and Bais*, and against the Muhammadan Imperial officials. In the time of Aurangzéb, the *Kanhpuriya* Rája Balbhaddra Singh served in the Mughal armies against the Mahrattas and the Ját Rája of Bhurtpur, and is said to have brought the Rája of Sattara, in an iron cage, before his Imperial master. For these services he was created a *Maniabdar* of 5,000.

History.

The *Kanhpuriya* clan is found only in Oudh. It has a male population of 10,000, and is settled chiefly in the Rai Bareli, Sultanpur, and Partabgarh districts.

Geographical distribution.

he special divinity of the *Kanhpuriyas* is Mahesha Rakshaha, the buffalo-demon, to which they sacrifice buffaloes at religious festivals, more especially when a wedding or a birth takes place in the Rája's family.

Religion.

The clan is divided into the two following branches, descended from Sáhas and Ráhas respectively—

Tribal divisions.

Tiloi. | Kaithanla.

Kanhpuriyas intermarry with the following clans :—

Give their daughters to	Take wives from
Tilokchandi Bais. Baghél. Bisen. Sombansi. Súrajbansi. Chauhan. Sirnet.	Bhalé Sultán. Bachhgoti. Bisén. Bi khariya. Bandhalgoti. Raghubansi. Kath Bais. Gargbansi. Palwar. Janwar. Nandwak.

KARCHULIYA.

Shown in map as 46.

The name of this clan is derived from *kar* 'a hand', and *chaldána* 'to make use of.' The title *Karchuliya* was bestowed on them by the Emperor Ala-ud-din Khilji in the 14th century, to mark his appreciation of their valour at the siege of Chitór. According to Sherring* the *Karchuliyas* are descended from the *Sissodiyas* of Hamirpur, who were themselves an offshoot of the royal clan of Meywar. They are said to have settled in the Ballia district about the 15th century, under the leadership of a chieftain named Hém Sáh. It would appear, however, from local enquiries, that the *Karchuliyas*, or *Karchuli* as they are more generally called, are of the same stock as the *Hayobans*. In Rewah the *Hayobans* are actually called *Karchuli*, and *vice versá*. This would make them members of the *Chandrabansi* or Lunar race.

Traditional origin and history.

* Hindu Tribes and Castes.

Karchuliyas are found chiefly in the Ballia, Ghazipur, and Gorakhpur districts of the North-West Provinces, also in the Rewah State.

Geographical distribution.

The clan is not a large one, but its exact numbers cannot be stated as they are not recorded in the last Census Report.

Karchuliyas contract marriages with Rájpúts of the following clans :—

Give their daughters to	Take wives from
Ujjaini.	Lautamiya.
Baghel.	Nikumbh.

KATHERIYA.

Shown in map as 47.

This clan derives its title from *Kattiawar*, which is regarded as the cradle of the race. It is more probable, however, that it is really a corruption of *Katehar*, the ancient name of Rohilkhund.

History.

The *Katheriyas* are supposed to have invaded Rohilkhund about 1174. The Kattiawar origin may be dismissed as a fable. It is probable that they were originally settled in Benares and Behar, and that they travelled up the Doáb and invaded Rohilkhund from the west, ejecting the aboriginal tribes. It is said that when Prithiráj *Chauhán* was reigning at Delhi, and Jai Chand *Ráthor* at Kanouj, a Rájpút of the *Surajbans* race was forced to fly from Benares. The exile settled in Katehar, and from him are descended the *Katheriyas.* The murder of their Rája, Bhim Sén, at Delhi, transferred the allegiance of the clan from the *Chauháns* to the *Ráthors.* In 1184, after the capture of Mahoba, Prithiráj sent a force against the *Katheriyas* which was defeated. There seems to have been a fresh influx of *Katheriyas* from Behar about 1339, for in that year two Rájpúts of Benares, named Bijairáj and Ajairáj, entered Rohilkhund with their followers, and conquered and expelled the Ahirs and Bhúinhárs.

Geographical distribution.

Katheriyas are found chiefly in the Etah, Bareilly, Budaun, Moradabad, and Shahjahanpur districts of the North-West Provinces. They have male population of 21,000.

Katheriyas contract marriages with Rájpúts of the following clans :—

Give their daughters to	Take wives from
Kachwáha.	Ahban.
Bhadauriya.	Ponwar.
Chauhán.	Janghára.
Baghél.	Chandél.
Janghára.	Gaharwar.
Katiyar.	Raikwar.
	Nikumbh.
	Bais.
	Ujjaini.

KATIYAR.

Shown in map as 48.

This clan is said to have derived its title of *Katiyars* or 'slaughterers,' from the ruthless manner in which they massacred all who ventured to oppose them. They claim to be of *Tonwar* origin. The *Katiyars* of Etah state that they emigrated into the district from Jullundur, about three centuries ago. The *Katiyars* of Hardoi give a totally different account of their origin. They state that they came into Oudh from Sonoriya in Gwalior, under Rája Devi Datta, towards the end of the 16th century, and settled on the banks of the Ganges in Farukhabad. Thence they fought their way westward, subduing all the aboriginal tribes they encountered. The head of the clan is the Rája of Dharampur in Hardoi. The Etah *Katiyars* belong to the *Bharaddwaj*, those of Hardoi to the *Vaiyagar gotra.*

History and traditional origin.

Katiyars are found in the Etah, Bulandshahr, and Hardoi districts of Oudh and the North-West Provinces. The clan is known to be a small one, but its exact numbers cannot be stated, as they were not recorded at the last census.

Geographical distribution.

Katiyars contract marriages with Rájpúts of the following clans :—

Give their daughters to	Take wives from
Chauháns.	Báchhal.
Bhadauriyas.	Nikumbh.
Ráthor.	Bais.
Sómbansi.	Gaur.
	Katheriya.
	Jangharа.

KAUSIKS.

Shown in map as 49.

The tribal title of this clan is said to be derived from the name of their ancestor Kúsha or Kúshika, whose son Gadhi was the reputed founder of Gadhipur, a town which has been identified with the modern Ghazipur. It is possible, however, that *Kausik* is simply a corruption of the Sanskrit *kushika*, 'squint-eyed,' a nick-name applied to some members of this race. The clan claims to be of *Sombansi* descent.

Traditional origin.

The *Kausiks* held their sway in the south-east of the Ballia district and were long notorious for their turbulent character. When Ballia became part of the British dominions, all the *Kausik* estates were sold up for arrears of revenue, and the clan acquired an evil reputation for insubordination, and the perpetration of violent crimes. During the disturbances of 1857-58, they gave much trouble. After the suppression of the Mutiny, arrangements were made for the restoration of the *Kausik* lands to their former owners, compensation being paid to existing proprietors. The transfer has been attended with the happiest results. The *Kausiks* are now among the most loyal and peaceful of the eastern Rájpúts.

History.

About 1350, a band of *Kausik* settlers from Barágáon in Gh$\acute{a}$zipur, established themselves under Rája Dhúr in Gorakhpur, whence they pushed out colonies into Azamgarh and Basti. The Rája of Gopálpur in Gorakhpur is now the head of the clan.

Kausiks are now found chiefly in the Ballia, Gorakhpur, and Azamgarh districts of the North-West Provinces. They have a male population of nearly 10,000.

Geographical distribution.

In ancient times the favourite god of the *Kausiks* was Indra. They now worship Débi, and sacrifice a he-goat to her annually, and at the births of sons. The clan takes its *Gúrús* or spiritual guides from a sect of monotheists, peculiar to Ghâzipur, called the *Bheka Sháhi.* The name of the tribal *gotra* is the same as that of the clan.

Religion.

Kausiks contract marriages with Rájpúts of the following clans :—

Give their daughters to	Take wives from
Hayobans.	Hayobans.
Ujjaini.	Ujjaini.
Nikumbh.	Nikumbh.
Raghubansi.	Raghubansi.
Sirnét.	Bais.
Bisén.	Séngar.
Gautam.	Palwár.
Súrajbansi.	Barwár.
Drigbansi.	Kinwar.
Chauhán.	Karchúliya.
	Gahawár.
	Donwár.

KHICHÁR.

Shown in map as 50.

The title of this clan is probably derived from Khichidara, the original home of Déogaj Singh, the founder of the race, who is said to have settled at Asothar in Fatehpur about 1543, and married the daughter of the Raja of Aijhi, to whose possessions he afterwards succeeded. The next member of the clan to attain any celebrity was one Aram

Singh, who after having been unjustly deprived of his property, became a wealthy man through the miraculous discovery of a hidden treasure while ploughing. His successor Bhagwant Rai organized a successful insurrection against one of the Muhammadan Emperors, but was finally killed by treachery in 1760. A few years later the *Khichars* were deprived of their possessions by Asaf-ud-daula, the Nawáb Wazir of Oudh, who however gave the Rája a small pension to compensate for his losses. On the cession of the Fatehpur district to the British, the Rája was guaranteed the continuance of the pension, and the guarantee was ratified in 1805 by a *sanad* which fixed the grant at Rs. 7,500 per annum, and declared it to be hereditary. The *Khichar* clan, which once ruled a great portion of Fatehpur, is now reduced to a very low ebb, and retains next to nothing of its once extensive possessions. The head of the tribe is the Rája of Asothar.

History and traditional origin.

Khichars are found chiefly in the Banda and Fatehpur districts of the North-West Provinces. They have a male population of about 2,000.

Geographical distribution.

Khichars are inclined to *Shákta* worship, Débi being their principal goddess. They also appear to have two local deities, Bajpharkarha Bábá and Gharram Bábá. They are of the *Gautam gotra*.

Religion.

Khichars contract marriages with Rájpúts of the following clans:—

Give their daughters to	Take wives from
Tilokchandi Bais.	Bisén.
Ráthor.	Kath-Bais.
Bhadauriya.	Sómbansi.
Bisén	Chande.
Améthiya.	Dikhit.
Sómbansi.	Súrkhi.
Kachhwáha.	Gautam
Bargújar.	
Sengar.	
Gautam.	
Súrkhi.	
Dikhit.	

Kinwár.

Shown in map as 51.

The title of this clan is said to be a corruption of the word *Dankin*, the name of a river near the early home of the race. They claim to be of *Dikhit* origin, and state that they are descendants of Rája Mán *Dikhit* who lived at Mánchatur Asthán on the Jumna, and established a kingdom at Padampur in the Carnatic. Two cadets of the family took service, one with the *Gáharwár* Rája, of Benares, the other with a *Gautam* Bhuinhár. Each married a daughter of his patron. The descendants of the former are the *Kinwar* Rájputs, while those of the latter are the *Kinwar* Bhúinhárs. Before accepting a recruit from this clan it should be ascertained by careful enquiry whether he is a Rájpút or a Bhúinhár, as the latter are very fond of passing themselves off as the former.

Traditional origin and history.

Kinwars are found in the Ballia, Gorakhpur, and Azamgarh districts of the North-West Provinces, but are most numerous in Sháhabad and other portions of Behar. They have a male population of about 4,000.

Geographical distribution.

The favourite *Kinwar* divinity is the goddess Parméshwari Débi, to whom they sacrifice a he-goat on the last day of the month of *Sáwan.* They are of the *Kassyap gotra.*

Religion.

Kinwars contract marriages with Rájpúts of the following clans:—

Give their daughters to	Take wives from
Barwár.	Barwár.
Ujjaini.	Ujjaini.
Nikumbh,	Nikumbh.
Bisén (of Deorhi).	Bisén (of Deorhi).
Hayobans.	Hayobans.
Karchuliya.	Karchuliya.
Séngar.	Séngar.
Bais.	Bais.
Kausik,	Kausik.
Sirnét	Mahrawar.
Rájkumár.	Sarwár.
Súrajbansi.	Gáharwár.
Monas.	

LAUTÁMIYA.

Shown in map as 52.

Very little is known of the history of this clan, and no explanation is obtainable as to the derivation of their tribal name. Their origin is doubtful, and they are said to rank low among Rájpúts. Their former possessions, which at one time included a considerable portion of the Ballia district, have passed into the hand of the Máhárájá of Dúmráon. Many of the clan, however, still hold a good deal of land as lessees of the Rája, and owing to the peculiar productiveness of the soil, have acquired considerable wealth.

Traditional origin and history.

They are a sturdy independent race generally of fine physique, and addicted to frays and feuds of a serious character. Not many years ago the clan had the reputation of being closely associated with certain gangs of dacoits and robbers; they nevertheless furnish the army with some excellent soldiers.

Lautámiyas are found chiefly in the Ballia and Gházipur districts of the North-West Provinces, also in Sháhabad and other portions of Behar. They have a population of about 3,500 males.

Geographical distribution.

Religion.

The favourite divinity of *Lautámiyas* is the goddess Débi. They are of the *Bharaddwáj gotra.*

Lautámiyas contract marriages with Rájpúts of the following clans :—

Give their daughters to	Take wives from
Tilaunta.	Tilaunta.
Dhekaha.	Dhekaha
Kachhaniya.	Kachhaniya.

MAHROR.

Shown in map as 53.

The name of this clan is derived from *Méhra*, a *kahár* or *pálki* bearer. They profess to be descended from Shiuraj Singh, a Kshatriya adventurer who settled in Oudh in the 15th century under the protection of the great *Bais* Rája Tilok Chand; it is however very doubtful whether they have any real claim to be considered Rájpúts. According to tradition, Tilok Chand was defeated on a certain occasion by his Musalmán enemies, and would have been killed but for the heroic devotion of his dooly-bearers, who beat off his assailants after his military followers had fled. As a reward for their valour, the Rája changed their name from *Méhra* to *Mahror*, and gave them the status of Rájpúts, because on that day "his Rájpúts became women and his Kahárs Rájpúts." This anecdote affords a striking example of how low-grade tribes, in spite of the restrictions of caste, have occasionally risen from their humble estate and obtained admittance into the Kshatriya or military order. *Mahrors* should rarely be enlisted, as they are looked down upon by Rájpúts of purer descent.

History.

Mahrors are found chiefly in the Unao and Gházipur districts of Oudh and the North-West Provinces. They have a male population of about 2,000.

Geographical distribution.

Tribal divisions. The clan is divided into two septs:—

Mahror proper. | Gamel.

The *Gamels* are descendants of a *Mahror* father by an Ahir woman.

Mahrors contract marriages with members of the following clans:—

Give their daughters to	Take wives from
Gahlot.	Gahlot.
Janwár.	Janwár.

MONAS.

Shown in map as 54.

The title of this clan is derived from the name of their *gotra*, *Maun*, which is peculiar to themselves. They claim to be the descendants of emigrants from Ambar in Rájpútána who settled at Bhadohi in the Mirzapur district about 600 years ago, after expelling the aboriginal Bhars. The founder of the clan was Sagar Rai, the father of three sons, who at their parent's death divided his property. A grandson of Sagar Rai, named Jodh Rai, obtained a *zamindári sanad* from the Emperor. Sháh Jáhán, but was killed not long afterwards, by the Governor of Allahabad. Upon this, the Emperor is said to have given a fresh *sanad* to Jodh Rai's widow, who delegated the management of her estates to a relative of her husband's named Madan Singh. The latter, in the usual fashion, robbed his employer, and in course of time came to be regarded as the actual head of the clan. On his death the *zamindári* was divided among his sons. The *Monas* seem to have been a quiet, contented, and law abiding race. About 1743 during the reign of the Emperor Muhammad Sháh, Jaswant Singh, a cadet of the principal *Mona* family, ousted the rest of his kinsmen, and proclaimed himself Rája. He was supported in these proceedings by Muhammad Khan Bangásh, the Afghán Governor of Allahabad, who had married one of his sisters. About 1739 he was attacked by Bán Singh, one of the relations whom he had robbed, supported by the Rája of Partabgarh, who captured his fort at Suriánwán, and carried him off as a prisoner. The Rája of Partabgarh had meanwhile become security for the payment of the annual revenue due from the Bhadohi estates. Arrears, however, rapidly accumulated, and in 1748 the property passed into the hands of Balwant Singh the Rája of Benares, who in return paid up the claims of the Imperial officials. After various disputes with the Nawábs of Oudh, Balwant Singh was confirmed in the possession of Bhadohi by Shuja-ud-Daula in 1756. On the rebellion of Balwant Singh's son Chét Singh, in 1781, his estates passed under British control. Bhadohi now forms part of the family domains of the Máhárája of Benares. In 1857 the *Monas* assisted the rebels, for they had not forgotten how they had been expelled from their lands in the previous century, and they naturally looked upon the Mutiny as a favourable opportunity for the resumption of their former possessions.

Traditional origin and history.

Monas are found in the Allahabad, Jaunpur, and Mirzapur districts of the North-West Provinces. They have a male population of 7,600.

Geographical distribution.

Monas contract marriages with Rájpúts of the following clans:—

Give their daughters to	Take wives from
Gáharwár.	Bais.
Bachhgoti.	Bisén.
Sómbansi.	Bhánwág.
Bilkhariya.	Baghel.
	Palwár.
	Chandél.
	Gargbansi.

The *Monas* of Bhadohi rank higher than the rest of the clan, and occasionally intermarry with tribes of higher grade.

NÁNDWÁK.

Shown in map as 55.

Traditional origin and history.

The title of this clan is derived from the name of their ancestor Náun Ráo, a *Kachwáha* Rájpút of Ulwar, who left his home early in the 16th century, on a pilgrimage to Gaya, and was attacked while passing through the Jaunpur district by the Bhárs. With the aid of the Governor of Oudh, he expelled them, and established his authority over two pergunnahs which he named after Mandil Gopál and Barsáthi, two *Rishis* or Hindu saints, reverenced by himself and his son. The *Nándwáks* built forts all over the Jaunpur district, which were either destroyed or captured by Rája Balwant Singh of Benares during the last century. On the district passing into the hands of the British, the *Nándwáks* were given back their former possessions, but were unable to retain them, and their land is now chiefly in the hands of Musalmán officials.

Geographical distributin

Nándwáks are found on the Azamgarh, Jaunpur, and Mirzapur districts of the North-West Provinces. The clan is a small one, and only numbers about 1,000 males.

Religion.

Nándwáks mostly worship Mahábir and Dúrgá. They belong to the *Kassyap gotra.*

Nándwáks contract marriages with Rájpúts of the following clans :—

Give their daughters to	Take wives from
Sómbansi	Kath-Bais.
Drigbansi.	Chandél.
Rájkúmar.	Rájkumár.

NÁNWÁG.

Shown in map as 56.

Traditional origin and history.

Very little is known of the history of this clan. They are possibly connected with the *Nándwáks.* It is stated by Sherring that they settled in

Jaunpur in the middle of the last century with the sanction of Rája Balwant Singh of Benares.

Geographical distribution.

The *Nánwág* clan is practically restricted to the Jaunpur district of the North-West Provinces. It has a population of about 4,000 males.

Religion.

Nánwágs worship Débi. They are of the *Kausil gotra.*

Nánwágs contract marriages with Rájpúts of the following clans :—

Give their daughters to	Take wives from
Bachhgoti.	Drigbansi.
Surwár.	Surwár.
Sónwán.	Gautam.
Ráthor.	

NIKUMBH.

Shown in map as 57.

The title of this clan is derived from the Sanskrit *Nikhumbha*, the 'croton plant.' The traditional ancestor of the clan was Kuvalayasva, one of the Solar kings of Ajudhya, who having conquered the demon Dhunda, acquired the title of Dhundumárá, and gave his name to

Traditional origin and history.

the country called Dhundhar or Jeypore. Here his descendants remained and were known as *Nikhumbhas.* They appear to have been among the earliest Aryan settlers in Rájpútána, and on being driven out of Ulwar and Jeypore about 1450, settled in Oudh. It is stated by some authorities that they are *Kachwáhas*; this is probably a mistake, though it is likely enough that they served the *Kachwáhas* after the latter had taken possession of Jeypore. The Farrukhabad colony was established towards the end of the 12th century by two *Nikumbh* adventurers from Oudh called Mán and Sahráj, who were invited by the Rája of Kanouj to expel the aboriginal Bhárs. Their descendants rendered valuable assistance to the *Sómbansi* Raja of Sandi, who conferred on them the title of *Nikumbh* or *Nék-kám*, 'good service.' The *Sirnet* clan is generally considered to be of the same stock as the *Nikumbhs.*

The *Nikumbhs* are no longer found in Rájpútána and the Punjáb.

Geographical distribution.

In the North-West Provinces they have a male population of 8,000, and are settled in the Farrukhabad, Jaunpur, Ballia, Azamgarh, and Hardoi districts.

Religion.

The *Nikumbhs* are inclined to ***Shákta*** worship, the goddess Débi being their principal divinity.

Nikumbhs intermarry with the following clans:—

Give their daughters to		Take wives from	
Eastern districts.	Farrukhabad and Hardoi.	Eastern districts.	Farrukhabad and Hardoi.
Bisén	Chauhán.	Bais.	Gaur.
Bais.	Bhadauriya.	Barwar.	Bais.
Digbansi.	Chandel	Gautam.	Dhakré.
Harihoban.	Ponwar.	Kausik.	Gaharwar.
Chauhán.	Katiyar.	Sengar.	janwár.
Raghubansi.	Báchhal.	Donwar.	Sómbansi.
Surajbansi.	Sengar.	Harihobans.	Ahban.
Ujjaini.	Sómbansi.	Gaharwar.	
Rajkumar.		Ujjaini.	
		Raghubansi.	

PARIHAR.

Shown in map as 58.

Traditional origin.

The name of this clan is derived from the Sanskrit *Parinára*, 'repelling.' It is one of the agnicular or fire tribes, an account of the origin of which will be found on page 111 under the heading of *Ponwar*.

The founder of the race is said to have established himself at Mandawar in Marwar, which was the ancient capital of the *Parihárs*. In 1194 the *Ráthor* refugees from Kanouj found an asylum in *Parihár* territory, but treacherously repaid the hospitality of their hosts by driving them out of their homes. A *Parihar* dynasty ruled over Gwalior from 1129 to 1211. In 1196 the Gwalior fortress was captured by Kutub-ud-din Aibeg, but was retaken by the Hindus who held it till 1232, when the *Parihár* dynasty became extinct. The story of how Paramál, the *Parihár* nephew of Téjpál, (the *Kachwáha* Rája of Gwalior) obtained his uncle's throne, has already been given on page 89. The *Parihárs* say that they preceded the *Chandels* and *Baghels* in Bundelkhund and Rewah.

History.

There is a large *Parihár* colony in the Etawah district. They inhabit the intricate and inaccessible network of ravines that abuts on the *Pánchnadi* or confluence of the Jumna, Chambal, Káli-Sindh, Kuári, and Pahúj. On the defeat of Anángpál of Delhi, in the 11th century, the head of the clan, Sumit Rai, fled with his followers into this wild region, to which he gave the name of *Parihára*. The *Parihárs* of the Doáb have always been lawless and desperate. In the early days of the British dominion they were notorious thugs and robbers, but the reputation of the clan has now much improved, and they have recently increased in importance through judicious marriages with *Séngars* and *Chauháns*. The *Parihars* of Unao claim to be emigrants from Kashmir who settled in Oudh in the reign of Humáyun. The eastern *Parihárs* are probably colonists from the Doáb. The head of the clan in the North-West Provinces is the self-styled Rája of Malhájini in Etawah.

Parihár settlements in Oudh and the North-West Provinces.

In Rájpútána the *Parihar* clan is scattered and of little importance. They number nearly 6,000 males and are found chiefly in Marwar and Bikaneer. In Oudh and the North-West Provinces they have a male population of 16,000, with settlements in the Agra, Etawah, Cawnpore, Hamirpur, Jhansi, Jalaun and Unao districts.

Geographical distribution.

In Rájpútána the tribal divinities of the *Parihars* are Gájan-mátá, Chaonda-mátá and Lakhmináth. In the North-West Provinces they mostly worship Débi.

Religion.

The principal *Parihár* septs are as follows:—

Parihar proper.	Lúlapota.
Ramawat.	Juda.
Nádhat.	

Parihárs intermarry with the following clans :—

In Rájpútána.		In Oudh and the North-West Provinces.	
Give their daughters to	Take wives from	Give their daughters to	Take wives rom
Ráthor.	Bhatti.	Chauhán.	Chandél.
Jádus.	Gahlot.	Ráthor.	Gautam.
Kachwáha.	Ráthor.	Kachwáha.	Dikhit.
	Chauhán.	Bhadauriya	Chauhán.
	Solanki.	Jadón.	Kachwáha.
			Ponwar.
			Baghel.
			Bais.
			Raikhwar.
			Jaiswar.
			Nikumbh.
			Gaharwar.
			Séngar.
			Gaur.

Tribal characteristics.

Parihárs are as a rule tall handsome men with athletic figures. In Rájpútána they show special preference for service in the cavalry. The Rájpútána *Parihár* differs from other Rájpúts of that country in that he will no eat pig.

PALWAR.

Shown in map as 59.

The title of this clan is derived from Pali, a village in Hardoi from which they are said to have emigrated about 600 years ago into Fyzabad. They claim as their ancestor a *Sómbansi* adventurer named Pithraj Deo, whose descendants established a colony in Azamgarh early in the 14th century. The *Sombansis* of Pali deny all connection with the *Palwars*, and the latter have consequently invented a story that their ancestors came from Pali near Delhi, once the seat of a *Sómbansi* dynasty. The *Palwars* were a brave and turbulent race. They had no Rája, but the different branches of the clan always united for the achievement of a common purpose. From their forts at Narani and Chahora on the Gogra they levied blackmail from all comers, and defied the efforts of the Lucknow Government to reduce them to order. When Oudh was annexed, they showed unmistakable hostility towards the British, and on the outbreak of the Mutiny, broke into open rebellion, plundering and fighting in Fyzabad, Azamgarh, and Gorakhpur. When the European fugitives from Fyzabad were escaping in boats down the Gogra, they were stopped at Narani by Udit Naráyan Singh, the eldest son of the *Palwar* chief and were insulted and robbed by his followers. On reaching Chahora, the fort occupied by Madho Parshad, another *Palwar* leader, they received some show of hospitality, and were handed over to an escort supplied by Máhárája Mán Singh. For the offence above mentioned, Udit Narayan Singh was subsequently tried, and sentenced to three years' imprisonment. Madho Parshad Singh, whose conduct at the outset was good, was the first to unfurl the standard of rebellion. Assembling his clan, he plundered the town of Manori, and attacked Azamgarh. The *Palwars* then passed over into Gorakhpur and joined the rebel *Názim* in that district. Here they were defeated by our Gúrkha allies under Jang Bahádur. While *en route* to Lucknow, the latter attacked the small fort of Berozpur in Fyzabad, which was bravely held by 34 *Palwars* who were all killed at their posts. On the re-occupation of Fyzabad, the *Palwar* chiefs postponed their surrender till the very last moment, but the only one ever called to account for his misdeeds was Udit Narayan Singh, to the circumstances of whose case allusion has already been made.

Traditional origin and history.

Palwars are found in the Gorakhpur, Azamgarh, and Fyzabad districts of Oudh and the North-West Provinces. They have a male population of 9,800.

Geographical distribution.

Palwars have much the same prejudices as the *Sómbansis*. They worship snakes and during the month of July they abstain from milk, give up washing and shaving, and lie on the bare ground. They belong to the *Baydgar gotra*.

Religion.

Palwars contract marriages with members of the following clans :—

Give their daughters to	Take wives from
Rájkumar.	Nikumbh.
Rájwar.	Donwar.
Bachhgoti.	Barwar.
Gargbansi.	Chandél.
Kanhpuriya.	Raghubansi.
Bhalé-Sultán.	Bais.
Súrajbansi.	
Sombansi.	
Raghubansi.	

PONWAR, PÁNWAR, PRAMÁR OR PUÁR.

Shown in map as 60.

The name of this clan is derived from the Sanskrit *Pramara*, or 'first striker'. It was the most powerful of the agnicular or fire tribes. The legend of their origin is very curious. In ancient times the Bráhmans were sorely persecuted by demons, who in spite of the sanctity of Mount Abu, desecrated their shrines, extinguished the sacrificial flames, and rendered their offerings impure. The harassed *Rishis* persevered, however, and reassembling round the *agni-kunda*,* rekindled the sacred fire, and prayed to Mahádéo for assistance. The god at once gave ear to their supplications, and there issued from the flames a figure of peaceful mien whom the Bráhmans appointed guardian of the gate, hence his name of *Prilhi-ka-dwára* or *Parihára*, 'earth's door.' After fresh invocations to the gods, a second figure came out of the fire, and being formed in the *chalu*, or palm of the hand, was called *Chalukya*. A third figure appeared in the same manner who was called *Pramára* or 'first striker,' as he was the first to go forth against the demons, who, however, proved too strong for him. At the fourth incantation

Traditional origin.

* The *Agni-kunda* was the altar on which was kindled the *agni* or sacred flame.

a terrible figure emerged from the fire, lofty in stature, fierce in aspect, clad in armour, and four armed, hence his name *Chauhán.* Fortified with the blessings of the Bráhmans, the latter was again despatched against the powers of darkness, and this time prevailed. He slew their leaders, and pursued the vanquished demons to the nethermost depths of hell. Such is the mythical origin of the four agnicular or fire tribes; they were in all probability really Scythian mercenaries who assisted the Bráhmans against their own people and obtained recognition as Kshatriyas as a reward for their services to Hinduism.

History.

The glory of the *Ponwars* has departed, but they cherish the memory of their former greatness At one time the clan ruled over the whole of India from the Sutlej to the sea. There is an ancient saying that "the world is the *Pramar's*". They were predominant in Rájasthán at the time of Alexander's invasion, who found in their Rája, Chandragúpta, one of his stoutest opponents. Their principal cities were Dhar, Ujjain Chitór, Abu, and Chandravati. The *Pramárs* or *Puárs* were expelled from Chitór about 714 by the *Gahlots.* Their traditions now seem to centre round Dhar, the Rája of which is a member of the tribe.

Ponwar settlements in Oudh and the North-West Provinces.

Ponwar colonies are scattered all over Oudh and the North-West Provinces. They settled in Agra and Bulandshahr after their expulsion from Ujjain by Shahab-ud-din Ghori in 1193. The Unao settlement dates from the time of Akbar, who gave the *Ponwars* land in the district as a reward for their services at the siege of Chitór. From Oudh they spread into Gorakhpur, where they dispossessed the *Biséns.* The *Ponwars* settled extensively in Cawnpore, Azamgarh, and Ghazipur, where they are known as *Ujjainis.* The head of the *Ujjainis* is the Rája of Dumráón. The *Ujjainis* of Cawnpore profess to be the descendants of Súr Sah *Ponwar* of Ujjain, who settled in the district by invitation of his relative Jai Chand, the *Ráthor* Rája of Kanouj, and drove out the aboriginal Bhars.

There is an inferior branch of the clan called *Khidmatiya* or *Chobdar* which is of servile origin as indicated by its name, and descended from a low caste woman. No high caste Hindu will eat anything touched by them. It is stated that a thousand men of this sept formed the Emperor Akbar's bodyguard, and though formerly notorious for their roguery, were transformed by Mughal discipline into reliable household troops.

The *Ponwars* of Lalitpur and Banda are still somewhat addicted to dacoity, and are described by Sleeman as "needy, proud as Lucifer, and always ready to eke out their means by robbery."*

Geographical distribution.

In Rájpútána and the adjoining districts of the Punjáb, the *Ponwar* males number 24,000. They are found chiefly in Marwar, Meywar, Dholpur, Jhind and Rohtak. The *Ponwars* of Dholpur, though numerous, have lost some of the characteristics of true Rájpúts, through association with Játs and Bundélas. In Oudh and the North-West Provinces, the *Ponwar* and *Ujjaini* population amounts to 45,000 males. They are found chiefly in the Meerut, Agra, Farukhabad, Moradabad, Shahjahanpur, Cawnpore, Banda, Lalitpur, Jaunpur, Ballia, Gorakhpur, Lucknow, Unao, Sitapur, Hardoi, Fyzabad, and Shahabad districts. A few *Ponwars* are also found in Central India and Guzerat.

Religion.

In Rájpútána the favourite *Ponwar* divinity is Gajânmata. In Oudh and the North-West Provinces *Ponwars* workship Debi or Dúrga,—the favourite god of most Rájpúts.

Ponwars are divided into the following septs:—

In Rájpútána, Central India and Guzerat.	In Oudh and the North-West Provinces.
Ponwar proper.	Dhar Ponwar.
Soda.	Ráj Ponwar.
Sankla.	Ujjaini.
Umeth (Central India).	Khidmatiya or Chóbdar } an inferior branch by a low caste woman.
Mulshi. } (Guzerat).	
Solora. } (Guzerat).	
Jaipál. } (Guzerat).	
Kargoah. } (Guzerat).	
Kabbha. } (Guzerat).	
Dor.	
Bhail.	

* A Journey through the Kingdom of Oudh.

Ponwars and Ujjainis intermarry with the following clans :—

In Rájpútána.		In Oudh, the North-West Provinces, and Bhojepore.*	
Give their daughters to	Take wives from	Give their daughters to	Take wives from
Kachwáha.	Gahlot.	Ráthor.	Chamar-Gaur.
Gaur.	Chuhán.	Chauhán.	Nikumbh.
Ráthor.	Tonwar.	Sombansi.	Raghubansi.
Gahlot.	Ráthor.	Kachwáha.	Janwár.
Chauhán.		Dikhit.	Raikwar.
Solanki.		Bhojepore: Bisen.	Ahban.
Parihar.		Bhojepore: Sirnét.	Gaharwar.
Jhalla.		Bhojepore: Rájkumar.	Bhojepore: Dikhit.
		Bhojepore: Súrajbans.	Bhojepore: Nikumbh.
		Bhojepore: Raghubausi.	Bhojepore: Barwar.
		Bhojepore: Sikarwar.	Bhojepore: Hariyobans.
		Bhojepore: Kalhans.	Bhojepore: Kinwar.
		Bhojepore: Hariyobans.	Bhojepore: Raghubansi.
			Bhojepore: Séngar.
			Bhojepore: Sakarwar.
			Bhojepore: Chandél.

Pundir or Purir.

Shown in map as 61.

This clan belongs to the ancient *Dahima* race, one of the 36 royal tribes, of which Tod says: "Seven centuries have swept away all re-collection of a tribe which once afforded one of the proudest themes for the song of the bard." The *Pundirs* were the most powerful vassals of the *Chauháns* of Delhi, and at one time held the Lahore frontier for Pirthiráj. The original home of the Punjáb *Pundirs* was Thanésar, and the country between Karnál and Umballa. They were eventually dispossessed by the *Chauháns* under Rána Har Rai

* Bhojepore is a portion of the Shahabad district of Behar.

and for the most part fled across the Jumna. The *Pundirs* of the Doáb state that their ancestors were emigrants from Saharanpur. Their chief settlement was in Aligarh. The *Pundirs* are described as a fine hardy race, and in former times were much given to helping themselves from the property of their neighbours. Confident in their power of combination, the *Pundirs* used to resist the police and revenue authorities by open force. They are still notorious cattle lifters, and are equally distinguished by their pride. In the famine of 1860-61, they preferred to die in their homes, rather than accept relief. The *Pundirs* of Aligarh under their leader Thákur Kundan Singh, were conspicuously loyal in the Mutiny. They protected the *Tahsildar* of Sikandra Ráo, and overawed the Muhammadan population of that town. In the end of August 1857, Kundan Singh having been made *Názim* of the *tahsil*, occupied Sikandra Ráo with 1,500 followers, reinstated the *Tahsildar*, and maintained him in that position till British authority was restored. He was rewarded by the grant of two villages.

History.

Pundirs are found in the Saharanpur, Muzaffarnagar, and Etawah districts, and have a male population of 17,000.

Geographical distribution.

Religion.

Pundirs are mostly Shiva worshippers.

Pundirs contract marriages with members of the following clans:—

Give their daughters to	Take wives from
Bargújar.	Bargújar.
Janghára.	Janghára.
Tonwar.	Tonwar.
Chauhán.	Chauhán.
Jatu.	Játu.
Ponwar.	Ponwar.
Indauliya.	Indauliya.
Gahlot.	
Kachhwáha.	

RAGHUBANSI.

Shown in map as 62.

This clan claims to be descended from Raghu, one of the *Surajbans* kings of Ajudhya. The *Raghubansis* of the Doáb say they came from Ajudhya, with Kúsha, son of Ráma. Those of the Benares district describe themselves as descendants of Déo Kumar who married a daughter of Rája Banár, a celebrated ruler of Benares. The Ghazipur colony is said to have settled there about 1543, during the reign of the Emperor Sher Shah. At the permanent settlement of Bengal in 1791, the *Raghubansis* were large landowners in Benares, but our revenue system and the growing desire of bankers, merchants and lawyers to acquire land, has led to the loss of a considerable portion of their ancestral possessions. "They remain for the most part a proud aristocracy of cultivating tenants, ever with a dangerously envious eye to the paternal estates, the possession of which, however originally acquired, has been legalized according to their ideas, far more completely than any decree of an alien judge can the usurper's."* They are a very fine race and would make excellent soldiers but for the fact that many are *bhagat*, *i.e.*, vegetarians, which takes away from their military value. The outward sign of a *bhagat* is the red *tilak* or forehead mark.

History.

Geographical distribution

Raghubansis are found in the Benares, Mirzapur, Jaunpur, Ghazipur, Azamgarh, and Sultanpur districts of Oudh and the North-West Provinces. They have a male population of 32,000.

Religion.

Raghubansis mostly worship Ráma. They are of the *Kassyap gotra*, but some of their communities profess to belong to the *Vasisht*.

Raghubansis contract marriages with members of the following clans:—

Give their daughters to	Take wives from
Bachhgoti.	Nikumbh.
Rájkumar.	Chaupat Khambh.
Rájwar.	Birwar.
Sirnét.	Nanwág.
Kahnpuria.	Chandél.
Bandhalgoti.	Bisén.
Palwar.	Gaharwar.
	Monas.

* Gazetteer of the North-West Provinces.

RAIKWARS.

Shown in map as 63.

The title of this clan is derived from Raika, the name of a village in the Kashmir hills near Jummoo, which is claimed as the original home of the tribe.

Traditional origin.

The *Raikwars* belong to the Solar race, and established themselves in Oudh early in the 15th century. They claim four *Ráthor* brothers as their ancestors, and state that the latter emigrated from Guzerat to Kashmir, about 300 years before the clan moved into Oudh.

The founders of the clan were three brothers named Partáb Sáh, Dundé Sáh and Bhairwanand, who about 1414 took up their abode at Ramnagar in the Bara Banki district. On Partáb Sáh's death, his two sons, Sáldéo and Baldéo, persuaded their uncle Bhairwanand that in accordance with the prophecy of a *Pundit*, it was necessary that he should allow himself to be killed by them, in order to ensure the prosperity of his race. To this he obligingly consented. The brothers Sáldéo and Baldéo then entered the service of two Bhár Rájas, and managed their estates so satisfactorily, that the Rájas in their pride began to resist the Muhammadans. The *Raikwars* took advantage of the opportunity, slew their patrons, and about 1450 possessed themselves of their estates. Such is the origin of the two great *Raikwar* houses of Ramnagar and Baundi. In 1590, during the reign of Akbar, the *Raikwar* chieftain, Harhardéo, was summoned to Delhi to explain a breach of good manners in levying toll from a lady of the Imperial family as she passed through his estates on a pilgrimage to the shrine of Sayyad Salár. He, however, rendered the Emperor such valuable assistance in suppressing a rebellion in Kashmir, that the latter bestowed upon him large grants of land in Bahraich, and the clan rose to high favour with the Mughals. In 1751 the *Raikwars* seem to have headed a great Hindu movement to shake off the Musalmán yoke in Oudh. Had the insurrection broken out at the time of the Rohilla invasion, it would have had every chance of success. As it was, they delayed matters until after Safdar Jang, the Nawáb Wazir, had disposed of the Rohillas by diplomacy, the result being that the Rájpúts were defeated by the Musalmáns with great slaughter at Chhéola Ghát, many of their Rájas being slain. After this the Ramnagar and Baundi estates were confiscated and the *Raikwars* remained in low circumstances until 1816, when they gradually recovered their possessions. The power of the clan was at its height in the thirty years which preceded the annexation of Oudh. It is yet a nystery why this tribe turned so bitterly against the British in the Mutiny. Of the rebel leaders, three—Narpat Singh of Rúia, Gúrbaksh Singh of Bhitauli, and Hárdatt Singh of Baundi—were *Raikwars*. These three chiefs led a force of 25,000 men even after the fall of Lucknow. Baundi for months sheltered the Queen of Oudh and her paramour Mámmu Khan. Bhitauli was the head-quarters of the rebellion. In Rúia the Moulvi of Fyzabad ensconced himself, and under its walls lie the remains of Adrian Hope, perhaps the most mourned of the English soldiers who fell in the campaigns of 1857-58. There are small *Raikwar* colonies in Fyzabad, Gorakhpur, and Azamgarh, which were established by emigrants from Oudh about seven generations ago.

Geographical distribution.

The *Raikwars* are found chiefly in the Unao, Hardoi, Bahraich, and Bara Banki districts of Oudh. They have a male population of 13,000.

Religion.

Raikwars to this day make an annual pilgrimage in the village of Chanda Sihali to worship a *chabutra* or platform erected to the memory of their hero Bhairwanand, who gave up his life to ensure the prosperity of his race. Unlike other Rájpúts, *Raikwars* cannot use tooth-brushes made of the wood of the *nim* tree.

Raikwars contract marriages with Rájpúts of the following clans :—

Give their daughters to		Take wives from	
Bahraich and Bara Banki.	Chauhán.	Bahraich and Bara Banki.	Chandél.
	Bhadauriya.		Bisén.
	Sirnét.		Janwár.
	Gargbansi.		Gahlot.
	Bhalé-Sultán.		Dikhit.
	Chandauriya.		
	Ráotar.		
	Bachhgoti.	Unao.	Gahlot.
			Mahror.

	Give their daughters to		Take wives from
Unao.	Dikhit.	Hardoi.	Bais.
	Gaharwár.		Ahban.
	Janwár.		Katheriya.
	Chauhán.		Gaur.
	Chandél.		Chandél.
Hardoi.	Sómbansi.		
	Chandél.		
	Gaur.		
	Chauhán.		
	Tonwar.		
	Ahban.		

RÁTHOR.

Shown in map as 64.

Their traditional origin.

The name of this celebrated clan is derived from the Sanskrit *ráshtra kúla*, 'a royal race.' The *Ráthors* claim to be descended from Ráma, king of Ajudhya, which would make them a sept of the Solar race. Their true origin, however, is lost in obscurity. It is not improbable that the *Ráthors* were *Gaharwárs* who adhered to Bráhmanism when the rest of the clan became Buddhists. The *Gaharwárs* to this day claim to be connected with the *Ráthors*, and there is evidence to prove that Kanouj was governed by a *Gaharwár* dynasty, before the *Ráthors* took possession of the place.

History.

In 1050 the *Ráthors* ejected the *Tonwars* from Kanouj, and there founded a kingdom which rivalled Delhi in power and magnificence. In 1191 the Afghán Muhammad Ghori captured Delhi, stormed Kanouj, and defeated Rája Jai Chand at Benares, where he was drowned in crossing the Ganges. After this crushing reverse, the Rája's nephew Sheoji emigrated with his vassals to Marwar and Bikaneer, where they seized and established themselves on a portion of the *Bhátti* territory. There the clan rapidly increased, and in less than three centuries regained its former prestige. The Máhárája of Jodhpore or Marwar is the head of the *Ráthor* clan, which also furnishes the reigning families of Bikaneer and Kishengarh, and the titular Rája of Rámpur in Etah.

Ráthor settlements in the North-Western Provinces.

The *Ráthors* of Mainpuri and Etah settled there after the fall of Kanouj. Parjan Pál, a descendant of Rája Jai Chand, founded Khor near Shamsabad in the Farukhabad district, which was attacked by the Musalmáns under Shamsuddin Altamsh in 1236, and only captured after a siege of 12 years. Being unable to make any impression on the *Ráthor* fortress, a Muhammadan *fakir* suggested that a large head of cows should be driven up to the gates, behind which the besiegers might advance in safety. The ruse was successful, and seeing that they could not repulse the enemy without endangering the sacred kine, the *Ráthors* abandoned the city, and retired by a postern gate. *Ráthor* refugees from Khor settled in Budaun, Farukhabad, and Etah, whence they expelled the aboriginal Méos and Bhars. The Azamgarh settlement was founded by colonists from the Doáb about 20 generations ago. The Rája of Rampur in Etah, a lineal descendant of Jai Chand, is the head of the clan in the North-West Provinces.

Geographical distribution.

In Rájpútána the *Ráthors* are the most numerous and powerful of the Rájpút clans, and are imbued with a strong national spirit. Their male population amounts to 102,000. In the North-West Provinces they number 35,000 males. The eastern settlements have fallen in social status through intermarrying with inferior clans, but the *Ráthors* of the Doáb pride themselves on the purity of their blood, and have pedigrees as flawless as those of their western brethren. In Rájpútána, *Ráthors* are found in Meywar, Dungarpur, Marwar, Jaisulmeer, Bikaneer, Jeypore, and Kishengarh. In the North-West Provinces they have settled in the Farukhabad, Mainpuri, Etawah, Etah, Bareilly, Budaun, Shahjahanpur, Cawnpore, and Azamgarh districts.

The following are the principal *Ráthor* septs:—

Mallináth.	Bidráwat.
Jódhá.	Champáwat.
Bika.	Kándalót.
Merthia.	

The tribal divinities of the *Ráthors* are Hanumánji, Rámdéo, and Nágnechi in Marwar; and Lakhmináth, Chutterbhúj, Nagnéchi and Karniji in Bikanir. They are of the *Kassyap* gotra.

Ráthors intermarry with the following clans:—

In Rájpútána.		In the North-Western Provinces.	
Give their daughters to	Take wives from	Give their daughters to	Take wives from
Kachwáha. Bhatti. Gahlot. Jhalla. Solanki. Ponwar. Chauhan. Tonwar Jádu.	Kachwáha. Bhátti. Gahlot. Jádu. Tonwar. Parihár. Jhalla. Solanki. Ponwar. Chauhán. Gaur. Bargújar.	Kachwáha. Chauhán. Bhadauriya.	Kachwáha. Chauhán. Bhadauriya. Parihar. Chandél. Dikhit. Ahban.

The *Ráthor* of Rájpútána is remarkable for his freedom from Hindu prejudices. In Bikaneer he will eat food and drink water without troubling to enquire by whom it is served. He will eat food cooked by Bráhmans, Banyas, Ahirs, Játs, Gújars, Nais, and the servant class; and can dispense with a *chauka* or prepared cooking place. The staunchness of the *Ráthor* warrior has always been proverbial. The Mughal Emperors owed half their conquests to the prowess of "the *lakh turwar Rathorin*," or '100,000 swords of the *Ráthors*.' They still make admirable soldiers, whether from Rájpútána or the Doáb, but the former are very difficult to enlist, as the *Ráthors* of Marwar will only serve in the cavalry, while those of Bikaneer will not take service at all.

RÁWATS.

Shown in map as 65.

The *Ráwats* call themselves pure *Bais*, but this is not generally admitted by their neighbours, who say that they are *fifth* sons of Rája Tilok Chand. The term 'fifth sons' is the common Rájpút eupheuism for bastards†. It is very probable that they are the offspring of Tilok Chand by an Ahir woman. They themselves assert that about 250 years ago the aboriginal Sunars, taking advantage of some festivities at Bithur, their principal village in Unao, rose and massacred the whole clan, only one woman, who proved pregnant, escaping. She was protected by an Ahir, and in gratitude called her son Ráwat* Béni Singh. On

History.

* Ráwat is a favourite title among Ahirs.

† See also page 28.

growing up to manhood Béni Singh entered the service of the Emperor of Delhi. There he rose to favour, and obtaining permission to recover his ancestral estate, led a force against the Sunars and massacred the entire tribe while they were keeping up the festival of Káli Débi, thus regaining his former possessions.

Geographical distribution.

Ráwats are found in the Unao and Fatehpur districts of Oudh. The clan is not a large one, but its exact numbers cannot be stated as they are not recorded in the last Census Report. *Ráwats* worship Debi, and belong to the *Bharaddwaj gotra*.

Religion.

Rawats contract marriages with members of the following Rájpút clans :—

Give their daughtsers to	Take wives from
Gaur.	Bais.
Chandél.	Banáphar.
Chauhán.	Janwár.
Kachwáha.	

SÉNGAR.

Shown in map as 66.

The origin of this clan is unknown; it is one of the 36 royal tribes and like the *Gautam* claims descent from Singhi Rishi.

Traditional origin and history.

The Bráhman Singhi Rishi was invited to the court of the *Gaharwar* Rája of Kanouj, and married his daughter, receiving as her dowry a grant of an immense number of villages, extending from Kanouj to Manikpur. Puran Déo, the grandson of Singhi Rishi, and founder of the *Séngar* clan, emigrated to the Dekhan. Several centuries later, the clan moved to Dhar in Málwa, and thence to Bándhúgarh in Rewah, and Jagmohanpur on the Etawah border of Jalaun. There in 1065 was born Rája Bisukh Déo, who married a daughter of Jai Chand, the *Ráthor* king of Kanouj. After the fall of that city, the *Séngars* took possession of the greater part of Etawah, and the river Basind was renamed the Séngar in their honour. The *Séngar* colony in Oudh was established in 1527 when the Emperor Bábar was engaged in subduing the independent chieftains of Hindustán. While so employed, many of the Afghán adventurers who had served the preceding Lodi dynasty, came in and tendered their services. Among these was Shaikh Bayazid, who was appointed Governor of Oudh. With the usual faithlessness of a Patháu, he shortly afterwards revolted, and raised a considerable army to oppose the Mughals. Among his followers were number of *Séngar* Rájpúts from Jagmohanpur, under two leaders called Jagat Sáh and Gopál Singh. after Shaikh Bayazid's defeat, the *Séngars* settled down quietly in Unao. Eleven generations later, the aboriginal Lodhs rose suddenly against the *Séngars*, and murdered the majority of the clan. The fugitives fled to their brethren at Jagmohanpur, and returning thence in force, recovered their possessions in Unao. Meanwhile Pathan settlers had begun to encroach upon the lands of the *Séngar* colonists, and the latter feeling themselves strong enough to oppose them, met them at Bani, and after a great fight drove them across the Sai. The head of the clan is the Rája of Jagmohanpur in Jalaun.

Geographical distribution.

The *Séngar* clan is very little known in Rájpútána. In Oudh and the North-West Provinces it has a male population of 32,000, distributed throughout the Etawah, Cawnpore, Jalaun, Ballia, and Unao districts.

Séngars intermarry with the following clans :—

Give their daughters to		Take wives from	
North-West Provinces.	Chauhán.	Oudh & North-West Provinces.	Parihár.
	Bhadauriya.		Chamar-Gaur.
	Ráthor.		Chandél.
	Kachwáha.		Gautam.
	Sisodiya.		Gaharwar.
	Chandél.		Panwar.
	Tonwar.		Gahlot.
	Jádon.		Baghél.
Oudh.	Chauhán.		Bisén.
	Ráthor.		Janwár.
	Parihar.		Bais.
	Tilokchandi Bais.		Sengar.

	Give their daughters to		Take wives from
Eastern Districts.	Bais.	Oudh.	Dikhit.
	Gahlot.		Sómbansi.
	Harihobans.	Eastern Districts.	Bisén.
	Ujjaini.		Donwar.
	Kausik.		Kákan.
	Sirnet.		Kausik.
	Rájkumar.		Nikumbh.
	Surajbansi.		Sakarwar.
	Parihár.		Harihobans.
	Kinwar.		Raghubans.
	Raghubansi.		
	Sómbansi.		
	Nikumbh.		
	Chauhán.		

SIRNÉT.

Shown in map as 67.

Traditional origin.

Various accounts have been given of the origin of the title of this clan. One authority derives it from *sira*, 'a head,' and *neta*, a 'leader.' Another explanation is that one of their chiefs was in the habit of wearing on his head a cloth of gold called *nét*, and the Muhammadan king in whose service he was, not choosing to recollect his Hindu name, called him *Sirnét*, or 'the man with the gold cloth on his head.' In the Ghazipur districts the *Sirnéts* call themselves *Nikumbhs* and say they got the name from their custom of raising the hand to the head without bowing, when making obeisance to a superior. One of the Muhammadan Emperors, annoyed by the apparent disrespect of some *Nikumbh* chiefs who were in attendance at his court, ordered that before their entrance a sword should be placed across the doorway in such a manner that they, on entering the presence, should be forced to stoop. Some of the *Nikumbh* chiefs, scorning to abandon their tribal customs, maintained their upright position and were decapitated. The Emperor, satisfied with this exhibition of determination, permitted them in future to make their *salám* in their own fashion, and gave them the title of *Sirnét*, which is said to be a corruption of the Persian *sarnist*, 'head less.'

The *Sirnéts* claim descent from Bharáta, the brother of Ráma of Ajudhya.

The founder of the clan was a *Súrajbans* or *Dikhit* Rájpút named Chandra Sén, who, after incurring the wrath of some Muhammadan Emperor, was forgiven at the intercession of a friendly Bráhman, and, after his release, accompanied the latter to his home in the country beyond the Gogra. After many adventures, Chandra Sén is said to have settled in Gorakhpur towards the end of the 12th century, and there established a kingdom which was called *Satási* because the circuit of his territories extended to 87 *kós*. As he appropriated land eastwards, he became involved in hostilities with the *Donwár* Rájpúts. They were on the point of compelling him to quit the district, when his Bráhman adviser suggested a stratagem which proved completely successful. Chandra Sén, being a pure Kshatriya, was deemed superior to the *Donwars*, who had sullied their lineage by intermarrying with Dóms and Bhárs. He therefore suggested that his daughter should marry the son of the principal *Donwar* Rája, on condition of his being allowed to retain a part of the country he had invaded. His proposal was gladly accepted. Immense preparations were made for the wedding, and Chandra Sén gained admission to the *Donwar* fort with a large body of followers. Then, seizing his opportunity, he treacherously murdered the *Donwar* chiefs, while his followers outside slaughtered as many of the clan as they could find. The power of the *Donwars* was crippled by this blow, and the *Sirnéts* became one of the most powerful clans in Gorakhpur.

History.

The *Sirnet* clan is found in the Gorakhpur and Basti districts of the North-West Provinces, and has a male population of nearly 10,000.

Geographical distribution.

The favourite *Sirnét* deity is the goddess Débi. The clan belongs to the *Bharaddwáj gotra*.

Religion.

Sirnéts contract marriages with Rájpúts of the following clans :—

Give their daughters to	Take wives from
Kalhans.	Súrajbans.
Súrajbans.	Baghél.
Chauhán.	Bisén.
Bhadauriya.	Rájkumar.
Baghél.	Bachhgoti.
	Kalhans.
	Gautam.
	Gaharwar.
	Dikhit.
	Kanhpuriya.
	Amethiya.

SIKARWARS OR SAKARWARS.

Shown in map as 68.

Traditional origin.

The title of the clan is derived from Fatehpur-Sikri in the Agra district, the present head-quarters of the clan. It is included by Tod amongst the 36 royal races and is supposed by some authorities to be a sept of the *Bargújars.* Like the latter, the *Sikarwars* claim descent from Láva, the son of Ráma, king of Ajudhya.

History.

According to tribal traditions it would seem that the *Sikarwars* on leaving Ajudhya, made the tour of Northern India. From Oudh they migrated to Lahore, by which perhaps is meant Laháwar in Gwalior; from Laháwar to Rajor in Ulwar; from Rajor to Rúpbás in Bhurtpur; and from Rúpbás to Fatehpur-Sikri. The migration from Gwalior territory is said to have taken place about 600 years ago. Towards the end of the 12th century, the tribe spread all over the Agra district, and must have established colonies in Oudh and Gorakhpur, shortly after the invasion of Shaháb-ud-din Ghori. The Ghazipur and Azamgarh branches claim to have emigrated from Fatehpur-Sikri, but say their ancestors were Bráhmans; they also claim a mythical personage called Rája

Gadh as their ancestor, and hence sometimes call themselves *Gadiyas.* The *Parbatiyas* of the lower Himalayas are said to be a branch of the *Sikarwars.*

Geographical distribution.

Sikarwars are found in the Agra, Ghazipur, Gorakhpur, Azamgarh and Hardoi districts of Oudh and the North-West Provinces, and have a male population of 18,000. The clan is also numerous in the Gwalior State, especially in the neighbourhood of the Chambal, where its members have a high reputation for bravery.

Religion.

Sikarwars are of the *Bharaddwáj gotra* and chiefly worship Mahádéo.

Sikarwars contract marriages with Rájpúts of the following clans:—

	Give their daughters to		Take wives from
Agra.	Bhadauriya.	Agra.	Bhadauriya.
	Chauhán.		Chauhán.
	Jádón.		Jádón.
	Dhákré.		Dhákré.
	Gahlot.		Gahlot.
	Ponwar.		Ponwar.
	Parihár.		Parihár.
	Pundir.		Pundir.
	Tonwar.		Tonwar
			Bargújar.
			Baresari.
			Indauliya.
Eastern districts.	Hayobans.	E. districts.	Hayobans.
	Ujjaini.		Ujjaini.
	Donwar.		Donwar.
	Kinwar.		Kinwar.
Oudh.	Chauhán.	Oudh.	Báchhal.
	Bhadauriya.		Raikwar.
	Ponwar.		Janwár.
	Sómbans.		Ahban.
			Gautam.

SOLANKI OR CHALUKYA.

Shown in map as 69.

This clan is one of the four agnicular or fire tribes, of which an account has been given on page 111 under the heading of *Ponwar*.

Traditional origin.

The title of *Chalukya* is derived from *challu*, because the founder of the race was formed in the *challu* or 'hollow of the hand' when the *Rishis* summoned their four Kshatriya champions from the flames of the *agni kunda* on Mount Abu.

The *Solankis* are said to have been settled on the banks of the Ganges before the *Ráthors* obtained possession of Kanouj, but according to their own traditions they held Lahore up to about the 8th century. They were among the first Rájpúts to become Muhammadans, and were the principal opponents of the *Bháttis* when the latter first settled in the Bikaneer desert. The *Solankis* were formerly princes of Kalyan near Bombay, whence they established a dynasty which ruled over Anhalwára Pattan, one of the richest and most warlike kingdoms in India, with dominions extending from the Carnatic to the Himalayas. Their capital Anhalwára Pattan was stormed by Mahmud of Ghazni, in 1024, but soon recovered its former prosperity.

History.

In the 8th century a band of *Solanki* adventurers left Tonk in Rájpútána and settled under the leadership of Rája Maldeo Sarmáni in the Etah district, where their descendants are still to be found, but in greatly impoverished circumstances. The colony in Budaun is probably an offshoot of the Etah settlement.

Solanki settlements in the North-West Provinces.

The *Solankis* are now a small clan, and in Rájpútána their male population only amounts to 7,000. They are found chiefly in Marwar, Jeypore Boondi and Rewah. In the North-West Provinces they number 8,000 males, and have settlements in Etah and Budaun.

Geographical distribution.

The principal *Solanki* divinities are Krishna and Ráma. The tribal goddess in Rájpútána is Chárbhujja.

Religion.

The principal tribal divisions are as follows:—

Solanki proper.	Rahallia.
Bhagél.	Chandáwat.
Khalats.	Bhutta.
Sojathia.	Dhaien.

Certain septs are also found in Guzerat and the Dekhan.

Solankis intermarry with the following clans :—

RÁJPÚTÁNA.		NORTH-WEST PROVINCES.	
Give their daughters to	Take wives from	Give their daughters to	Take wives from
Bhátti. Jádu. Ráthor. Kachwáha. Pónwar. Parihar.	Ráthor. Pónwar.	Chauhán. Bhadauriya.	Katiyar. Tomar. Ráthor. Báchhal. Bais. Gaur. Pundir. Bargújar. Chauhán.

SÓMBANSI.

Shown in map as 70.

The title of this clan is derived from the Sanskrit *Soma*, 'the moon,' from which the *Sómbansi* like the *Chandarbansi* claim to be lineally descended. From a generic name applied to all tribes belonging to the Lunar race, *Sómbansi* has come to be the title of a particular clan. The same thing has happened in the case of the *Súrajbansi*, and it is probable from the number of its *gotras* that the *Sómbansis* of the present day are descended from remnants of various Kshatriya tribes, claiming a Lunar origin, who banded themselves together for mutual protection, and adopted the title of *Sómbansi* as the distinctive appellation of their brotherhood.

Traditional origin.

The *Sómbansis* claim a mythical personage called Púr as the founder of their clan. Their most ancient traditions attribute the northern shores of the Ganges as their original home, but historical researches prove that by the 13th century they were settled at Jhúsi near Allahabad. There the *Sómbansi* Rája Bhai Sén was visited by a Muhammadan *fakir*, who ordered him to abandon his fort. On this demand being refused, the *fakir* murdered the Rája, but consoled his Ráni, who was pregnant at the time, by assuring her that her unborn child would become a warrior of great renown. The Ráni then left Jhúsi and settled near Partábgarh in Oudh, where in due time she gave birth to a son called Lákhan Sén, who about 1258, expelled the Bhars and the *Ráikwar* Rájpúts from the district, and established a kingdom of his own. The sons of Lákhan Sén quarrelled over their heritage, and one of them secured the favour of the Muhammadan Emperors by becoming a Musalmán, and marrying a lady of the Imperial family. In the reign of Akbar, Rája Sultán Sáh served with his tribal contingent in the Múghal army then fighting in the Dekhan. As a reward for his services, the paternal estate was conferred on him in *jaghir* tenure, the only condition of the grant being that the *Sómbansis* should escort the annual tribute of Bengal to Delhi. One of Sultan Sáh's successors, the Rája Jai Singh, defeated and captured a *Bundéla* outlaw named Chatur Sál, for which the Emperor conferred upon him the privilege of wearing a *topi* in *darbar* in lieu of the usual *pagri*. In the reign of the Emperor Muhammad Shah (1738-48) Rája Pirthipat Singh murdered the son of a Manikpur banker who had enough influence at Delhi to obtain the issue of an order to Safdar Jang, the Subadar of Oudh, to punish the murderer. This was eventually accomplished by treachery, the Rája being assassinated in *darbar* and his estates confiscated. This was the end of the Partábgarh Ráj, for the property was shortly afterwards divided. The head of the clan is now the Rája of Bahlolpur. The *Sómbansis* of Farrukhabad claim descent from Randhir Singh, an adventurer from Oudh, who settled in the Doáb about 300 years ago. The Chand dynasty of Kumaun is an offshoot of a younger branch of the *Sómbansis* of Jhúsi, from whom the *Rautélas*, another tribe of hill Rájpúts, also claim descent.

Geographical distribution.

Sómbansis have a male population of 43,000, which is scattered through the Farrukhabad, Bareilly, Shahjahanpur, Allahabad, Jáunpur, Azamgarh, Rai-Bareli, Sitapur, Hardoi, Gonda, and Partabgarh districts of Oudh and the North-West Provinces.

Religion.

The *Sómbansis* are snake-worshippers. During the *Nág-Panchmi* festival in July-August, *Sómbansis* give up shaving, wear dirty clothes, and abstain from milk, meat and fish. Their favourite divinities are Mahádéo and Káli. The *Sómbansis* have as their family heroes, five saints—four of them princes of *Sómbansi* blood, and the fifth a *Gaharwár* Rája of Benares. The principal of these, Alá Rikh, gave his name to Aláukhpur, contracted into Aror, and since named Partábgarh.

Sómbansis are divided into the three following gotras:—

Baiyagar. | Sankirat. | Atri.

Tribal divisions.

The *Sómbansis* of Sandi in the Hardoi district rank higher than any other branches of the clan.

Sómbansis contract marriages with Rájpúts of the following clans:—

District	Give their daughters to	District	Take wives from
Hardoi.	Chauhán.	Hardoi.	Raikwár.
Hardoi.	Ráthor.	Hardoi.	Katiyar.
Hardoi.	Kachwáha.	Hardoi.	Gaur.
Hardoi.	Bhadauriya.	Hardoi.	Báchhal.
Partabgarh.	Améthiya.	Hardoi.	Bais.
Partabgarh.	Bais.	Hardoi.	Janwár.
Partabgarh.	Baghél.	Hardoi.	Chandél.
Partabgarh.	Gautam.	Hardoi.	Ponwár.
Partabgarh.	Kalhans.	Hardoi.	Gaharwar.
Partabgarh.	Parihár.	Hardoi.	Sakarwar.
Partabgarh.	Súrajbansi.	Hardoi.	Ahban.
Partabgarh.	Sirnét.	Hardoi.	Nikumbh.
Partabgarh.	Chauhán.	Partabgarh.	Dikhit.
Partabgarh.	Kachwáha.	Partabgarh.	Bachgoti.
		Partabgarh.	Rájkumar.
		Partabgarh.	Rájwar.
		Partabgarh.	Bisén.
		Partabgarh.	Kanhpuriya.
		Partabgarh.	Janwár.
		Partabgarh.	Durgbansi.
		Partabgarh.	Bandhalgoti.
		Partabgarh.	Nandwak.

SURAJBANSI.

Shown in map as 71.

The title of this clan is derived from the Sanskrit *Surya*, 'the sun' and *vansha*, 'a race.' The Solar races claim descent from Ikshváku, the grandson of the sun, who founded Ajudhya and established the dynasty from which sprang Ráma, the hero who was afterwards deified as an incarnation of Vishnu. The modern *Surajbansi* must not be confounded with the Solar

Traditional origin.

race of the epic period of Hinduism, as though admittedly connected with the latter, it is probable that the existing clan originated in a congerie of degraded members of various tribes claiming a Solar origin, who banded themselves together for mutual protection, and gradually formed a new sept, which adopted the title of *Súrajbansi* as its distinctive appellation.

All the Solar tribes except the *Súrajbansi* claim descent from Láva and Kúsha, the sons of Ráma. The latter, however, claim Bhárat, the brother of Ráma, as their ancestor, and state that he left Ajudhya to assist his uncle, the ruler of an Aryan principality in the Himalayas or Kashmir, in repelling an invasion of barbarians from China and Tibet.

History.

Bhárat never returned, and is credited with having founded Srinagar in Garhwál. The *Súrajbansis* of the Basti district are supposed to have come from Kumaun under their chiefs Alak Déo and Tilak Déo, and to have expelled the aboriginal Ráj-Bhárs and Tárus. There is a widely received tradition among Rájpúts that a *Súrajbansi* leader named Kanak Sén left Ajudhya about 224 with a large following, and migrated westward to Guzerat, and from thence to Chitór in Rájpútána. The *Surajbansis* of the Fyzabad district claim descent from Lálji Singh, an adventurer from Kumaun, who settled in the district about 350 years ago and entered the service of a wealthy grain dealer. On the latter's death, Lálji Singh seized his property and became a great landholder. There seems to be an undoubted connection between the *Súrajbansis* of the plains and certain hill tribes of Garhwál, Kumaun, and Nepál, who lay claim to a Kshatriya origin. Besides the settlements made in prehistoric times by Bhárat, there is a tradition, confirmed by Tod in his Annals of Rájasthán, that towards the end of the 12th century a band of *Sisodiya* Rájpúts of the *Súrajbansi* or Solar race escaped from Chitór, and after cutting their way through the Muhammadan hosts, took refuge in the hills of Nepál, where they were hospitably received by the aboriginal hill tribes. To this day *Khás* Gúrkhas often describe themselves as *Súrajbans* Rájpúts, and the Malla Rájas of Nepál claim to be descended from Ansuvárma, a member of the *Súrajbans* family which ruled over Visáli near Patna, at the time of the Buddhist dominion. The *Pahári Súrajbansis* of Khairagarh in the Kheri district, are emigrants from Kumaun who were driven out of their native hills by the Gúrkhas towards the close of the 18th century. From about 1790 to 1830 they wandered about the border subsisting on the charity of their fellow Kshatriyas, and fighting for the British against their old enemies the Nepalese. In 1830

districts. Their exact numbers are not recorded in the Census Report.

Marriages.

Tánks intermarry with clans of the highest grade.

TARKÁN OR TARKAR.

Shown in map as 74.

The title of this tribe is said to be a corruption of *tark kiyá* thrown aside,' because the founders of the clan, who were notorious Bráhman dacoits, were offered pardon if they would abandon their evil courses. They did so, and to show how completely they had severed from their old caste, they threw aside their Bráhmanical *Janéos*, hence their name. They have thus no claim whatever to be considered Rájputs; they claim affinity however, with the *Dikhits*, and say that these latter excommunicated them for having adopted *kardo* or widow marriage. They are turbulent, of poor physique, and generally unsuitable for enlistment. Among Rájpúts they hold a very low place, being regarded as *Gaurúas* (q. v.)

Traditional origin and history.

Tarkáns are found in the Muttra and Agra districts of the North-Western Provinces, and have a male population of about 3,500.

Geographical distribution.

Tarkáns contract marriages with members of the following clans :—

Give their daughters to	Take wives from
Báchhal.	Báchhal.
Gaur.	Gaur.
Jádon.	Indauliya.
Janghára.	Baresari.
Kachwáha.	
Indauliya.	
Baresari.	

TILAUNTA.

Shown in map as 75.

This is a small tribe of *Tonwar* origin. They say that their ancestors emigrated from Delhi into the Shahabad district in the time of Rája Bhoj.

History.

Considering its small numbers, the clan furnishes a good many recruits to the Native Army.

Geographical distribution. *Tilauntas* are found only in the Shahabad district of Behar.

Religion. *Tilauntas* worship Débi. They are of the *Kassyap gotra.*

Tilauntas contract marriages with members of the following clans:—

Give their daughters to	Take wives from
Chauhán.	Dhekaha.
Lautamiya.	Lautamiya.

TONWAR, TOMAR, OR TUAR.

Shown in map as 76.

The name of the clan is derived from the Sanskrit *tomdra*, 'an iron club.' The *Tonwar* belong to the Lunar race, and are usually reckoned among the 36 royal tribes.

Traditional origin.

The *Tonwar* were at one time very powerful, and furnished Delhi and Kanouj with a celebrated dynasty. The last of the *Tonwar* Rájas was Anangpál, who abdicated in favour of his *Chauhán* grandson Pirthiráj, during whose reign the Musalmáns conquered India. A *Tonwar* dynasty ruled over Kanouj from 736 to 1050, when it was taken from them by the *Ráthors*, who compelled them to return to the neighbourhood of Delhi. In the reign of Ala-ud-din Khilji, a *Tonwar* Rájpút, called Bir Singh Déva, declared his independence, and founded the *Tonwar* kingdom of Gwalior, which was a powerful and wealthy state up to the time of its capture by Ibrahim Lodi in 1519. The *Tonwar* are now of little account, but they still hold a portion of the Jeypore state called Torawatti,* and have a titular Rája who lives at Pattan, the principal town.

History.

* Also called Tonwarwatti.

Tonwar settlements in Oudh and the North-Western Provinces.

The *Tonwars* of Budaon are emigrants from Delhi who settled in Rohilkhánd about 1202, during the reign of Shahab-ud-din Ghori. The Bareilly *Tonwars* came from Budaun in 1388, and expelled the aboriginal Gwálas, Ahirs, and Bhils. Some of the Rájpúts of Garhwál claim to be of *Tonwar* origin. The eastern settlements of the clan are probably offshoots of the Budaon and Bareilly branches. The latter have now almost entirely dispersed.

Geographical distribution.

The *Tonwar* of Rájpútána have a male population of 13,000. They are found chiefly in Meywar, Marwar, Jeypore, Dholpur, and Bikaneer, also in the adjoining Punjáb districts of Hissar, Nabha, and Patiála. In the North-West Provinces and Oudh they number 18,000 males, and their settlements are scattered through the Muttra, Farrukhabad, Mainpuri, Etawah, Etah, Budaun, and Sitapur districts.

The *Tonwars* belong to the Lunar race and are consequently Krishna worshippers. In Rájpútána their tribal divinities are Jógmaiya or Sárúng.

The principal septs of the *Tonwars* are as follows :—

In Rájpútána and the Punjáb.	In Oudh, the North-West Provinces, and the Gwalior State.
Tonwar.	Nicoop.
Kallia.	Bájpanna.
Játu.	Himkar.
Borahan.	Gawalera.
Beágas.	Jasraiyah.
Jarroata.	Jerah.

The *Tonwar* proper of Tonwarwátti has three sub-divisions, *Asoji, Udoji*, and *Kelorji*. The *Játu* sept through poverty have intermarried with Játs and Gújars, and many families have been outcasted. This is especially the case with those residing in the Hissar and Bhiwani district who should be only enlisted after careful enquiry. A *Tonwar* origin is claimed by several Mahratta chiefs.

Tonwars intermarry with the following clans:—

In Rájpútána.		In Oudh and the North-West Provinces.	
Give their daughters to	Take wives from	Give their daughters to	Take wives from
Chauhán.	Chauhán.	Tilokchandi Bais.	Ahban.
Kachwáha.	Gaur.	Chauhán.	Gau
Ráthor.	Ponwar.	Bhadauriya.	Báchal.
	Bargújar.	Ráthor.	Janwár.
	Ráthor.	Kachwáha.	Ponwar.
	Solanki.	Parihár.	Chauhán.
	Parihár.		Bhadauriya.
	Jádú.		Ráthor.
	Bhátti.		Kachwáha.

Udmattia.

Shown in map as 77.

The title of this tribe is derived from the name of their supposed ancestor, a *Rishi* named Udiálak Múni. The clan professes to be descended from *Súrajbans* emigrants who left Oodeypore about three centuries ago, in the service of one of the early Muhammadan Emperors, and settled in Azamgarh after expelling the aboriginal Bhárs.

History.

Udmattias are found in the Azamgárh and Gorakhpur districts of the North-West Provinces. They have a male population of 28,000.

Geographical distribution.

Udmattias worship Débi. They belong to the *Batas Gotra.*

Religion.

Udmattias contract marriages with members of the following clan:—

Give their daughters to	Take wives from
Kákan.	Pachtoriya.
Bais.	Barhaiya.

UJJAINI.

Shown in map as 78.

Traditional origin and history.

The title of this clan is derived from the city of Ujjain in Rájpútána whence their ancestors migrated into Oudh, Behar, and the eastern districts of the North-West Provinces, during the reign of Jai Chand, the *Ráthor* king of the Kanouj. They are really a sept of the *Ponwars*, of whom an account has been given on page 111. Koer Singh of Jugdespur, one of the three rebel leaders who showed marked military talent in the Mutiny, was a *Ujjaini*, and a near relative of the late Rája of Dumráón the head of the clan.

Geographical distribution.

Ujjainis are found chiefly in the Cawnpore, Ballia, and Azamgarh districts of Oudh and the North-West Provinces, and in the Shahabad district of Behar. They have a population of about 3,000 males.

Religion.

Ujjainis are of the *Saunak* gotra and are *Shákta* worshippers, their principal deity being Káli.

Ujjainis contract marriages with the following clans:—

Give their daughters to	Take wives from
Bisen.	Nikumbh.
Sirnet.	Barwar.
Rajkumar.	Hayobansi.
Surajbans.	Kinwar.
Raghubans.	Raghubans.
Sakarwar.	Sengar.
Kalhans.	Sakarwar.
Hayobans.	Chandel.
	Kákan.
	Narauni.

CHAPTER III.

RELIGION, CUSTOMS, AND RELIGIOUS FESTIVALS.

The religion of the Rájpúts does not differ in any essential particular from that of other classes of high caste Hindus. In Rájpútána and the Eastern Punjáb it is of a simple type, closely resembling the primitive faith of the Aryans, modified, however, by certain usages (such as the worship of the Sun) introduced by Scythian tribes now included in the Kshatriya caste. The nearer we approach to Ajudhya and Benares, the more is the Rájpút dominated by the ceremonial restrictions of the Bráhman, and the more bigoted is the character of his beliefs. Rám Chandar, Mahádéo, and Káli or Débi are perhaps his favourite divinities ; but, as has been noted in Chapter II, nearly every Rájpút clan has its own patron deity, to which its members pay special respect, and look for protection and favour.

The Hindu religion may be said to have passed through the three following stages, which will be briefly described—

1. Védism. 2. Bráhmanism. 3. Hinduism.

VÉDISM.

The religion brought by the Aryans into India from their homes in Central Asia was a simple form of Nature-worship. The deities of the early Hindus were Surya, Agni, and Indra, or Sun, Fire, and Rain, the minor divinities of the earth, air, and sky, being regarded merely as associates of this elemental triad. The traditions of this primitive period are contained in the *Védas*, a series of hymns and texts expressing the wants and beliefs of the people, and their manner of invoking and praising their gods. The *Védic* hymns contain no interdictions against widow-marriage or foreign travel, nor do they insist upon child marriage, or the vexatious restrictions of caste, all of which owe their origin to the Bráhmans. The gods of the *Védic* epoch were bright and friendly. There were no blood-drinking deities to propitiate. Sacrifice was merely a symbol, representing the gratitude of the people to their divine protectors. The ordinary offerings consisted of the sacred *homa*, or rice, milk, butter, and cruds, with animal sacrifices, particularly of the horse,* on occasions of special solemnity.

BRÁHMANISM.

The gradual formation of a special class devoted to religious meditation and austerities, led to the organization of a regular priesthood, who officiated at the sacrifices, and moulded the vague Nature-worship of the *Védas* into a definite philosophical creed, made manifest by an elaborate ritual. The deepest thinkers felt that all material things were permeated by a divine spirit. This vague, mysterious, all-pervading power, which was wholly unbound by limitations of personality, at last became real. The breath of life received a name. They called it ***brahman***, from the Sanskrit *brih* 'to expand,' because it expanded itself through space, diffusing itself everywhere and in every thing. The old *Védic* triad disappeared. Agni, Indra, and Surya gave way to Brahma, Vishnu, and Síva. In other words, the forces of Nature were identified with a vague spiritual power which, when manifested as a Creator, was called *Bráhma;* as a Preserver, *Vishnu;* as a Destroyer, *Siva;* and found its human manifestation in the sacred order of Bráhmans, who were thus raised immeasurably above the rest of mankind. The *Védic* idea of sacrifices was that they were thanks-offerings to the gods; but as *Védism* developed into Bráhmanism, the whole theory of sacrifice changed. It was considered that the gods required to be nourished by the essence of the food offered up, and that their worshippers should take advantage of their being pleased and invigorated, to obtain from them the boons they desired. This idea was further developed into a belief that super-human powers were to be attained by sacrifices, which as a natural result became more and more complicated. According to the true theory of Bráhmanism, all visible forms on earth are emanations of the Almighty. Stones, rivers, plants, and animals, are all progressive steps in the infinite evolution of His Being. The highest earthly emanation is man, and the highest type of man is the Bráhman, who is the appointed mediator between gods and humanity. In the *Trimurti* or Hindu Trinity, all three persons are equal, and their functions interchangeable. All three are imbued with the same divine essence, and as the latter is all-pervading, they may be worshipped through the medium of inferior gods, goddesses, ancestors, heroes, Bráhmans, animals, and plants.

---

* The *Aswamédha* or horse sacrifice was practised by the Solar Rájpúts on the banks of the Ganges and Sárju 12 centuries B. C. "It was a martial challenge which consisted in letting the horse which was to crown the royal triumph at the year's end go free to wander at will over the face of the earth, its sponsor being bound to follow its hoofs, and to conquer or conciliate the chiefs through whose territories it passed." At the end of the year the horse was brought back, "led round the sacred fire and immolated with the sacred scimitar whilst Bráhmans chanted the *Védic* hymns. The carcase was then cut up and different portions of the flesh committed to the flames, while the *hotris* or sacrificial priests recited appropriate *mántras* or texts."—Encyclopædia Britannica, and History of India—*Talboys Wheeler.*

HINDUISM.

We now arrive at the third stage of Hindu religious thought, and the modern forms of Hindu worship. The main point of difference between Bráhmanism and Hinduism is that the latter subordinates the worship of the Creator Bráhma to that of Vishnu, Siva, and the wives of these divinities, allowing each sect to exalt its favourite god above and in place of all others.

"Hinduism is based on the idea of universal receptivity. It has, so to speak, swallowed, digested, and assimilated, something from every creed. It has opened its doors to all comers. It has welcomed all, from the highest to the lowest, if only willing to admit the spiritual supremacy of Bráhmans, and conform to the usages of caste. In this manner it has held out the right hand of fellowship to fetish-worshipping aborigines; it has stooped to the devil-worship of various savage tribes; it has not scrupled to encourage the adoration of the fish, the boar, the serpent, trees, plants, and stones; it has permitted a descent to the most degrading cults of the Dravidian races; while at the same time it has ventured to rise to the loftiest heights of philosophical speculation. It has artfully appropriated Buddhism, and gradually superseded that competing system, by drawing its adherents within the pale of its own communion."*

Hindus are now divided into five principal sects:—

1. Shaivas or worshippers of Siva.
2. Vaishnávas, or worshippers of Vishnu.
3. Shaktas, or worshippers of the *female* personification of energy, as typified by the wives of the gods.
4. Ganapatyas, or worshippers of Ganapatti or Ganésh, the god of good fortune.
5. Sauras or worshippers of Surya, the Sun God. Of these, *Shaktism* and the worship of Ganésh are both mere offshoots of *Shaivism;* while Bráhmans, whether *Shaivas* or *Vaishnávas*, both worship Surya or Suraj Narayan, invoking him daily in the *gayátri*, the most popular of the *Védic* prayers. The members of these various sects are tolerant of each other's creeds, and all appeal to the *Puránas* † as their special

* Bráhmanism and Hinduism.—*Monier Williams.*

† "The *Puránas* are so called because they profess to teach what is ancient. They are 18 in number and are ascribed to a sage called Valmiki, the first Indian poet after the *Védic* epoch. "It is probable, however, that they were really written by various authors between the 8th and 15th centuries. In the present state of Hindu belief the *Puránas* exercise a very general influence. Portions of them are publicly read and expounded by Bráhmans to all classes of people; observances of feasts and fasts are regulated by them, and temples, towns, mountains and rivers, to which pilgrimages are made, owe their sanctity to the legends they contain."—Cyclopædia of India.—*Balfour.*

bible. All, however, show marked points of difference, some of which will now be noticed. The great bulk of Rájpúts are either Shaivas or Vaishnávas.

SHAIVISM OR SIVA-WORSHIP.

Siva is less human and far more mystical than the incarnated Vishnu. He is generally worshipped as an omnipotent god who has replaced Bráhma the Creator, and granted new life to all created things, but only through death and disintegration; hence his title of 'Destroyer.' He is not represented by the image of a man, but by a mystic symbol—the *linga** or phallus—the emblem of creative power, which is supposed to be in a state of perpetual heat and excitement, and to require to be refreshed by constant sprinklings of cold water, and the application of cooling *bilva* leaves. Siva is also known as Rudra and Mahádéo, and his worship is generally associated with Nandi, the sacred bull, and favourite attendant of the god.

An important difference between *Shaivas* and *Vaishnávas* may here be noticed. Siva-worshippers eat meat, a privilege which is generally denied to the followers of Vishnu.

VAISHNAVISM OR VISHNU-WORSHIP.

Vishnu is the most human and humane of the gods. He sympathises with men's trials, and condescends to be born of human parents. He is usually represented by the complete image of a well-formed human being, either that of Krishna or Ráma (his two principal incarnations) which every day is supposed to be roused from slumber, dressed, decorated with jewels, fed with offerings of grain and sweetmeats, and then put to sleep again like an ordinary man, while the remains of the food offered are eagerly consumed by the priests. *Vaishnávism* is the most tolerant form of Hinduism. It has an elastic creed, capable of adaptation to all varieties of opinion and practice, and can proclaim Buddha, or any remarkable man, to be an incarnation of the god. The chief characteristic of Vishnu is his condescension in infusing his essence into animals and men, with the object of delivering his worshippers from certain special dangers.

The incarnations of Vishnu are ten in number. In the first he appeared as a fish; in the second as a tortoise; in the third as a boar; in the fourth as a man-lion; in the fifth as a dwarf; in the sixth as

* "The *linga* or phallus represents the male organ. The emblem—a plain column of stone, or sometimes a cone of plastic mud—suggests no offensive ideas. The people call it *Siva* or *Máhádéva*."—Classical Dictionary of Hindu Mythology—*Dowson*

Paráshu or the axe-armed Ráma, the champion of the Bráhmans, and their saviour from their Kshatriya oppressors; in the seventh as the high-born Ráma, king of Ajudhya, and hero of the *Ramáyana* of which an account has already been given; in the eighth as Krishna, a Kshatriya of the Lunar race, who was brought up humbly among cowherds, and whose life is described in the *Mahábhárata;* in the ninth as the sceptical Buddha. The tenth incarnation has yet to come. It is to take place when the world is wholly depraved, when the god will appear in the sky, to redeem the righteous, destroy the wicked, and restore the age of purity.

SHÁKTISM OR GODDESS-WORSHIP.

Sháktism, in the simplest acceptation of the term, is the worship of *Shákti*, or female force personified as a goddess. The male nature of the Hindu triad was supposed to require to be supplemented by the association of each of the three gods with a *Shákti* or type of female energy. Thus Sáraswáti, the goddess of speech and learning, came to be regarded as the *Shákti* or consort of Bráhma; Lakshmi the goddess of beauty and fortune, as that of Vishnu; and Parvati, daughter of the Himalayas, as that of Siva.

Hindus, whether *Shaivas* or *Vaishnávas*, are separated into two great classes. The first, called *dakshina márgis* or 'followers of the right hand path,' are devoted to either Siva-Parvati or Vishnu-Lakshmi in their double nature as male and female. The second, called *vama márgis* or 'followers of the left hand path', are addicted to mystic and secret rites, and display special preference for the *female* or left hand side of each deity. The bible of the latter is the *Tántras*, which are believed to have been directly revealed by Siva to his wife Parvati. It is these *Sháktas* or left hand worshippers who devote themselves to the worship of Parvati rather than Siva, and of Lakshmi rather than Vishnu: in the same way the sect shows greater reverence for Radha and Sita—the two incarnations of Lakshmi—than for Krishna and Ráma, the contemporaneous incarnations of her husband. Another favourite deity of the *Sháktas* is Amba or Débi, the mother of the universe, the mighty mysterious force whose function is to control and direct two distinct operations—*viz.*, (1) the working of the natural appetites and passions whether for the support of the body by eating and drinking, or for the propagation of life through sexual cohabitation; and (2) the acquisition of supernatural faculties, whether for a man's own individual exaltation, or for annihilation of his opponents.

Parvati under her other names of Débi, Káli, Bhawáni, or Dúrga, is the principal goddess of *Sháktism.* She is described as a terrible blood-drinking divinity, black in colour, fierce in temperament, besmeared with gore, wreathed with skulls, and only to be propitiated by animal or even human sacrifices. She was probably an aboriginal deity adopted by the Bráhmans to popularize Hinduism among the non-Aryan races.

THE WORSHIP OF GANÉSH AND VILLAGE AND HOUSEHOLD DEITIES.

Ganapatti or Ganésh is the god of good luck and the remover of difficulties. He is considered as a kind of king of the demons, ruling over good and bad alike, and controlling the malignant spirits who are continually plotting against the peace of humanity. This deity is represented by the grotesque figure of a short, fat, red-coloured man, with a big belly, and the head of an elephant. No public festivals are held in his honour, but his image is in every house, and he is always worshipped prior to the commencement of important business.* On writing a book his aid is always invoked, and his picture is frequently drawn over the doors of shops and houses, to ensure success and good fortune to the owners.

Village gods.

Under this heading a few of the minor godlings may be noticed. Hanumán, the monkey god, is worshipped throughout India. He owes his popularity to the fact that he assisted Ráma to recover his wife Sita from Rávana the Demon-King. The Aryans habitually referred to the aboriginal tribes or *Dasyus*† as "black complexioned, flat-nosed, and *monkey like;*" thus Hanumán, who was really an aboriginal chief who rendered Ráma valuable assistance in his expedition to Ceylon, was transformed by popular tradition first into a monkey general, and eventually into a monkey god. Sitála Dévi is the small-pox goddess, and is held in the utmost dread. *Bhuta* are the spirits of men who have died violent deaths either by accident, suicide, or capital punishment, without the subsequent performance of proper funeral ceremonies. *Préta* are the spirits of deformed and crippled persons. *Pisácha* are demons created by men's vices. All these demons are propitiated by offerings of food and the incantation of *mántras.* Nearly every village has two or three divinities of its own. These are

Demons.

---

* According to Tod the Ráipúts of Rájpútána adore a goddess called Asapúrna or the 'fulfiller of desires,' who is invoked previous to any undertaking in much the same way as Ganésh.

† *Dasyu* in Sanskrit means 'a slave.'

generally deceased local celebrities, deified for the occasion, and worshipped in the shape of a mound of earth or stone, at the foot of a *pipal* or some other sacred tree.

THE WORSHIP OF SURYA, THE SUN GOD.

The adoration of Surya or Suraj Narayan is a *Védic* survival of the greatest antiquity. Although there are but few temples dedicated to his service, he is worshipped by all Hindus, irrespective of sect. He is generally regarded as a manifestation of all three persons of the Hindu Trinity. In the east, at morning, he represents Bráhma or Creation; overhead at noon, he typifies Vishnu or Preservation; in the west at evening, Siva or Destruction. The *gayatri* or morning prayer of the devout Hindu is an invocation to the Sun's vivifying essence—"let us meditate on the excellent glory of the divine Sun: may he enlighten our understanding."

In Rájpútána "Har or the Sun is the patron of all who love war and strong drink, and is especially the object of the Rájpút warrior's devotion; blood and wine accordingly, are the chief oblations to this god." *

MINOR FORMS OF WORSHIP.

First and foremost comes the worship of the cow. "Of all animals it is the most sacred. Every part of its body is inhabited by some deity. Every hair on its body is inviolable. All its excreta are hallowed. Any spot which a cow has condescended to honour with the sacred deposit of her excrement is for ever consecrated ground, and the filthiest place plastered with it is at once cleansed and freed from pollution, while the ashes produced by burning this substance are of such a holy nature that they not only make clean all material things, but have only to be sprinkled over a sinner to convert him into a saint."†

The worship of the cow.

Serpent-worship was practised originally by Scythians and aborigines and was probably adopted from them by the Bráhmans. Images of snakes are generally found coiled round the *Linga*, or stretched out as a canopy over it.

Serpent-worship.

The trees, plants, and fruits reverenced by Hindus are the *túlsi* or holy basil; the *pipal*; the *bilva* or *bel*; the *váta* or banyan; the *amra* or mango the *nim*; the lotus; the cocoanut; and the *kusa* or sacred grass.

Plant and tree worship.

* Annals of Rájasthán.—*Tod.*

† Bráhmanism and Hinduism.—*Monier Williams.*

The planets are worshipped and give names to the days of the week. Thus Monday is named after *Soma*, the moon; Tuesday after *Mangala*

Planet worship.

Mars; Wednesday after *Budh*, Mercury; Thursday after *Vrihaspati*, Jupiter; Friday after *Shukra*, Venus; Saturday after *Sani*, Saturn; and Sunday after *Surya*, the Sun god.

Many rivers are worshipped by Hindus. The Ganges is supposed to flow from Vishnu's foot, and to fall on Siva's head. The river is considered so sacred, that there is no sin, however heinous, which cannot be atoned for by bathing in its sacred stream; hence the traffic in Ganges water, which is transported in small bottles to the most distant parts of the country. The *tribéni* or confluence of the Ganges, Jumna and Sáras-

River Worship.

wáti * at Allahabad, is one of the most popular places of Hindu pilgrimage. The Ganges lost its sanctity in 1895, when the Nerbudda replaced it as the holiest of Indian rivers. The mere sight of the Nerbudda is said to purify the soul from guilt. The dead may be cremated on both of its banks, whereas only the north bank of the Ganges should be used for this purpose.

It is well known that the Hindu doctrine with regard to a future state is a belief in the transmigration of the soul. Most of the gods have their own heavens, and as thousands of years may elapse between each of

The Hindu heaven.

his reappearances upon earth, the prayer of the devout Hindu is that he may be permitted to pass these periods of peace in the heaven of the deity which he has selected as the object of his particular devotion.

Besides heavens of various degrees of felicity, Hindu mythology provides a number of hells, of different degrees of horror, the roads to which are long and painful, over burning sands, and pointed red-hot stones. Along these, amidst showers of scalding water, and through caverns filled with

The Hindu hell.

all sorts of terrifying objects, the Hindu sinner threads his way to the judgment seat of Yáma, whose throne is surrounded by a terrible river called Vaitaráni—the Styx of the Hindu hell. Here he is tried by the God of Death, and consigned to a heaven or a hell, according to his conduct during life.

All Hindus go through their daily devotions alone, either in their own

Daily devotions.

houses, or at any temple, tank, or stream in convenient proximity to their homes.

* The Sáraswáti no longer exists, and its former course is merely indicated by a dry water course. It ran at one time into the Indus, but since its disappearance is believed by Hindus to flow under ground, and join the Ganges and Jumna at Allahabad.

Shaivas, Vaishnávas, and *Sháktas,* the three principal sects of Hindus, are recognisable one from the other by the peculiar caste marks, called *tiláka* or *pundra,* with which they decorate their foreheads. That of *Shaivas* consists of three horizontal strokes, made with the white ashes of burnt substances, to represent the disintegrating forces of Ṣiva; that of *Vaishnávas,* of three upright marks, close together, red or yellow in the centre and white at the sides, to represent the footprint of Vishnu; that of *Sháktas,* of a small semi-circular line above the eyebrows, with a small round patch in the middle. The branding of the arms, breasts, etc., is also different for each sect. *Shaivas* brand themselves with the sign of the trident and *linga,* the weapon and symbol of Siva; *Vaishnávas* with that of the club, the discus, and the conch shell, the special attributes of Vishnu.

Caste marks.

Shaivas and Vaishnávas both wear rosaries of beads round their necks. The *Shaiva* rosary is a string of 32 or 64 rough berries of the *rudráksha* tree, while that of the *Vaishnávas* is made of the wood of the sacred *tulsi* plant, and consists of 108 beads.

Rosaries.

CUSTOMS.

The principal phases in the life of a Rájpút are celebrated by twelve appropriate ceremonies called *Karams.* These commence from a period anterior to his birth, when the Kshatriya mother first indulges in the hope of offspring, and continue through almost every incident of his career, until the thirteenth day after death, when his soul is supposed to wing its flight to another world. Only the most important of these *Karams* need be mentioned, *viz.,* those relating to—

(*a*) Birth.

(*b*) Initiation into the twice born order by investiture with the *janéo* or sacred thread, a ceremony resembling the Christian rite of baptism.

(*c*) Marriage.

(*d*) Death.

Ceremonies relating to Birth.

On the birth of a male child, the father or a relative at once summons the *parohit* or family priest, and enquires of him whether the infant was born at a propitious moment. The *parohit,* with many forms and ceremonies, then consults the stars, keeping a note of his observations for subsequent record in the *janam-patri,* or horoscope, which is an elaborate statement of

Jat Karam or birth.

every particular relating to the child's birth, parentage, ruling constellations, and future prospects.

If the *parohit's* reply is favourable, the *nai* (family barber) is sent round to summon relations and friends, who thereupon tender their congratulations to the family, while the *parohit*, assisted by five other Bráhmans, goes through the rites prescribed for the occasion.

After a week of feasting and rejoicing, the *parohit* is asked to fix upon a propitious day for the naming of the child. This is done after consultation of the *janam-patri* and other formalities requiring the attendance of Bráhmans.

Nám Karam or naming.

About 40 days after birth the infant is carried outside the house and *mántras* or sacred texts are repeated to Surya, the Sun God. When the child is about two years old, an auspicious day is selected for the ceremony of tonsure, which is performed twice. On the first occasion the hair is entirely removed, but at the second shaving a small tuft called the *churki* or *choti* is left at the top of the head.

Múran or tonsure.

If the infant is born in the 19th or lunar division of the zodiac * called *múl*, the mother is secluded for 27 days, and the father is not permitted to see his child except as a reflection in a mirror, or a vessel filled with melted *ghi*. Omission of this precaution would, it is considered, result in the child's death within a year. During this period no strangers are admitted into the house, and the father neither shaves nor sends his clothes to the wash. On the 27th day the *parohit* is sent for, and a most elaborate ceremony is gone through, called the *ná-páki púja*, in which many Bráhmans assist, involving the parents in great expense. The *parohit* concludes the rite by announcing that the incubus of the *múl* or unpropitious birth has been removed, and the establishment is at last purified.

---

* "The zodiac is an imaginary zone of the heavens within which lie the paths of the sun, moon, and principal planets. The zodiac of modern astronomers is divided into 12 signs marked by 12 constellations. The Hindu zodiac is a lunar one and is divided into 27 mansions called *nakshatras*, a word originally signifying stars in general, but appropriated to designate certain small stellar groups marking the divisions of the lunar track. The 27 *nakshatras* are supposed to correspond with the 27½ days in which the moon revolves round the earth. A special *nakshatra* is appropriated to every occurrence in life. One is propitious to marriage; another to entrance upon school life; a third, to the first ploughing; a fourth, to laying the foundations of a house. Festivals for the dead are appointed to be held under those that include but one star."—*Encyclopædia Britannica.*

On the birth of a daughter all feasting and rejoicing is dispensed with, only the bare rites being observed. Among the higher clans of Rájpúts the birth of a daughter is regarded as a positive misfortune.

CEREMONIES RELATING TO RELIGIOUS INITIATION OR INVESTITURE WITH THE *Janéo.*

The *janéo* or sacred thread is the emblem worn by the three highest castes of Hindus to symbolize their second or spiritual birth, and to mark the distinction between themselves and the once-born Sudras. It consists of three strings of spun cotton, varying in length, according to caste. The length of a Rájput *janéo* is 95 *chúas*, a *chúa* being the circumference of four fingers of the right hand.

The *Janéo* or sacred thread.

Once invested with this hallowed symbol, the Rájpút never parts with it. Thenceforth it serves as a constant reminder of his aristocratic origin, and of his duties as a member of the warrior caste. It is usually worn over the left shoulder and under the right arm, and its triple form is supposed to symbolize Bráhma, Vishnu and Siva, the three persons of the Hindu Trinity, and Earth, Air, and Heaven, the three worlds pervaded by their essence. The *janéo* must always be made by Bráhmans, and should be renewed once a month.

The investiture of a Rájpút with the *janéo* represents his formal admission into the ranks of the twice-born. It usually takes place at the same time as marriage, so that the two ceremonies are combined, and one expenditure suffices for both. The *Purbiah* or Hindustáni Rájpút takes almost as much pride in his *janéo* as a Bráhman, but in Rájpútána and the eastern districts of the Punjáb, where Rájpúts are freer from Bráhmanical influences, they seldom wear the thread, and regard it more as the symbol of a priest than of a warrior. The ceremony of initiation is rather elaborate. At the moment of investiture, the officiating *pundit* whispers a verse from the *Védas* into the neophyte's ear. The family *parohit* then addresses the young Rájpút, and after inculcating various precepts for his religious and moral conduct, dismisses him with an *asirbád* * or Bráhmanical blessing.

Upanyana or Initiation.

CEREMONIES RELATING TO MARRIAGE.

Among Rájpúts, the ceremonies attending the marriage rite are even more elaborate than those relating to birth and investiture

* Bráhmans are addressed by other castes with the respectful salutation of *pailagi*, "I place myself humbly at your feet." The Bráhman in return bestows his *asirbád* or blessing—"may your riches increase."

with the *janéo.* It is the ambition of every Rájpút to add distinction to his family pedigree by forming alliances with illustrious houses. Owing, however, to their peculiar marriage customs, this is no easy matter, and the higher the clan the greater the difficulty. In the first place Rájpúts are exogamous, *i.e.*, they must marry into their own tribe, but out of their own clan. Marriage within the clan is impossible, and in fact would be regarded as incest. Besides this, although a Rájpút lad may accept a bride from a clan inferior in status to his own, a similar privilege is denied to the Rájpút girl, whose husband must be her equal, and if possible, her superior. The result of these restrictions is a surplus of women in the higher septs, leading to a competition for husbands, and an enormous increase in the cost of getting a daughter married. It is this question of expense, that is the cause of the female infanticide which is so prevalent among Rájpúts. The field of matrimonial selection is further limited by the fact that Rájpúts, in common with most respectable classes of Hindus, bar marriage within the following degrees of kinship :—

Chachera or the family of the paternal uncle.
Mamera „ „ „ „ „ maternal uncle.
Phuphera „ „ „ „ „ paternal aunt.
Mausera „ „ „ „ „ maternal aunt.

A Rájpút, moreover, will never marry into any family with which any of his own relations have contracted marriages within living memory.

When a Chhatri boy is about 11 years old, his father deputes a *ghataka* or professional matchmaker to negotiate a promise of marriage with the parents of a girl belonging to some suitable clan.† In making a selection, caste equality is considered of greater importance than wealth. Nevertheless, says Sleeman,* "all is a matter of bargain and sale. Those who have money must pay in proportion to their means in order to marry their girls into families a shade higher in caste than themselves, or to get brides from them, when such families are reduced to the necessity of selling their daughters to inferiors." In some parts of northern India the *lagi* or matchmaker is the *nai* or family barber ; but among the higher grade clans he is more often a Bráhman, who goes about from one family to another until he discovers an eligible girl. The formalities gone through in the case of a daughter are very much the same as for a son. The first move is made by the girl's father who, when his daughter is about 8 years old, inquires after a suitable lad among his friends and relations. Having made his

Barricha, Saggai, or Betrothal.

* A Journey through the Kingdom of Oudh.

† Many of the highest Rájpút families in Rájpútána obtain wives from the Hill Rájpúts of Kangra and Jummoo. This is partly due to the undoubted purity of their blood, and partly to the beauty and fair complexions of their women.

choice, he proceeds to the boy's village, accompanied by his *nai*, *parohit*, and the *ghataka*, or *lagi*, and there arranges for an introduction to the lad's relations.

The emblem of marriage among Rájpúts is the cocoanut. It is generally sent by the father of the bride to the father of the bridegroom, and signifies that the former makes an offer of his daughter's hand. If the proposal is accepted, the cocoanut is retained; but if the alliance is declined, it is returned, an insult which the bride's family will never forgive.

As soon as preliminaries have been settled, the lad's father brings his son dressed in his best clothes for inspection by the girl's relations. The next step in both cases is an investigation of genealogies and a verification of the pedigrees of both parties. This is conducted by the family *Bháts* or *Chárans.** If these inquiries are satisfactory, a *pundit* is engaged to scrutinise the boy's *janampatri*, and the constellations are consulted to decide whether the lunar mansions in which both parties were born combine propitiously. On a favourable reply being received, a *tilak* or *téka*† is affixed to the lad's forehead, and the question of dowry or *dahaez* is then gone into. As soon as this matter is disposed of, relations and friends are informed of the engagement, and the betrothal called *Saggai* or *Barricha* is complete.

In Rájpútána *Saggai* and the subsequent ceremony called *Beeah* are more or less merged into one, and the ages of bride and bridegroom have been fixed at 13 and 18 respectively. A regular scale of expenditure has also been determined, suitable to the means of the parents. In Oudh and the North-West Provinces it is still a point of honour among Rájpúts to spare no expense over marriages. The most reckless extravagance is permissible, and not only are the whole savings of a lifetime wasted over a single wedding, but money is borrowed at the most exorbitant rates of interest without thought of the ruin which such imprudence must inevitably entail. This is a serious social evil, and is gradually reducing the Rájpút yeoman of these provinces to the position of a dependent of the Banya or Mahájan to whom he has mortgaged his ancestral property.‡

---

* The *Bhát* is generally a genealogist and historian; the *Cháran* is a bard and herald and composes verses in honour of famous ancestors.

† Some *tékas* are marked with *dhai* or milk curds; others with a kind of red earth called *roli* or *sandur*.

‡ A girl's marriage costs from Rs. 100 to Rs. 150 to her father, and a boy's from Rs. 70 to Rs. 180 to his father; so the average expenditure from both sides on a wedding is from Rs. 170 to Rs. 250. Among the wealthier classes the expenses of a wedding run to thousands.

The next step is to select an auspicious date for the *Beeah* or marriage ceremony. This as a rule involves numerous references to the stars, and every hitch in the proceedings has to be got over by propitiatory gifts to the *pundits*. It is customary to notify the date finally decided on in a letter written on yellow paper, which is called the *lagan*. This is sent round to all the relations and friends of both families by the party receiving the first intimation of the date from the *pundits*.

The most favourable season for marriages is the spring, but marriage may take place in any of the following months, each of which possesses peculiar attributes—

Mágh, *i.e.*,	from about	10th January	to 10th February.
Phágan, *i.e.*,	,, ,,	10th February	to 10th March.
Baisakh, *i.e.*,	,, ,,	10th April	to 10th May.
Jeyt, *i.e.*,	,, ,,	10th May	to 10th June.
Asarh, *i.e.*,	,, ,,	10th June	to 10th July.

The marriage season.

The month of *Mágh* is said to bring a wealthy wife; *Phágan*, a good manager; *Baisakh* and *Jeyt*, a dutiful helpmate; while marriages in *Asarh* are reputed to be very prolific.

Special Rájpút marriage days.

In ancient days, constant wars made it very difficult for a Rájpút to carry out all the ceremonies prescribed for the rite of marriage. Seven days were therefore appointed on which weddings could be celebrated without the interference of Bráhmans. They are as follows:—

Janam Ashtmi, *i.e*,	about	3rd September.
Deo-uthán, *i.e.*,	,,	20th November.
Chárandi or Dolandi, *i.e.*,	,,	1st March.
Akatiz, *i.e.*,	,,	19th April.
Phalera Dhuj, *i.e.*,	,,	18th February.
Basant Panchmi, *i.e.*,	,,	22nd January.

This custom is peculiar to Rájpúts, and is one which Bráhmans are very loth to admit, as by it they can be totally ignored. It is well suited to the necessities of a warlike race, and is freely made use of by soldiers who are prevented by circumstances from obtaining leave during the regular marriage season.

As soon as the actual date of the marriage is settled, friends and relations are invited to take part in the *Barát* or wedding procession, and all are asked to bring their retinues so as to add to the dignity of the occasion.

The *Barát* or Marriage Procession.

On the morning of the bridegroom's departure for the bride's house, he is dressed in yellow, adorned with jewels, wreathed in flowers and his feet dyed red. He then mounts his *palki*, with his younger brother or cousin as best man. Before starting, offerings are made at the village shrines, and a visit is paid to the village well. Here the bridegroom's mother pretends that she will throw herself in unless her son repays her for the love and care bestowed upon him since his birth. The lad thereupon seizes her, and swearing eternal devotion, implores his mother to prolong her life for his sake. To this she of course consents, and the *Barát* having meanwhile formed up, a start is made for the bride's house. It is generally arranged that the procession should arrive towards evening, its approach being invariably announced by the *nai* or family barber.

As the bridegroom's party draws near, the bride's friends form themselves into a procession, and with torches, drums, and singing, welcome the arrival of the *Barát*. After an exchange of salutations the bridegroom is ceremoniously conducted to the bride's door, where he is received by her relations. A religious ceremony follows, accompanied by a general distribution of presents, and money is thrown out, and scrambled for by the crowd outside. The bridegroom now returns to his camp, which is usually pitched in a neighbouring tope of trees.

Meanwhile his father escorted by his *pundit* and *nai* proceeds to the bride's house with the wedding presents, and after they have been inspected by the family, all retire to rest.

Suddenly the bride's *pundit*, who is supposed to have been watching the heavens, announces that the hour for the wedding has arrived. This is the signal for general activity. The bride and bridegroom meet once more, and after being seated opposite and near one another, the ceremony of joining hands is gone through. As soon as this is finished, the bride's father bestows various gifts on his son-in-law, and presents are received from the friends of the family who offer their congratulations and good wishes. The concluding ceremonial, called the *agni púja*, completes the marriage rite. A fire of mango wood is lit with much ceremony, and the young couple are made to stand up, facing east, with their garments tied together. They then march round the sacred fire three times, each circuit being made in seven steps, while the *pundits* chant prayers and texts from the *Védas*. Loud singing and beating of drums accompanies almost every portion of the marriage ceremony, as a curious idea prevails that the efficacy of all religious rites is greatly enhanced by noise.

***Beeah* or marriage.**

After three more days spent in feasting, rejoicing, and settling the dowry accounts, the bride starts with her husband for his home. Here she makes a stay of a few days, and then returns to her father's house where she remains until old enough to cohabit with her husband.

The last of the ceremonies relating to marriage is the *Gaona* or home-taking. This usually takes place when the bridegroom is about 15 or 16 and the girl about 12. A propitious day is selected, in consultation with the *parohit*, and the husband then pays a short visit to his wife's family, which is made the occasion for more rejoicing and feasting. The final leave is then taken, and the young people start for home, this time to commence life together in earnest. In the unavoidable absence of the bridegroom, the bride may be taken home by either her husband's father or brother.

Gaona, Mukhlawa or home-taking.

Plurality of wives is permissible among western Rájpúts, and they may be married either by the full, or among clans which practice it, the irregular forms called *Shádi* and *Karáo*. Three or four wives are not uncommon, but usually only one is *beáta*, or married by the orthodox rites.

Plurality of wives.

Western Rájpúts keep concubines, but the practice is not common except in Rájpútána. Three descriptions of concubinage are recognized. The first class consists of women called *Khawás*, generally Játnis or Gújarins, who are kept in the seclusion of the *Zanána*. Their offspring, called *Khawáswáls* or *Suretwáls*, are treated as Rájpúts, but are not allowed to put their mouths to the *hukah* of an *asl* or pure born man, nor to actually eat off the same dish, though the true Rájpút will eat food cooked by them. The second and third classes are called *Daroghi* and *Goli*. The former are usually bought women who work about a Rájpút's house, but never leave it; the latter are generally of low caste, draw water from the wells, work in the fields, and are, as their name implies, practically slaves. The male progeny of the two last named are called *Daroghas* and *Golas* respectively. They generally assume the name and clan of the master of the house, though, as a matter of fact, they may be anybody's children.

Concubinage.

CEREMONIES RELATING TO DEATH.

When death is approaching, a *pundit* is sent for. The sick man is laid with his bedding on a layer of *kusa* grass on a spot which has previously been leeped, or encircled by a ring of cowdung. A sprig of the *tulsi* plant, a piece of gold, or a few drops of Ganges water are placed in his mouth, failing which a little mud from a sacred stream may be plastered on his forehead. The object of these precautions is to detain the messengers of Yáma, the God of Death, until the proper propitiatory ceremonies have been carried out. A cow is then brought to the dying man's side, and he is made to grasp its tail, the idea being that by the sacred animal's assistance

Ceremonies on the approach of death.

he will be safely transported across Vaitarani, the Styx of the Hindu hell. The cow is of course presented to the *pundit*, who, after repeating appropriate *mántras* or texts, calls upon the dying man to repeat one of the names of Vishnu, such as Rám, Narayan, or Hari. This done, salvation is assured.*

After death, the body is covered with a white cloth, and is carried to the burning place, which is generally on the banks of a stream. The funeral rites are always conducted by Maha-Bráhmans, a despised sect, specially entrusted with the performance of funeral rites. On the way, the mourners chant various verses,† and on arrival the body is shaved, washed, and either decorated with flowers or plastered with Ganges mud. Clean clothes are put on, and the corpse is then laid on the funeral pile facing north. The latter, strictly speaking, should be constructed of *tulsi* and sandal-wood, but as a matter of fact all descriptions of wood are used. Five *pindas* or balls of rice are placed on the body. The eldest son of the deceased, or his representative, now sets fire to the pile, reciting a text from the *Rig Véda*. When the corpse is half burnt, a relative of the deceased should crack the skull by a blow, delivered with a stick, composed of some sacred wood. By this the soul is supposed to be released from the body. Oblations of *ghi* and grain are offered up, and as soon as the cremation is over, all purify themselves with ablutions, and again make oblations of water and sesamum, muttering the name of the deceased.

Kiria karams or funeral rites.

If a man dies in a remote place, or if his body is not found, his son should make an effigy of the deceased with *kusa* grass, and then burn it on a pile with similar rites. This procedure is very generally observed by the relations of sepoys who die on service.

The period of mourning is ten days, during which the members of the deceased's family are not allowed to shave, wear shoes, or eat cooked food. On the last day, all near relatives should have their heads shaved.

Period of mourning.

On the third day after cremation, the bones and ashes, called *Phul*, are collected and placed in a vessel, which is thrown into the Ganges, or some acred river. If this cannot be done at once, the remains are buried, pending a favourable opportunity for their disposal.

On the eleventh day after death, the *Shráddha* ceremonies commence. These are reverential offerings to ancestral spirits. *Pindas* of rice, *ghi*, and sugar are scattered about, and a vessel of water is hung on a *pipal* tree, for the use of the soul of the deceased until its final departure for another world, which is supposed to take place on the thirteenth day.

*** Needless to say these ceremonies would only be observed in full in the case of a man dying at his home.**

† They generally say "*Rám Nám sackh hai*," "the name of Rám is true."

On this occasion, friends, kinsmen, and an *odd** number of Bráhmans must be fed.

The *Shráddha* ceremonies are repeated in a simple form every month for a year, and afterwards twice a year—on the anniversary of the death, and again in the month of September. Bráhmans have to be fed on each occasion. No marriage can take place in the family of the deceased until after the *che máshi*, or six months after death. In Rájpútána and the Eastern Punjáb, the *che máshi* rites are usually observed about three months after cremation, so as to avoid the inconvenience which would be caused by delaying marriages for the full period.

On the first anniversary of the death Bráhmans and friends are feasted, and a male calf is offered up by the chief mourner to the spirit of his departed relative. He washes the animal and brands it with the impression of a trident, the badge of Vishnu, and then sets it free to wander about the country in the form of a Bráhmani bull.

There are certain occasions when Rájpúts and other orthodox Hindus forego the observance of these rites. If a Rájpút lad dies before he has undergone the ceremony of tonsure, or before he is five years old, his body is *buried* instead of being burnt. In the same way, if the deceased child be under a month old, the body is at once *buried* near the place of its birth, generally in the *angan* or courtyard of the father's house.

LEAVE.

The amount of leave required by a Rájpút sepoy to enable him to take part in any of the ceremonies previously described, will depend upon the distance at which he is quartered from his home, and the proximity of the latter to a railway. The number of days granted must be sufficient to cover the time spent in travelling to and fro, in addition to the minimum period required for each rite, which is as follows :—

	Days.
(*a*) *Jútkaram* (birth) ; *Námkaram* (naming)	3
(*b*) *Upanyána* (investiture with the *janéo*)	3
(*c*) *Barát* or *Becah* (marriage)	10†

When granting leave for these ceremonies, consideration must be taken of the distance of the bridegroom's house from that of the bride. Allowing for a stay of 4 days and 6 days for the journey there and back 10 days' leave will generally suffice.

(*d*) *Gáona* (home-taking)	10
(*e*) *Kiria Karams* (funeral rites)	15

The period of leave should be reckoned from the date of death.

* It is usual to feed an *odd* number of Bráhmans on occasions of grief and mourning, and an *even* number at weddings and other rejoicings.

† This period would not be sufficient for a Rájpútána Rájpút, who, owing to the distance and inaccessibility of his home, would generally require about six weeks' leave.

HINDU FESTIVALS.

There are about 142 Hindu festivals during the year. An account of the more important ones will be found below. Lists of festivals, showing the exact dates on which they fall, are published annually by Provincial Governments, and copies can be obtained for reference on application to the Civil authorities.

Name of festival.	Month in which it usually falls.	Remarks.
Makár Sankrant ...	January ...	The celestial sign *Makár* answers to *Capricorn.* On that day the sun is said to begin his journey northward. To the early Aryans, living in a cold region, the approach of spring was an occasion of the greatest joy, and the commencement of the sun's northward progress could not pass unmarked, for then opened the auspicious half of the year. The sun especially is worshipped at this festival. Bathing in the sea is prescribed whenever it is possible. Rejoicings abound in public and in private. Great gatherings take place, as at Allahabad, where the Ganges and Jumna mingle; and at Gunga-Sagar, where the Ganges meets the Ocean.
Mauni Amáwas ...	January-February ...	A minor holiday. Persons observing this festival do not speak to any one until they have performed the ablutions prescribed for the occasion. Bathing may take place in the nearest large river or tank, but it should be carried out in the Ganges, if pössible, and especially at Hardwár.
Basant Panchmi ...	January-February ...	A spring festival. In Bengal, Sáraswáti, goddess of arts and learning, is worshipped at this time. No reading or writing is permissible, and the day is observed as a holiday in all public offices. Both sexes should wear *basanti* or yellow clothing and celebrate the festival with music and rejoicings.
Sheo-Rátri, properly Máha-Siva-ráti, the great night of Siva.	February-March ...	Commemorates the birth of Siva. A fast is observed during the day and a vigil is kept at night when the *linga* or phallus (the emblem of Siva) is worshipped.

Name of festival.	Month in which it usually falls.	Remarks.
Holi ...	February-March ...	This festival, identified with the *dola-yatra,* or the rocking of the image of Krishna, is celebrated, especially in the Upper Provinces as a kind of Hindu Saturnalia or Carnival. Boys dance about the streets, and inhabitants of houses sprinkle the passers-by with red powder, use squirts, and play practical jokes. Towards the close of the festival about the night of full moon, a bonfire is lighted, and games, representing the frolics of the young Krishna, take place around the expiring embers. During the Holi women are addressed with the utmost familiarity, and indecent jests at their expense are considered permissible.
Rám Naumi ...	March-April ...	This is commemorative of the birthday of Ráma. It is kept as a strict fast. The temples of Ráma are illuminated and his image adorned with costly ornaments. The *Ramáyana* is read in the temples, and nautches are kept up during the night. At noon of this day the *pujári,* (*i.e.,* the Bráhman who conducts worship at a temple) exihibits a small image of the god and puts it into a cradle. The assembly prostrates itself before it. Acclamations arise all round; handfuls of red powder are flung in token of joy; and all go home exulting.
Baisákhi-Amáwas, also called Satuahi Amáwas.	April-May ...	A minor Hindu festival in which *sattu* or ground barley and gram is distributed to Bráhmans before the feast.
Dasehra-Jeth ...	May-June ...	Commemorates the birthday of Gunga, goddess of the Ganges. On this day all Hindus who are able to do so, bathe in the Ganges, and give alms to the Bráhmans living on its banks. By so doing they secure the benefits of *dasehra, i.e.,* ten-removing sins; an attribute of the goddess Gunga "who effaces ten sins, however heinous, of such as bathe in her holy waters."

Name of festival.	Month in which it usually falls.	Remarks.
Nág-Panchmi ...	July-August ...	The festival is in honour of the *Nágas* or snake gods. The figure of a serpent is made of clay, or drawn on the wall, and worshipped. Living serpents are brought and fed with milk and eggs. All this is done to deprecate the wrath of the venomous reptile.
Sitála-Saptami ...	July-August ...	A minor festival, held two days after the *Nág Panchmi*. It is observed in honour of Sitála, the small-pox goddess. During this festival only cold food can be taken.
Raksha-Bandhan ...	July-August ...	A minor Hindu festival on which Bráhmans invoke protection for their clients against all evils during the year by binding coloured thread or silk round their wrists.
Janam-Ashtmi, properly Krishna-Janam Ashtmi.	August-September...	Celebrates in the birth of Krishna. It is one of the greatest of the sacred seasons. The worshippers fast the whole day. At night they bathe, worship a clay image of the infant Krishna and adorn it with leaves of the *tulsi* plant. Next day is a great festival for all keepers of cattle as Krishna spent his boyhood among cowherds.
Ganésha-Chatturthi	August-September...	A minor festival in commemoration of the birthday of Ganesh, god of wisdom. Clay figures of the deity are made, and after being worshipped for a few days, are thrown into the water.
Anant-Chaudas ...	August-September...	Commemorates the commencement of the winter season.
Pitr-Páksh, properly Pitri-Páksha or the fortnight of the Pitris or divine fathers; also called Mahaláya Amáwas.	September ...	This name is applied to the sixteen consecutive lunar days which are devoted to the performance of *Shráddhas* or ceremonies in honour of ancestors and deceased relatives.

Name of festival.	Month in which it usually falls.	Remarks.
Daséhra, Naorátri, Dúrga-Púja, or Rám-Lila.	September-October	This is the longest and most important of all Hindu festivals. It lasts ten days. It is celebrated in various parts of India, especially in Bengal, and is connected with the autumn equinox. It nominally commemorates the victory of Dúrga or Káli, wife of Siva, over a buffalo-headed demon. The form under which she is adored is that of an image with ten arms and a weapon in each hand, her right leg resting on a lion, and her left on the buffalo demon. This image is worshipped daily until the end of the festival, when it is cast into a river. The fourth is the sacrificial day, on which buffaloes, male goats, and sheep, are decapitated before the idol, to which the heads and blood of the victims are presented as offerings. The tenth day is called *Dasa-hara* or *Daséhra.* In Upper India the *Rám-Lila* or sports of Ráma take place on the same days, as the *Dúrga Púja* in Bengal. They commemorate the victory gained by Ráma over Rávana, King of Ceylon. A pageant is gone through consisting of an out-door theatrical representation of the storming of Rávana's castle. Conspicuous in the midst of the fortress is the giant himself, a huge figure with many arms, each grasping a weapon, and bristling with fireworks. Beside him sits Sita, the wife of Ráma, whom the giant has abducted. Without stands the indignant Ráma, demanding restitution of his wife, which being refused, the besiegers advance to the attack. Conspicuous among the assailants is Hanumán with his army of men dressed up as monkeys. The assault is at first repulsed, but is speedily renewed, this time with success. Síta is rescued, and Rávana is on the point of being captured, when he blows up, thus finishing a *tamásha* which is much appreciated by natives of every creed.
Diwáli or the feast of lamps.	October-November...	Commemorates the birth of Lakshmi, wife of Vishnu, goddess of wealth and fortune. Houses are freshly leeped. white-washed

Name of festival.	Month in which it usually falls.	Remarks.
		and illuminated. Gambling is permitted, almost enjoined during the feast. Fire-works are displayed. The Banyas and traders close their accounts for the year, and get new ledgers and books, which are consecrated and worshipped. It is the Hindu New Year's Day. Thieves are particularly active during this festival; as they consider a successful robbery committed then to be very auspicious, and to promise good luck during the year just commenced.
Déo-uthán-Ekadasi...	October-November...	This festival commemorates the awaking of Vishnu from four months' sleep. The image of the god is placed on a chair and rocked.
Gunga-Asnán ...	November ...	The great festival of the Ganges held in honour of Síva's victory over the demon Tripurasura. Large gatherings take place at Gurmukhtesar, Bithur, Allahabad, Sonepur, and other places. All should bathe in the Ganges or some sacred river.
Somwári-Amáwas ...	Any month ...	The fifteenth of any Hindu month falling on a Monday. It is observed as a religious festival for bathing and giving alms.
Suraj-Girhan ...	Any month ...	A day on which a solar eclipse occurs.
Chandar-Girhan ...	Any month ...	A day on which a lunar eclipse occurs.

CHAPTER IV.

CHARACTERISTICS.

"The Rájpút race is the noblest and proudest in India. With the exception of the Jews there is perhaps no people of higher antiquity or purer descent. They form a military aristocracy of a feudal type. They are brave and chivalrous, keenly sensitive to an affront, and especially jealous of the honour of their women."* In disposition they are manly, simple, and honest, and as a rule have none of the cunning and intrigue of the Bráhman. The chief characteristics of the true Rájpút are pride of race and inordinate extravagance. In Rájpútána he is easily recognised by his haughty bearing. There the chieftains of his tribe have ruled from time immemorial, and he feels himself free, and a member of the ruling race. Among the Rájpúts of Hindustán these peculiarities are very much modified, many defects disappear, and there only remain those traits which in a soldier command admiration and respect. "Indeed it is amongst the Rájpúts of our Army that we find the best specimen of Hindu character, retaining its individuality while divested of many of its faults. Here we acquire a clearer conception than elsewhere of their high spirit when roused, their enthusiastic courage and generous self-devotion, so singularly combined with gentleness, and an almost boyish simplicity of character"†. In no part of the world has the devotion of soldiers to their immediate chiefs been more remarkable than among the Rájpúts. The Mutiny, no doubt, was a striking example to the contrary, but even then "while some of the sepoys fought against us with their whole heart, the bulk of them, who had simply followed sheep-like some truculent and self-appointed guide, felt that they were fighting in a bad cause, and against their habitual leaders of whom they naturally stood in awe. Under such circumstances their conduct in the field could not draw out their military qualities in a true light; whereas those who remained true to their salt were the real representatives of the valour and fidelity of their race".‡

General character.

A Rájpút is generally a frugal liver. His ambition, as a rule, is to save as much money as he can until a marriage occurs in his family, when his extravagance knows no bounds. He however takes considerable pride in his appearance, and spends a good deal of his pay on clothes. Rájpútána Rájpúts are more liberal and open handed than their brethren of Hindustán; they feed better, and are far less anxious to save.

Thriftiness.

---

* History of India—*Talboys Wheeler.*

† Hinduism—*Harris.*

‡ Lucknow and Oudh in the Mutiny—*McLeod Innes.*

In matters relating to food and cooking there is a marked difference between the Rájpúts of Rájpútána and the eastern Punjáb and those of Hindustán and Behar. The former will not only employ Bráhmans as their cooks, but Banyas, Játs, Gújars, Ahirs, and Nais. They will all feed out of the same dish, use the same cooking utensils, and even dispense with a *chauka* or prepared fireplace. They will take meat *halláled* by a Musalmán, and will eat each other's cooked food whether fresh or stale. Moreover their freedom from ceremonial restraints enables them to dispense with the stripping, bathing, and other formalities, which to a Hindustáni Rájpút are indispensable preliminaries of a meal. They are in fact as little troubled by Hindu prejudices as the Sikhs. "They slay buffaloes, hunt and eat the boar,* shoot ducks and wild fowl†," and owing to their being in the habit of feeding together in messes, they require comparatively few cooking pots, and their wants on service are easily satisfied.

The customs of the Western or *Dési* Rájpúts in matters relating to their food.

Many of the Rájpúts of Oudh and the North-West Provinces are of doubtful descent, and it is probable that the extreme exclusiveness of some of the higher clans in matters relating to food and cooking, arises from a fear of falling in grade through association with those whom they consider to be their social inferiors. For this reason each man generally cooks for himself; but as a matter of fact, there is no reason why any Rájpút should not take food prepared by any Bráhman, by any one of his own clan, or any one of any clan which habitually intermarries with his own. For example, the *Tilókchandi Bais* often take wives from the *Kanhpuria*: any *Tilókchandi Bais*, therefore, should be able to eat at the same *chauka* as any *Kanhpuria*, all that is necessary being that each party should be a *bonâ fide* member of the clan to which he professes to belong.‡ The establishment of messes is thus perfectly feasible *so long as the men are of the same or of allied clans*, and matters are greatly facilitated by the employment of Bráhman cooks. The Rájpúts of Hindustán, however, have hitherto been too much under Bráhmanical influence to permit of their cooking in common; they would do so no doubt *on service*, but in the

The customs of the Eastern or *Purbiah* Rájpúts in matters relating to their food.

* Except *Parihars* and *Shaikhdwat Kachwáhas*.

† Annals of Rájasthán—*Tod*.

‡ In further illustration of this custom the following note has been communicated by the Officer Commanding 8th Bengal Infantry. "I find from enquiry that if a Rájpút, say a *Parihar*, marries into a *Gautam* family, and this *Gautam* family marries into a *Rájkumar* family, all these three clans can cook and eat *Kachi*, *i.e.*, food cooked in water together, provided they are personally known to each other. They will not go beyond this; for if the *Rájkumar* family marries into some other lower one, the *Parihar* will refuse to eat *Kachi* cooked by the lower-grade man, although the latter will eat food prepared by the *Parihar*. This holds good with all Rájpúts."

lines they generally prefer to feed separately, in much the same fashion as a Bráhman. It must be remembered that all the food prejudices of Hindus are with reference to what is called *kachi khána, i. e.*, food cooked in *water*. *Pakki khána* or food cooked in *ghi* does not give them much concern. All Rájpúts, even those most susceptible to Bráhmanical influence, can eat *pakki* cooked by *Halwais,** away from the *chauka*, and at any time. *Pakki* generally takes the form of *púris*, and even in Benares and Sháhabad, where the Rájpúts are nearly as strict as the Bráhmans, they will buy these cakes in the bazaar, and eat them at any time, without bothering to take off their shoes, or going through the smallest ceremony.†

Cooking.

For cooking, a space is marked off, about five feet square, called the *chauka*, within which is the *chula* or fireplace. The whole is then *leeped* with mud or cowdung. The materials for the meal being placed within the *chauka*, the Rájpút steps outside, and purifies himself by washing his feet. Before cooking he always bathes, and while in the water changes his *dhoti* or loin-cloth. If possible, he should immerse himself at least twice, repeating certain prayers as he faces the east. While eating, the clean *dhoti* is the only garment worn,‡ but a handkerchief may be thrown over the shoulders, for wiping the face and hands. It is essential also to wear the *janéo*,§ which indeed is never laid aside. Dinner over, the *chauka* is left, hands and feet are again washed, and *Pán*‖ and tobacco may be indulged in. Should anyone not a Rájpút touch the *chauka* after it has been prepared, all the food within its limits is defiled, and must be thrown away. As a rule, only one meal is eaten, about midday; but sometimes another is taken towards sunset. All food is eaten with the fingers, and only the right hand is used.

The articles of food which a Rájpút is permitted to enjoy vary according to circumstances. In Rájpútana and the eastern Punjáb he will eat pig, sheep, goat, deer, game-birds, and sometimes even the domestic fowl. Fish he cannot indulge in, not because it is prohibited, but because it is seldom

* "Halwáis, also called Mithaiyas, are Hindu confectioners. Their use of *ghi* in making sweetmeats renders food prepared by them pure."—"Ethnographical Hand-book."—*Crooke.*

† Among local prejudices relating to food may be mentioned the following peculiarity brought to notice by the Officer Commanding 16th Bengal Infantry. "The clans of Baiswára (roughly speaking Unao, Lucknow, and Rai Bareli,) will not intermarry, or eat at the same *chauka* with the clans of Banodha (*i.e.*, Fyzabad, Sultanpur, and Partabgarh.) Even men of the same clan from opposite banks of the River Sai or the Chuab will not, as a rule, mess together."

‡ On service, or in a cold climate where exposure of the naked body would be likely to cause sickness, clothes may be worn while cooking, ***provided they are made of wool.*** Bathing under these circumstances would be limited to washing the face, feet, and hands.

§ Except among Western Rájpút.

‖ *Pán* or *Pán Supári* is a well known masticatory which to some extent takes the place of opium, tobacco, and other narcotics. Slices of the areca nut are wrapped in the fresh leaves of the betel-pepper vine, with a small quantity of quicklime. It has an aromatic and astringent taste. All classes, male and female, chew it, and they allege that it strengthens the stomach, sweetens the breath, and preserves the teeth. It gives the lips, tongue, and teeth a reddish tinge."—Cyclopædia of India—*Balfour.*

procurable. In Hindustán he will eat sheep, goat, deer, fish, and game-birds, but pig and the domestic fowl are generally held in abhorrence. Meat, however, whether in Rájpútána or Hindustán, is too dear to be anything but an occasional luxury; the staple food of the Rájpút is *chapatis* or unleavened bread, rice, *dál*, spices, and all sorts of vegetables, except turnips, beetroot, and onions. Nearly everything is cooked in *ghi* or clarified butter, and various seasonings are added as a relish.

Food.

There is a marked difference between western and eastern Rájpúts in regard to what they drink. The Western Rájpút has a decided partiality for liquor, and "the *piála* or cup is a favourite with all who can afford it."* He will drink without hesitation from the ordinary *mashak* or *pakhal* of a Muhammadan *bhisti*. Men of equal grade will drink from each other's *lotahs*, and a superior, though unable to actually apply it to his lips, will take water without objection from the earthenware vessel of an inferior. The material of the drinking vessel is also a matter of indifference. It may be made of brass, iron, copper, zinc, leather, or wood.

Customs of the *Desi* or Western Rájpút in matters relating to water-supply.

The Eastern Rájpút is far more particular in every way. He is extremely abstemious, and as a rule takes nothing but water, milk, and sherbets. He has a rooted aversion to the water skin, and can only drink from *mashaks* made of canvas or goatskin, and carried by Hindu water-carriers. Even these are seldom used, and most regiments find it more convenient to provide themselves with zinc or copper water tins, specially constructed for transport on mules. Each man has his own brass *lotah*, and if it is lent to an inferior, it must be purified by being passed through the fire before the owner can again make use of it.

Customs of the *Purbiah* or Eastern Rájpúts in matters relating to water-supply.

Rájpúts are rather partial to drugs, and indulge in *gánja*, *bhang*, *post*† and opium. They are also addicted to the use of tobacco, which they both chew and smoke. The Rájpúts of Rájpútána are large consumers of opium. "A Rájpút," says Tod, "is useless without his opium, and I have often dismissed their men of business to refresh their intellects by a dose, for when its effects are dissipating, they become mere logs. Opium to the Rájpút is even more necessary than food."

Use of drugs.

Rájpút cooking utensils are made of metal so that they may be readily purified by scouring. In a regiment this duty is generally entrusted to a special class of company servants called *gúrgas*.

* Annals of Rájasthán.—*Tod.*

† *Bhang* is a powerful stimulant extracted from wild hemp. *Post* is an infusion of poppy heads.

Cooking pots.

The names of the different utensils and their respective uses are as follows:—

Batlohi.—A vessel used for cooking rice and *dál.*

Táwa.—An iron plate on which *chapátis* are baked.

Thali.—The brass platter in which *atta* is kneaded into *chapátis,* and from which food is eaten after it has been cooked.

Lotáh.—A brass drinking vessel.

Chamach.—A brass spoon for use with *dál* and rice.

Karhai or Karahi.—An iron vessel used for cooking vegetables and *púris, i.e., chápatis* made with *ghi* instead of water.

Katori.—A small brass cup in which *ghi* is placed.*

Clothing.

The principal and never-omitted article of dress with a *Rájpút* is the *dhoti* or loin-cloth, of which there are always two. It is changed daily while bathing before the mid-day meal, and is generally washed by the wearer. Next the skin is worn a short jacket called a *mirzai,* and over it another of thicker material called an *anga.* In every case the opening is on the *right* side in contradistinction to Muhammadan clothing, of which the opening is on the *left.* This applies to all classes of Hindus. As a matter of fact, however, there is a growing tendency to wear loose coats, of semi-European pattern buttoning down the centre. In native undress, sepoys as a rule wear white cotton blouses called *kurtas.* The head dress is invariably the *pagri* or turban, which each clan ties in its own particular fashion. In Oudh and the North-West Provinces caps are preferred to *pagris* by certain classes of Rájpúts. The favourite colour of the Rájpút is yellow, and in ancient days the donning of a saffron coloured robe indicated that the wearer intended to fight to the last, neither giving nor expecting quarter.

Education.

In the matter of education, Rájpúts are a long way inferior to Bráhmans. Few educated men spring from their ranks, and the vast majority of our Rájpút recruits are absolutely illiterate when they join. They generally manage after a time to acquire enough of the Nágri or Kaithi character to indite a very simple and not easily deciphered epistle to their homes, and to spell out with difficulty a similar effusion from their friends.

Wherever the Rájpút has preserved his nationality and independence, he accepts the Bráhman as a necessity, but declines to consider him as a superior in aught but a spiritual sense. At sacrifices, marriages, deaths, and for casting horoscopes, the Bráhman is indispensable. As a *parohit*

* **Many of these cooking pots could be dispensed with by Western Rájpúts.**

or family priest his advice is sought for, especially by the women; but meddlesome interference is not tolerated, and his sphere of influence is always restricted within reasonable bounds.

Religious observances.

This is specially the case in Rájpútána, where the Rájpút "worships his horse, his sword, and the sun, and attends more to the martial songs of the bard than to the prayers and litanies of the Bráhman."* The nearer we approach Ajudhya and Benares, the more susceptible is the Rájpút to Bráhmanical influence, and the more rigid his adherence to the forms of the Hindu religion. Like the Bráhman, the Rájpút performs his devotions alone, generally on the banks of the stream or tank in most convenient proximity to his home. There are three daily periods for devotion called *trikal*, one hour before and after sunrise, one hour before and after noon, and one hour before and after sunset.

The Rájpút except the *Bhattis* and *Ráthors* of Bikaneer, pays nearly as much attention to his personal cleanliness as a Bráhman. Daily shaving† is almost a religious duty. A barber is always employed, and the operation is gone through out of doors

Personal habits.

Teeth are cleansed with a twig, generally of the *ním* tree. After its application to the teeth the twig serves to clean the tongue, a fresh twig being used on each occasion. No words can express the abhorrence of a high caste Hindu for the European practice of retaining a tooth brush after use, as saliva is of all things the most utterly polluting. When a *Purbiah* Rájpút visits the latrine, and goes into the fields for purposes of nature, he invariably hangs his *janéo* over his *right* ear, so that his business may be known to his neighbours

Taking them as a class, Rájpúts are remarkably free from debauchery. They are rarely infected with venereal diseases, and considering the style of clothing in use by both sexes, their morality is highly commendable. Nudity is held in especial abhorrence and is strictly prohibited. In marked contrast

Morality.

with this however, is the extraordinary license they give to their tongues. The grossest terms are used in conversation between men and women without exciting the least surprise. This may be attributed to that "simplicity which conceives that whatever can exist without blame may be named without offence."‡

As has before been mentioned, an extreme sensitiveness on all points relating to the honour of their women is a marked feature in the Rájpút character. Except in certain clans which have fallen in status, their

* Annals of Rájasthán—*Tod.*

† The shaving here alluded to, refers to the armpits rather than to the face, for beards are generally worn.

‡ Hinduism—*Harris.*

widows may not remarry, and as the honour of every family demands that its daughters should be married into the highest possible clans, girls are regarded as a burden, and female infanticide is regrettably common. For this reason also, the higher the grade of Rájpút, the commoner is the crime, owing to the greater difficulty of obtaining suitable husbands. Sleeman in his 'Journey through the Kingdom of Oudh" makes the following reference to infanticide :—" After the murder of every infant the family considers itself an object of displeasure to the Deity, and on the 12th day after birth they send for the *parohit* or family priest, and by suitable gratuities obtain absolution. This is necessary whether the family be rich or poor ; but when the absolution is given, nothing more is thought or said about the matter. The lower clans who can unite their daughters to those of higher grade commit less murders of this kind than others, but *all* Rájpút clans are more or less addicted to female infanticide. It is the dread of sinking in substance from loss of property, and in grade from loss of caste, that alone leads to the destruction of female infants."

Female infanticide among Rájpúts.

Among Rájpúts, as with most classes of Hindus, the women do not join in the society of the men, and are not admitted to an equality with them. Even when walking together, the woman always follows the man, although there may be no obstacle to their walking abreast. The household duties of a Rájpútni do not differ from those of women of other classes. She grinds the corn, cooks the food, spins, and brings in wood, fuel, and water, but owing to her being secluded after the Muhammadan fashion, she is not, except among the poorest classes, available for agricultural labour, and, unlike the Játni, can take no part in the outdoor work of the fields. " Altogether, Rájpút females are a very unsatisfactory institution, and this goes far to weigh down and give a comparatively bad name to men who are often industrious enough."*

Position of Rajpút women.

Certain classes of Rájpúts called *Gaurúa,* and found chiefly in the Eastern Punjáb and the districts bordering on the Jumna, practise what is called *karáo*, or the marriage of widows with the brother of a deceased husband. It is only younger brothers who form these connections, elder brothers being prohibited from marrying their younger brother's widows. When the laws of Mánu were enacted, there appears to have been some doubt as to whether *karáo* was permissible. From a consideration of all the discussions on

Karáo or widow-marriage.

* Ethnology of India—*Campbell.*

the subject, it appears that failure of issue was the point on which its legality turned. All the modern schools of Hindu law prohibit the practice entirely, and a Rájpút clan adopting it, is at once degraded and regarded as impure. In Rájpútána *karáo* was first practised by *Chauháns* in Marwar, and is permissible among certain *Ponwars*, *Parihars*, *Chauháns* and *Ráthors*, who are called *Natráyat* Rájpúts.

Rájpúts were formerly particularly addicted to *Sati*, or the self-immolation of widows on the husband's funeral pyres. Lord George Bentinck suppressed the practice in British India in 1829; but the custom, though happily now abandoned, lingered on for some years later in Rájpútána and Bundelkhund. "The slaughter of a wife at the obsequies of a deceased husband seems to have been a Scythian custom. It was an outgrowth of a belief in ghosts. The dead man was supposed to need the society of his wife in the world of shades. The Aryans appear to have had no such custom. If a man died childless, his widow was expected to bear a son to his nearest kinsman; but otherwise the widows of a Rája continued to live in the royal residence, under the immediate protection of his successor. The original distinction between the Scythian and Aryan usages is thus obvious. The Scythians buried their dead; the Aryans burned them. The Scythians slaughtered a living female to enable her to accompany the dead man; the Aryans placed the widow in charge of the new head of the family. Both usages found expression among the Rájpúts. The dead man was burnt according to the Aryan fashion, but the living widow was burnt with him, in order that she might accompany her husband to the world of spirits. The rite of *Sati* as practised by the Rájpúts may thus be described as a Scythic usage modified by Aryan culture. The female was no longer slaughtered as an unwilling victim to the selfish sensuality of a barbarian, but was the widow of a high-souled Rájpút, the reflex of his chivalrous devotion, prepared to perish with him in order that she might accompany her husband to a heaven of felicity. *Agni* or fire was the purifying deity, the divine messenger that carried the sacrifice to the gods, and the sanctifying flame that bore the widow and her lord away to the mansions of the Sun. In this manner the horrible rite so revolting to civilization and humanity was imbued with an element of religion, and elevated the distracted widow into a courageous and self-sacrificing heroine. Such was the Rájpút rite of *Sati*. It was the expression of the highest conjugal affection combined with the lowest state of female degradation. The unhappy widow had no way of escape from a joyless life of servitude except by the most horrible of sacrifices. The honour of

The Rájpút rite of *Sati*.

the family depended upon the heroism of the woman, and the widow was too often condemned to the pain of martyrdom when the heroism was altogether wanting."*

Closely akin to the rite of *Sati* was the horrible sacrifice called *Johur*, where the females were immolated on the occasion of a defeat, to preserve them from pollution or captivity. At the famous siege of Chitór in 1303, the Rájpúts being driven to the last extremity, determined to destroy their women rather than they should fall into the hands of Allá-ud-din Khilji and his Muhammadan soldiers. "They were conveyed to a great subterranean retreat where, in chambers impervious to the light of day, the funeral pyres were lighted, and the Ráni and several thousand women sought security from dishonour by committing themselves to the flames."† Perhaps the most recent example of a sacrifice of this kind was in 1803, when at the siege of the rock fortress of Gawalgarh in Berar, by Sir Arthur Wellesley, the Rájpúts forming the garrison, finding all hope of saving the place to be vain, collected their wives and daughters, and having slain them, sallied forth to the attack of the besiegers with no other hope but that of selling their lives dearly.

The Rájpút rite of *Johur*.

The Rájpúts are styled the royal race of India, of which they were for many centuries the rulers. The great Hindu families, descendants of mighty potentates, are still in the main of Rájpút blood. Combining from the earliest times the functions of ruling and fighting, no houses in India can boast of longer pedigrees or more splendid histories. At the present time the profession of arms is universally regarded as a natural and legitimate one for members of this caste. The physique of the Rájpút fits him for the profession of a soldier. A fine up-standing muscular man, combining as he does a love of athletic sports with a military carriage, it is not surprising that amongst the younger members of a family, the military profession should be very generally sought after. As has been said before, the Bengal army was at one time almost entirely composed of this class, and the profession of arms has consequently become a tradition among them. Though the Rájpúts of Rájpútána as a rule lack the height of their brethren of Hindustán, they are generally sturdier and often better limbed, and as far as physique is concerned, the former are perhaps better suited for the cavalry, and the latter for the infantry. Rájpúts are extremely fond of wrestling, and exhibit great strength in

Love of the military profession, physique, and skill in manly sports.

* History of India—*Talboys Wheeler*.

† Annals of Rájasthán—*Tod*.

weilding enormous clubs. They are also fond of single stick, running, jumping, and indeed take kindly to all sports requiring skill and vigour.

The Rájpúts of Hindustán are mostly yeomen, cultivating their own lands; but though nearly all are addicted to agriculture, there is among most clans a rooted aversion to the actual handling of the plough, which is considered a menial and degrading office, incompatible with their status as Kshatriyas. In Rájpútána they despise all agricultural pursuits and leave them to Játs, Gújars, Ahirs, and Minas. The Rájpút of the Eastern Punjáb differs but little if at all from the Rájpút of Rájpútána. He is an inefficient husbandman, and much prefers the care of cattle, whether his own or other people's, to agriculture. He still retains his pride of birth which leads him to look down on the Ját, who is immeasurably his superior in industry. He has an innate instinct for cattle-lifting, and has reduced this pursuit from a romantic pastime to an absolute science.

The Rájpút as an agriculturist.

It is a general custom among Rájpúts, subject of course to exceptions, for brothers to live together so long as their father is alive, and to separate at his death. We may thus find four or five brothers with their families living in separate houses arranged round a common courtyard, the whole forming but one household. The general practice among the yeoman classes which furnish the majority of our sowars and sepoys is for the elder brothers to remain at home, cultivating the ancestral lands, while the younger ones take service in the army and police, and contribute to the family purse by savings from their pay, and the pensions granted to them on retirement. The death of an elder brother often compels a soldier to ask for his discharge, not from any dissatisfaction with the service, but simply in order to enable him to look after his land. The establishment of an Active Reserve has done much to lessen this difficulty, and has on many occasions enabled the sepoy to retain his connection with the army, without sacrificing his agricultural interests.

Family life.

The main laws of inheritance among Rájpúts are as follows. Succession goes first to the sons and their male offspring, *i.e.*, if a son dies, the share which he would take goes to his sons, and so on. If a son dies leaving a widow, she takes a life interest in the share which would have come to him. Thus the nearer male descendants do not exclude the more remote, but all share according to the position which they occupy in relation to the deceased. In the absence of sons the widow takes a life interest in the deceased's estate, but where sons succeed, she has a claim to suitable

Laws of inheritance.

maintenance only. On the death of a widow, or in her absence, or on her remarriage,* the father, if alive, succeeds. This of course rarely happens, as it is not often that the son separates from the father during his life time, and still less often does a separated son obtain a separate part of the family land on partition before his father's death. Daughters and their issue have no customary right to succeed; they are only entitled to maintenance, and to be suitably betrothed and married.

Litigiousness.

Litigiousness is one of the peculiar characteristics of Rájpúts as of other classes of Hindus. A determination to prosecute a case to its farthest limits, in spite of adverse decisions and friendly counsels, is a common cause of ruin to the Rájpút suitor. Rather than abandon his cause he will appeal from court to court, until his expenses far exceed the amount for which he is contending. This love of litigation is productive of much perjury.

Pancháyats.

Pancháyats now play a less important part in the social regulations of the people than they did in former times. A *pancháyat* may be described as a court of arbitration for the settlement of disputes, which are also cognizable by law, without having recourse to the courts for justice. It generally consists of from three or five persons, one of whom acts as chairman, decisions being arrived at by the opinion of the majority. A *pancháyat* deals generally with caste matters, and, though it has no legal authority, is a powerful tribunal, whose decisions are seldom appealed against. It passes sentences of various degrees of severity. Sometimes the offender is ordered to give a feast to his brotherhood, sometimes to pay a fine, and if refractory, may be excluded from social intercourse with his caste fellows. In grave cases he may incur the most terrible penalty of all—total excommunication.

The village community.

Next to caste there is no institution in India more permanent than the village community, which dates back to the time of the early Aryan settlements. In Northern India, the headman of every village is called a *Lumbardar*. He is a recognized official, and is directly responsible to the *Zaildar* or *Tahsildar* for the collection of the revenue due from the village and its lands. The typical village is divided into wards, each of which is in charge of elders, who form the *pancháyat* or village council. Grazing grounds are held in common; the income derived from grazing dues, hearth-fees, and the rent paid by persons cultivating the common lands are credited

* Among *Gaurúa* Rájpúts only.

to a general fund; and certain common charges, such as the cost of entertaining subordinate officials, travellers, and beggars, are debited against it, forming a primitive system of local self-government. The *pancháyat* settle all questions relative to the general well-being of the village, they audit the accounts of the village fund, and all matters affecting the community as a body, such as breaking up jungle land and cutting down trees, must invariably be submitted to their decision. The *zamindars* or landholders consider themselves immeasurably superior to the traders and village menials, the distinctive sign of whose inferiority is their liability to pay hearth-fees.

Village menials.

Village menials are divided into two classes—those connected with agriculture, such as the blacksmith, carpenter, and *chamár*,* and those connected with household matters, such as the weaver, potter, waterman,† barber, *dhobi*, and sweeper. They are paid chiefly in kind, receiving a certain fixed percentage of the yield of each harvest, and eke out a scanty subsistence by pursuing their special callings.

* The *Chamár* is a leather dresser. He skins animals and acts as a village drudge and watchman. He is of course an outcast, but is not quite so degraded as the *Bhangi* or sweeper, for he will not act as a scavenger.

† The waterman of the higher castes is the *Kahar* or dooli-bearer. His social position is not a high one, but he is regarded as a person of respectability as Brahmans and Rájpúts can take water from his hands, and he is even permitted to prepare their *chapatis* up to the point when they are placed on the fire for baking. In a Rájpút regiment most of the Native Officers' servants are *Kahars*.

CHAPTER V.

RECRUITING.

Fighting capacity depends not only on race but also on hereditary instinct and social status, therefore it is essential that every effort should be made to obtain the very best men of that class which a regiment may enlist.

General.

Men of good class will not enlist unless their own class be represented in the regiment, and if once a good recruiting connection be established, little, if any, difficulty will be experienced in obtaining recruits of the same stamp in the future; and the converse equally applies, for where the companies are commanded by native officers, who, as regards race and breeding, are not altogether desirable, they will naturally try to bring into the regiment men of their own kind, who in their turn are eventually promoted to be non-commissioned and native officers, and a ring, very difficult to break through, thus becomes established, which acts as a powerful deterrent to the good class whom it may be desired to introduce into the regiment.

It is an inducement to a good man to enlist in a regiment, where he knows he will be surrounded by men who know him and come from his neighbourhood, for it at once places him in touch with his home and belongings, and if he be unable to obtain leave or furlough, those who do on their return bring him news of his home, he is consequently more likely to be happy and contented, his interests are in the company, and a spirit of *esprit de corps* becomes engendered in him—a powerful factor in the efficiency of every regiment.

Selection of recruiting party.

The men composing the party should be of the same tribe and sub-division or clan as it is desired to recruit from, and, if possible, of the same district. The strength of the party should be regulated by the number of recruits required, probably ⅛ to ¼ would be a sufficient proportion, and in this way the work is more likely to be quickly and consequently economically performed.

Commander of the party.

The native officer or non-commissioned officer in charge of the party should be a good man as a recruiter, possessed of tact and likely to treat recruits considerately. A native officer of influence and property in the district, it is desired to recruit from, would be the best, and a regiment possessing such a one would probably monopolize the best recruits from his neighbourhood; for the men have the advantage of knowing under whom they are going to serve, and feel their interests will consequently be looked after. Recruiting parties should not be away from their regiments on this duty for more than three months, as the men are apt to become stale, and disheartened if from any cause they are unable to obtain recruits.

A non-commissioned officer, with hopes of promotion, has everything to gain by bringing good recruits, and this incentive will cause him to work all the harder.

There are many non-commissioned officers and men in regiments of good class, who, though they do not shine as particularly smart soldiers, still have the faculty of procuring good recruits whenever detailed for the duty, where others of equally good class, though much smarter soldiers, fail to obtain the same stamp of man; this is probably due to their social qualifications and a taking manner, which enables them to induce men to enlist, for there can be no doubt that where difficulty may exist in procuring men of a certain class, they are prevailed on to enlist by the tales of pleasant times before them, good pay, little work, etc., etc.

Men of the party.

However good the commander of the party may be, he is likely to fail unless supported by good men, who should be generally of active habits and a genial disposition, and the selection might be left to him unless they happen to be men known as good recruiters, who have previously done good service; he is responsible to the Commanding Officer for his work, and would know the men most likely to give him the best assistance.

Reward to recruiters.

A really good recruiter is invaluable and as worthy of reward, if not more so, than a soldier who excels in his military duties, when it is considered how the regiment benefits by his efforts; for as the material is so will the regiment be, and no amount of training will make a man into a good soldier if in the first instance he is a man of bad class.

Every encouragement should be given to men who do well on recruiting duty, an entry made in their sheet roll to this effect or such public recognition as the Commanding Officer may deem best, so as to render the duty a popular one; it is perhaps hardly politic to punish those who do badly, though they need not be employed again, for, if men see they are liable to punishment for failure, they are likely to be chary in volunteering for the duty, through fear of failing to attain good results.

Responsibility of recruiters.

The men should be held responsible that the recruits they bring are of the right stamp and what they represent themselves to be, for, though this may possibly make the work slower, still it ensures better material finally, and it should be impressed on the party that a *few really good recruits of the right sort are better than a number who only just come up to the required standard.*

Recruiting by leave and furlough men.

Men returning from furlough and leave should be encouraged to bring back a recruit or two with them, as thus recruited singly by their friends, they are likely to take more interest in the regiment, and are probably of finer physique than if obtained in the ordinary way. But men expressing a desire to bring recruits from their homes should be warned of the responsibility they incur in the matter of defraying the travelling expenses of any who may be found unfit physically or for any other reason.

System of working the party.

When it has been ascertained from the District Recruiting Officer when and where the party are to present themselves, they should be warned to leave their address at the post offices and police stations of the places through which they pass, so that the District Recruiting Officer can at any time, if necessary, communicate with them. They should work in twos and threes and not singly. All recruits need not be taken to the District Recruiting Officer, those obviously unfit from such defects as enlarged spleen, defective vision, knock knees, prominent varicose veins or any other noticeable physical defect can be rejected at once prior to his visit.

It is an important thing to examine recruits as near their homes as possible, it thus saves them long marches and secures recruits who might otherwise be lost to the service; it has the further advantages that final rejections are reduced to a minimum, time and expense are saved, and the discontent and trouble, entailed on rejected men having to return long distances to their homes, is done away with.

Seasons for recruiting Rájpúts.

The best season is from October to the end of May, April and May being perhaps the best months. June sometimes affords favourable results, though not generally a good month. July, August, and September are bad months, and recruiting during this period might almost be entirely suspended, for ordinarily the country roads are knee deep in mud and slush, and it is raining most of the time, thus hindering the movements of recruiters who prefer to remain under shelter and keep dry, whilst recruits are equally averse to moving long distances abroad in wet and mud; and in addition, there is in many parts of the country a superstition about making journeys in the monsoon, leaving their homes at this season being considered unlucky.

After a recruit joins his regiment, the usual descriptive roll to verify his caste, etc., is sent to the civil officer of his district, but it is necessary to establish his identity, if possible, at the time of enlistment, for it sometimes happens that a recruit having first possibly squared the village authorities to whom his verification roll will be ultimately sent, misrepresents his caste and enlists, though detection, sooner or later, is inevitable through the men of his company, whose suspicions are sure to be aroused; if, however, recruiters be held responsible there is little likelihood of this.

Verification of recruits.

The following valuable notes on the identification of Rájpút recruits have been furnished by Captain Newell, District Recruiting Officer.

Verification of a Rájpút recruit.

A Rájpút should be asked the following questions:—

(1) What clan he belongs to and what district.
(2) What his gotra is.
(3) What clan his mother came from.
(4) From what clans male members of his family have taken wives.
(5) Into what clans female members of his family have been married.
(6) What food he will eat, by whom cooked, and from what vessels he will drink.

If satisfactorily answered and the replies agree with the information contained in the clan history and marriage tables, the recruit is a true Rájpút.

Sometimes a Brahman tries to pass himself off as à Rájpút, but there is a difference in the '*janeo*' worn by both, that of the Rájpút is shorter, and is worn only after he is married, whilst the Brahman always wears it. There is a difference also in the knot, and some people can by examining it distinguish a Rájpút from a Brahman.

Difference between Brahman and Rájpút janeo.

Among Eastern Rájpúts smoking from the same '*hukka*' is permissible only to those who can eat '*roti*' together, and drinking is prohibited.

Eastern and Western Rájpúts.

Western Rájpúts are much more lax in these observances, and can eat food cooked by Jats, Ahirs, etc., whilst they can drink and smoke with other castes.

With practice a Western Rájpút can be easily recognised, but with a Rájpút from the extreme east, Arrah or Shahabad, it is more difficult, as the mixture of blood and impurity of descent have destroyed the purity of the type.

Careful observation and practice can do wonders, and in a short time an observant officer will, in nine cases out of ten, be able to distinguish Rájpúts, Brahmans, and Eastern and Western Muhammadans simply by looking at them.

Race characteristics of the Rájpút.

One peculiarity of the country Rájpút is his simplicity. He is a straightforward, guileless, honest, gentlemanly fellow and his manners betray him. As a class Rájpúts are comparatively speaking the straightest people in the country and generally speak the truth.

They have not the astuteness of the Brahman, nor the deceit and cunning of the bunniah, for whom they are no match, and in many cases their money and lands pass into the hands of the money-lender.

These characteristics are mentioned, as in conversation with Rájpúts or Brahmans they are easily discerned, whilst conversation on various topics brings out their racial characteristics in an extraordinary manner.

Clans to be enlisted.

There is a considerable difference between the Western and Eastern Rájpúts, both in character, customs, and intensity of religious feeling; the former having fewer caste prejudices in regard to eating and drinking, and generally the Rájpúts of the West rank higher than those of the East. Marriage is the true test of the Rájpút, and an intimate acquaintance with the permissible clan marriages is therefore necessary to any one enlisting them, tables are given in the history of each clan in the text, showing to and from what clans wives are given and taken.

Exogamy.

The first test is that of exogamy; and endogamous Rájpúts as well as those that practise '*karao*' or widow marriage (*vide* page 169) are looked down upon and should not be enlisted, though any septs of a clan which are exogamous should be enlisted.

Classes to enlist.

For instance, among the Jádons or Jádubánsis are many spurious branches to be carefully avoided, but true exogamous septs such as Bhatti, Chhoukar, Barésari, and Jaiswar should be enlisted, and practically there seems no reason why Rájpúts, who are received in marriage by the higher clans, should not be enlisted.

Gaurava is the general term applied to all Rájpúts who have lost caste by practising '*karao*,' and these should be avoided.

The Rájpúts from Arrah and the east of Oudh are called "Bhojpuriyas," as the country they live in is called Bhojpur; they are looked down on by the Oudh men, as the majority are of low grade, a list of some of these clans is given in Appendix B.

Captain Newell, the District Recruiting Officer, says of them :—

Character of Bhojpuriyas.

"I personally do not think much of these men, they have magnificent physique, but are not generally credited with valour. However, I doubt much whether their want of courage has been proved. They are very intelligent and make smart soldiers, but are, however, tricky and more difficult to deal with than their western brethren."

"With all their magnificent physique, I do not believe that they have much stamina, but to give them their due a large number have always been in our ranks, and many of them have distinguished themselves by good and faithful service.

Buinhars.

Buinhars are also mostly found in Bhojpur and should not be enlisted in Rájpút regiments unless kept in separate companies; they will all eat together. Captain Newell gives his opinion of them in the following words :—

"They are of magnificent physique, but their character is against them. They are very tricky and intriguing, exceedingly litigious and quarrelsome; it is impossible to get to like these men, there appears to be no redeeming point about them, except their physique which is superb. A regiment of these men on parade would certainly take the eye, they are tall and heavily built, but I do not believe in them at all. I doubt whether they possess either stamina or courage, they make good wrestlers and tug of war teams, but personally I do not think they are good for much else."

A tabulated statement of the Western and Eastern Rájpúts, giving their clans, sub-divisions, numbers, locality, and qualifications as soldiers, will be found in Appendices A and B in numerical order.

Recruiting grounds.

A list of the various districts and their value from a recruiting point of view is given in Appendix C, as well as the principal clans found in each district.

Fairs.

Good recruits can be enlisted at fairs, the only thing against it being the difficulty sometimes of verification, for unless they happen to belong to the same district as the recruiters, the latter is unable to verify their caste and antecedents, though they would of course be eventually detected after joining the regiment; and in this case, after being fed for two or three days by the party, the recruit may change his mind and bolt, knowing there is no probability of his coming across them again. Many young men, however, attend fairs for the express purpose of enlisting, because either their parents will not allow them to enlist at home, or a party may not have visited the neighbourhood lately.

A list of fairs in the Rájpútána district is given in Appendix D, as well as some of the principal fairs in North-Western Provinces and Oudh.

Leading families of the district.

The District Recruiting Officer should endeavour, as far as possible, to gain the friendship and assistance of the native princes and the leading and influential men of the district. Retired native officers and soldiers can also assist to a very great extent in recruiting, but it is necessary in the first instance to be on a friendly footing with them and obtain their good will, and how this can be best effected is a matter for the District Recruiting Officer to decide; but showing an interest in their affairs, a respect for their customs and listening readily to their troubles and grievances will go far to produce the desired result, whilst visiting them and conversing on current topics of interest about their history and traditions, etc., will do much to render them willing to afford assistance when required.

District Recruiting Officer.

He should strive to make himself popular and well known in the district, and thoroughly acquainted with the feelings and characteristics of the tribes enlisted, by studying their customs, traditions, manners, etc., and by thus showing a friendly and sympathetic interest in them and their affairs will ingratiate himself with them and gain their respect and esteem.

Touring.

In the cold weather the District Recruiting Officer is enabled to make short tours in the district, and can thus keep in touch with and superintend the parties working at the time. Should the Medical Officer be living at some considerable distance from the place where the recruits are enlisted, the District Recruiting Officer can often save them the trouble of going so far by a prior physical examination, the eyesight can be examined by test cards, and those recruits suffering from any obvious physical defect rejected on the spot.

In the case of regiments actually stationed in the district, or those that are met with on tour, much good can be effected by a personal interview with the Commanding Officer, and by thus becoming acquainted with the officers and native officers, studying the composition of the regiment, looking at the recruits, and acquiring a general knowledge of the men, the requirements of a regiment will be better understood, and this all tends to make recruiting run smoothly and produce the best results. Special sepoys of the regiment can also be interviewed and recruiters selected.

Employment of Pensioners.

If a District Recruiting Officer can succeed in obtaining employments for the pensioners, of his district, it will have a beneficial effect on recruiting generally and conduce greatly to his popularity. It is a good plan to see the employer and point out the advantages of taking pensioned sepoys, besides writing to the different heads of civil departments.

Regulations. The recruiting regulatious and orders on the subject of recruiting are laid down in Section XIX, Arm Regulations, India, Volume II, which has been recently revised.

Note.—Much valuable information for the compilation of this Chapter has been furnished by Captain Newell, District Recruiting Officer, whilst, in addition to the list of authorities already quoted at the beginning of the book, the following authorities have been consulted :—

Précis of Orders and Notes on Gurkha Recruiting by Captain Vanstittart, 1-5th Gurkhas.

Notes on Sikhs by Captain W. R. Falcon, IV Sikhs.

Memorandum on Recruiting of the Regiments of the Bengal Command by Brigadier-General G. E. Young.

APPENDIX A.

AREA I.—WESTERN RÁJPÚTS, PAGE 29 OF TEXT.

Clans.	Rájpútána.		Oudh and North-Western Provinces.		Qualifications as soldiers.	Remarks.
	Sub-divisions.	Locality and numbers.	Sub-divisions.	Locality and numbers.		
Chauhan (royal race).	Bhadauriya, Golwal ... Bagore, Khichi. Chitha, Hara. Deora, Mori. Dhundhoti, Nirbhan. Purbiya, Sanchora. Sonagirra, Tak.	(42,000) Bikanir, Bundir, Gurgaon, Jeypore, Kotah, Marwar, Meywar, Sirrohi, Rohtak.	Bhadauriya, Deora. Bijai, Hara. Bhahu, Khichi. Ball, Khera. Banaphar, Kanji. Chaleya, Kamodari.	42,000 Meerut Division; 42,000 Agra do.; 18,000 Delhi do.; 50,000 { Lucknow do., Rohilkand do., Fyzabad do., Allahabad do., Benares do., Gorakhpur do. }	Very good ...	Pages 62-63 of text for particulars and list of clans with whom marriage is permissible.
Ponwar (royal race)	Ponwar, Soda, Sankla	(24,000) Marwar, Meywar, Rohtak, Dholpur, Jhind.	Dhar, Ponwar, Raj, Ponwar, Ujjaini. } Chobdar, an inferior branch.	(45,000) Meerut, Agra, Farukhabad, Moradabad, Shahjahanpur, Cawnpore, Banda, Jaunpur, Ballia, Gorakhpur, Lucknow, Fyzabad, Rohtak districts.	Ditto ...	Page 113 for clan marriages. Ponwars in Dholpur not so good quite.
Rathor (royal race)	Bidrawal, Bika, Jodha. Chanpawat, Kandalot. Mallinath, Merthia.	(102,000) Bikanir, Marwar, Meywar, Dungarpur, Jeypur, Jaisalmeer.	As given under Rájpútána	(35,000) Agra Division, Rohilkhand Division, Cawnpore, Azamgarh districts.	Ditto ... Marwar Rahtors only serve in the cavalry.	Pages 120-121. Rathors of Rájpútána free from Hindu prejudice.
Kachwahas (royal race).	Balbhadarot, Khangarot. Banbirpota, Khampawat. Chatarbhojot, Khambani. Kalyanot, Nathawat.	(68,000) Jeypur, Ulwar, Shaikawatti, Torawati.	Ditto ...	(31,000) Meerut, Muzaffarnagar, Muttra, Agra, Etawah, Cawnpore, Jalaun districts.	Very good ...	Pages 90-91.

AREA I.—WESTERN RÁJPÚTS, PAGE 29 OF TEXT—*contd.*

Clans.	Rájpútána.		Oudh and North-Western Provinces.		Qualifications as soldiers.	Remarks.
	Sub-division.	Locality and numbers.	Sub-division.	Locality and numbers.		
Tonwar (royal race)	Beagas, Jarrota ... Borahan, Khallia. Jatu, Tonwar.	(13,000) Bikanir, Dholpur, Marwar, Meywar, Jeypur.	Nicoop Gawalera, Bajpanna, Jasraiyah, Himkar, Jerah.	(18,000) Agra Division, Budaun, Sitapur, Rohtak districts.	Very good ...	Page 136.
Bargujar (royal race)	*Nil.*	(2,200) Jeypore, Ulwar	Ahmed Khani, Lal Khan, Bikram Khan, Rai Mani, Kamal Khani.	(17,000) Aligarh, Bulandshahr, Etah, Budaun, Moradabad.	Ditto ...	Page 46.
Jadons, Jadu, Jadubansi.	Jadus (of Kerowlee), Mudecha, Jarecha (of Kutch Bhuj), Bitman, Soha, Sumecha.	(9,000) Jeysulmeer, Jeypore, Bhartpur, Kerowlee.	Bhatti, Chhoukar, Baresari, Jaiswar, Bargala, Jasawat, Porch Uriya, Nara.	(35,000) Aligarh, Bulandshahr, Muttra, Agra, Etah.	Good ...	Page 83. 16,000 are Jadons, 19,000 Jadubansi. Exogamous septs should only be taken.
Parihar (royal race)	......	(6,000) Bikanir, Marwar.	Parihar, Nadhat, Lulapota; Ramawat, Juda.	(16,000) Agra, Etah, Cawnpore, Hamirpur, Jhansi, Jalaun, Unao districts.	Do. ...	Page 108. Closely allied with the Solanki. Special preference for cavalry in Rájpútána.
Solanki ...	......	(7,000) Marwar, Jeypur, Boondi, Rewah.	Solanki, Baghel, Khalats, Sojathia, Rahallia, Chendawat, Bhutta.	(8,000) Etah, Budaun ...	Do. ...	Page 128.
Bhattis ...	Kelan, Khlanh, Jaisalmeria, Pugalliya, Meldot.	(31,000) Marwar, Meywar, Jaisalmeer, Bikanir.	Bhatti, Jaiswar ...	(5,000) Bulandshahr, Etah, Bareilly.	Do. ...	Page 53. Bhattis of North-Western Provinces claim to be Jadons.
Gahlot (royal race).	Gahlot, Sisodiya, Ahara, Manguliya, Kailwa, Mohar.	(41,000) chiefly Meywar	As given under Rájpútána	(2,000) Meerut and Agra divisions scattered about.	Very good ...	Page 75.
Bargala ...	*Nil.*	*Nil.*	......	(5,400) Gurgaon and Bulandshahr districts.	Undesirable ...	Page 45. Spurious branch of the Jadhubansi ranked as impure. Ill-conducted tribe permits "Karao" or widow marriage.
Gaurava ...	*Nil.*	*Nil.*	Tarkar, Jasawat, Jais, Jaiswar, Bhal, Bargala, Indauliya, Bachhal, Nare, Porch Uriya, Mahedwar.	Agra, Muttra, Bulandshahr, Delhi districts.	Ditto ...	Page 80. Rájpúts of fallen grade permit "Karao" or widow marriage.

APPENDIX B.

EASTERN RÁJPÚTS.

Area II.—Page 29 of text.

Clans.	Sub-divisions.	Locality.	Qualifications as soldiers.	REMARKS.
Bisen (51,000).	Parasar, Bharradwaj, Sandil, Batas.	Benares and Gorakhpur divisions; Allahabad, Fyzabad, Gonda, Bahraich districts.	Good ...	*Vide* pages 55-56. For clan marriages. Rajah of Majhauli of Gorakhpur, head of the clan.
Bais (147,000) (royal race).	Tilokchandi. Rao, Raja, Sainbaisi, Sept Naihasta, Chotbhaiya, Gudaraha, Madhour.	Farrukhabad, Mainpuri, Budaun districts; Allahabad, Benares, Gorakhpur, Lucknow, Fyzabad divisions.	Do. ..	Pages 40-41. 360 subdivisions, of which Tilokchand sept takes first place. Other septs marry into 3rd grade clans. Some 700 already enlisted.
Sombansi (43,000).	Baiyagar, Sankirat, Atri.	Farrukhabad, Bareilly, Shahjahanpur, Allahabad, Jaunpur, Azamgarh, Rai Barelli, Sitapur, Hardoi, Gonda, Partabgarh districts.	Do. ...	Page 130. Those of Sandi in Hardoi rank highest.
Gautam (41,000).	Rajah, Rao, Rana, Rawat.	Budaun district; Allahabad, Benares, Gorakhpur divisions.	Do. ...	Pages 79-80. Rajah of Argah, Fatehpur, head of clan. Should be ascertained they are not Bhuinhar Brahmans.
Gaur (39,000).	Chamar-Gaur, Bhat-Gaur, Brahman-Gaur, Amethiya, Gaurahar.	Farrukhabad, Etawah, Etah, Budaun, Shahjahanpur, Moradabad, Cawnpore, Hamirpur, Unao, Sitapur, Hardoi districts.	Very good ...	Pages 77-78. Gaurahar sept have lost status through inferior marriages.
Chandel (38,000).	......	Shahjahanpur, Cawnpore districts; Benares, Gorakhpur divisions; Unao, Hardoi districts.	Good ...	Pages 59-60.
Dikhit (33,000).	......	Fatehpur, Banda, Hamirpur, Ghazipur, Gorakhpur, Azamgarh, Jalaun, Unao, Rai Barelli districts.	Do. ...	Page 68. Valuable assistance in mutiny.
Sengar (32,000) (royal race).	......	Etawah, Cawnpore, Jalaun, Balliah, Unao districts.	Very good ...	Page 122. Closely allied with Bhadauriya.
Surajbansi (23,000).	Savaran, north of Gogra; Bharradwaj, south of Gogra; Kassyap, south of Gogra.	Bulandshahr, Mirzapur, Ghazipur Basti, Kheri, Fyzabad, Barabanki districts.	Good ...	Pages 132-133.
Bachhgoti (19,000) or Rajkumar (13,000).	Bachhgoti proper, Rajkumar, Rajwar.	Jaunpur, Sultanpur, Allahabad, Fyzabad, Partabgarh districts.	Do. ...	Pages 34-35.
Bhadauriya (16,000).	Athbaiya, Kulhaiya, Mamu, Tasseli, Raut.	Agra, Etawah, Cawnpore districts and Gwalior State.	Very good ...	Pages 40-50. A loyal clan not so troubled by caste prejudices as other Rájpúts of Oudh. Serve readily in Gwalior Army.
Pundirs (17,000) (royal race).	......	Saharanpur, Muzaffarnagar, Etawah.	Good ...	Pages 114-115. Aligarh Pundirs very loyal in the mutiny.

Area II.—Page 29 of text—contd.

Clans.	Sub-divisions.	Locality.	Qualifications as soldiers.	Remarks.
Sirkarwars (18,000) (royal race).	......	Agra, Ghazipur, Gorakhpur, Azamgarh, Hardoi districts.	Very good ...	Pages 126-127. Should be ascertained, they are not Bhuinhar Brahmans.
Janwars (12,000).	......	Lucknow division, Gonda District.	Good ...	Page 88. Rajah of Gonda loyal in the mutiny.
Khanpuriya (10,000).	Tiloi, Kaithania ...	Rai Barelli, Sultanpur, Partabgarh.	Do. ...	Page 94.
Bhalé Sultan (9,000).	......	Sultanpur, Bulandshahr districts.	Do. ...	Page 51. Give some 200 men to Rájpút Regiments.
Améthiya (5,000).	......	Gorakhpur, Rai Barelli, Barabanki.	Do. ...	Pages 31-32.
Gaharwar (28,000).	......	Farrukhabad, Etah, Cawnpore, Allahabad, Mirzapur, Ghazipur, Hardoi.	2nd grade, but permissible.	Page 72.
Katheriya (21,000).	......	Etah, Bareilly, Budaun, Moradabad, Shahjahanpur.	2nd grade, but permissible.	Page 96.
Dhakré (6,500).	......	Agra district	Permissible ...	Page 65. Gave trouble in the mutiny.
Bachhals (11,000).	......	Bulandshahr, Muttra, Moradabad, Shahjahanpur, Sitapur, Kheri districts.	2nd grade ...	Pages 33-34.
Jhangara (10,000).	Bhur clan Tarai, Jangharа.	Bareilly, Budaun, Shahjahanpur.	Ditto ...	Pages 85-86. Turbulent and warlike tribe. Tarai practises "Karao" fallen in status.
Raghubansi (32,000).	......	Benares, Mirzapur, Jaunpur, Ghazipur, Azamgarh, Sultanpur districts.	Permissible ...	Page 116.
Raikwars (13,000).	......	Unao, Hardoi, Bahraich, Barabanki.	Ditto ...	Page 118. Troublesome in the mutiny.
Sirnet (10,000).	......	Gorakhpur, Basti districts ...	Ditto ...	Page 124.
Kalhans (12,000).	......	Bahraich, Gonda, Basti ...	Ditto ...	Page 93.
Bandhalgoti (6,000).	Bikram Shahi, Sultan Shahi.	Sultanpur district ...	Ditto ...	Page 42.
Gargbansi (5,000).	......	Azamgarh, Fyzabad, Sultanpur.	Ditto ...	Page 76.
Nikumbh (8,000).	......	Farrukhabad, Jaunpur, Ballia, Azimgarh, Hardoi districts.	Ditto ...	Page 106.
Palwars (9,800).	......	Gorakhpur, Azamgarh, Fyzabad.	Ditto ...	Page 110.
Ahbans (3,000).	Ahbans, Kunwar Ahbans.	Oudh, Hardoi, Kheri districts.	Undesirable ...	*Vide* page 30. Cunning and treacherous clan.
Bundelas (4,800).	......	Jhansi, Lalitpur districts ...	Ditto ...	*Vide* page 58. Turbulent and troublesome race, spurious descent.
Tarkhans (3,500).	......	Muttra, Agra	Ditto ...	*Vide* page 35. Turbulent, poor physique, practise "Karao."

Area II.—Page 29 of text—concld.

Clans.	Sub-divisions.	Locality.	Qualifications as soldiers.	Remarks.
Kakans, page 92 (6,000). Kausiks, pages 98-99 (10,000). Tilaunta, page 135. Udmattia, page 138 (28,000). Lautamiya, page 102 (3,500). Dhekaha, page 66 (2,000). Donwar, page 71. Sarwar, page 134 (3,000). Nandwak, page 105 (1,000). Birwar, page 48 (9,500). Mahrawar, page 102.	......	Jaunpur, Ballia, Ghazipur, Azamgarh, Gorakhpur, Mirzapur and Shahabad districts. Generally known as the Bhojpur district, the great bulk of the clans residing there being low grade and of spurious descent.	Generally undesirable as soldiers, though there are a considerable number in the ranks now.	Tilaunta and Lautamiya have a good many men enlisted. For description of Bhojpuriyas—*vide* the text.

APPENDIX C.

RECRUITING GROUNDS SHOWING CLANS IN EACH DISTRICT AND VALUE OF DISTRICTS.

Division.	District.	Clans.	Value.
MEERUT	Dehra Dun ...	Chauhan and Gahlot generally.	
	Saharanpur ...	Pundir.	
	Muzaffarnagar ...	Kachwahas, Pundir ...	Fair.
	Meerut ...	Ponwar, Kachwaha ...	Do.
	Bulandshahr ...	Bargujar, Jadons, Jadubansi, Bargala, Surajbansi, Bhalé Sultan, Gaurava, Bachhals.	Very good.
	Aligarh ...	Bargujar, Jadons, Jadubansi.	
AGRA	Muttra ...	Chauhan, Rathor, Tonwar, Gahlot. Kachwaha, Jadon, Bachhals, Gaurava, Tarkhan.	
	Agra ...	Ponwar, Kachwaha, Jadons, Parihar, Bhadauriya, Sirkarwars, Dhakré, Tarkhan.	
	Farrukhabad ...	Ponwar, Bais, Sombansi, Gaur, Gaharwar, Nikumbh.	Good.
	Mainpuri ...	Bais	Do.
	Etawah ...	Kachwaha, Parihar, Gaur, Sengar, Bhadauriya, Pundir.	Good, especially along banks of the Chambal.
	Etah ...	Bargujar, Jadon, Solanki, Bhatti, Gaur, Gaharwar, Katheriya.	Good.
ROHILKHUND	Bareilly ...	Chauhan, Rathor. Bhattis, Sombansi, Katheriya, Janghara.	Rohilkhund on the whole is a bad ground, as a large number of the Rájpúts are spurious.
	Bijnor ...	......	
	Budaun ...	Tonwar, Bargujar, Solanki, Bais, Gautam, Gaur, Katheriya, Jhangara.	
	Moradabad ...	Ponwar, Bargujar, Gaur, Katheriya, Bachhals.	
	Shahjahanpur ...	Ponwar, Sombansi, Gaur, Chandel, Katheriya, Bachhals, Janghara.	
	Pilibhit ...	......	
DELHI	Delhi ...	Chauhan. Gaurava.	
	Gurgaon ...	Bargala	Gurgaon very fair district.
	Karnal ...		
	Hissar ...		
	Roh ...	Ponwar, Tonwar ...	Hissar and Rohtak excellent districts, furnishing some of the best Rájpúts in the service. Punjab Cavalry recruit from Rohtak.

N.B.—The clans are given in the order of the Appendices A—B.

Recruiting grounds showing clans in each district and value of districts—contd.

Division.	District.	Clans.	Value.
RÁJPÚTÁNA ...	Jeypore ...	Chauhan, Rathor, Kachwahas, Tonwar, Bargujars, Jadons, Solanki.	All the best clans live in Rájpútána, but unfortunately at present the established connection with the district is small, only some 35 recruits being enlisted from there in 1896.
	Ulwar ...	Kachwaha, Bargujar.	
	Bikanir ...	Chauhan, Rathor, Tonwar, Parihar, Bhattis.	
	Meywar ...	Chauhan, Ponwar, Rathor, Tonwar, Bhattis.	
	Marwar ...	Chauhan, Ponwar, Rathor, Tonwar, Parihar, Solanki, Bhatti.	
	Dholpur ...	Ponwar, Tonwar.	
	Jaisalmeer ...	Rathor, Jadons, Bhattis.	
	Sheikawatti, Torawati.	Kachwahas.	
ALLAHABAD...	Cawnpore ...	Ponwar, Rathor, Kachwaha, Parihar Gaur, Chandel, Sengar, Bhadauriya, Gaharwar.	Good.
	Fatehpur ...	Dikhit, Chauhan	Do.
	Banda ...	Ponwar, Dikhit, Bais	Do.
	Hamirpur ...	Parihar, Gaur, Dikhit, Gautam ...	Do.
	Allahabad ...	Bisen, Sombansi, Rajkumar, Gaharwar throughout the division.	
	Jhansi ...	Parihar, Bundelas.	
	Jalaun ...	Kachwaha, Parihar, Dikhit, Sengar	Very good ground. Parihars and Sengars from here excellent material.
LUCKNOW ...	Lucknow ...	Chauhan, Bais, Janwars. — Ponwar.	
	Unao ...	Parihar, Gaur, Chandel, Dikhit, Sengar, Raikwars.	Unao and Rai Barelli form the Baiswara country and furnishes a large number of recruits.
	Rai Barelli ...	Sombansi, Dikhit, Kanhpuriya.	
	Sitapur ...	Tonwar, Sombansi, Gaur, Bachhals.	
	Hardoi ...	Sombansi, Gaur, Chandel, Sirkarwars, Gaharwar, Raikwar, Nikumbh, Ahbans.	Good district.
	Kheri ...	Surajbansi, Bachhals, Ahbans.	Kheri and Sitapur have never furnished many soldiers.

N.B.—The clans are given in the order of the Appendices A—B.

Recruiting grounds showing clans in each district and value of districts—concld.

Division.	District.	Clans.		Value.
FYZABAD ...	Fyzabad ...	Chauhan, Bais.	Ponwar, Bisen, Surajbansi, Rajkumar, Gargbansi, Palwars.	Partabgarh, Sultanpur, with the southern and eastern slice of Fyzabad comprises the "Banandha" district, a very good recruiting ground.
	Gonda ...		Bisen, Sombansi, Kathans.	
	Bahraich ...		Bisen, Raikwar, Kalhans.	
	Sultanpur ...		Bandhalgoti, Gargbansi.	
	Partabgarh ...		Sombansi, Rajkumar, Kanhpuriya.	Bahraich has never furnished many soldiers.
	Barabanki ...		Surajbansi, Raikwar, Bisen, Amethiya.	Gonda men are wanting in stamina.
GORAKHPUR ...	Gorakhpur ...	Chauhan, Bisen, Bais, Gautam, Chandel.	Ponwar, Dikhit, Sirkarwars, Sirnet, Palwar.	
	Basti ...		Surajbansi, Sirnet, Kalhans.	Barabanki bad for the Bais clan, but good for the 4 clans mentioned.
	Azamgarh ...		Rathor, Sombansi, Dikhit, Sirkarwar, Raghubansi, Gargbansi.	Bulk of the clans are of spurious descent.
BENARES ...	Benares ...	Chauhan, Bisen, Bais, Gautam, Chandel, Raghubansi.	Surajbansi, Gaharwar ...	East of Oudh. Extensive recruiting is not advocated.
	Mirzapur ...		......	
	Jaunpur ...		Ponwar, Rajkumar, Nikumbh.	In Ballia and Ghazipur the physique of the Thakur is very good and as regards physique it is generally good throughout these districts (*vide* remarks on Bhojpuriyas).
	Ballia ...		Ponwar, Sengar, Nikumbh.	
	Ghazipur ...		Dikhit, Surajbansi, Sirkarwars, Gaharwar.	

N.B.—The clans are given in the order of the Appendices A.—B.

APPENDIX D (1).

RÁJPÚTÁNA FAIRS AND TIRÂTS (PILGRIMAGE).

State.	Place.	Occasion.	Approximate date.	Remarks.
Jodhpur or Marwar.	Tilwarra ...	In honour of the god Malli ...	March ...	For 15 days.
	Pokarn ...	In honour of Ramdeoji ...	August ...	For 15 days.
	Parbatsar ...	In honour of Tejaji, great goddess of the Jats.	2nd October ...	No tirât held on account of scarcity of water.
	Rampuri ...	......	24th October.	
	Mandwa ...	Assemblage of 30,000 ...	December.	
Bikanir ...	Múkám ...	In honour of Jamaji ...	16th February ...	No tirâts.
	Guganmeri ...	......	18th—19th September.	
	Deshnok ...	In honour of Karmji, patroness of the Bikanir Rathor.	17th—18th October...	12 miles south of Bikanir.
	Koláth ...	......	23rd November ...	18 miles west of Bikanir City.
Alwar ...	Chuhar Sidh, Dehra Pergunnah.	In honour of a Meo saint assemblage of 80,000.	February ...	8 miles north-west of Alwar.
	Bilali Bansur district.	In honour of Sitla Devi ...	March and April ...	Largely attended.
	Rajgarh ...	Jagarnath's festival ...	June ...	Tirât.
Jeypore ...	Dausa ...	......	22nd January.	
	Madhopur ...	In honour of Parwarji Chauth	6th January. 28th October.	
	Ditto ...	In honour of Chumkariji ...	12th March. 8th October.	
	Kurita (Hindaun Tehsil).	In honour of Mahadeoji Khundela.	4th February ...	3 days' duration.
	Chaksu ...	......	12th March.	
	Nawai ...	In honour of Ranjhorji ...	3rd and 4th March.	
	Lohargarh between Udepur and Sikar.	In honour of Malket ...	30th April ... 25th September ...	Tirât.
	Chandla ...	In honour of Mahabir ...	April.	
	Bailpur ...	In honour of Gukni Seriji Mahadeo.	15th April.	
	Diggi, Tehsil Málpura.	In honour of Seri Kallanji ...	26th April.	
	Sai Tehsil ...	In honour of Mata Sunkbarji	3rd September.	
	Budda ...	In honour of Khakali Mata	October.	
Kishngarh ...	Kishngarh ...	In honour of Tejaji Rewari Balaji.	20th, 21st, 22nd and 23rd September.	
	Do. ...	In honour of Bhan Sathmi ...	24th January.	
	Do. ...	In honour of Sil Sathmi ...	10th March.	
	Do. ...	In honour of Sindhara Gangor.	20th March.	
	Do. ...	Dasserah	28th March.	
	Salimabad in Rupnagar Tehsil.	In honour of Janam Ashthmi	4th September.	
	Sirsira ...	In honour of Tejaji ...	20th September.	
	Adhor ...	In honour of Khadan Mataji	20th October.	
Ajmer-Merwara	Ajmer ...	In honour of Urs and Hazrat Khwajah Sahib.	20th January ...	6 days. 15,000 visitors.
	Beawar ...	Called Teja-ka-Mela ...	19th September ...	3 days. 10,000 visitors.
	Pushkar ...	......	19th November ...	5 days. 30,000 visitors.

APPENDIX D (2).

FAIRS IN NORTH-WESTERN PROVINCES AND OUDH.

Gatherings of 20,000 and upwards.

Name of Mela.	Place where held.	Date.	Object of fair.	Which class predominates.	Numbers attending.	Duration in days.
Maghmela ...	Allahabad ...	January	Bathing in Ganges ...	Hindus	150,000	30 days.
Sheo Rathri ...	Bagh Pat ...	February and March ...	Worship of Shiva ...	Hindu	20,000	1 day.
Garhwara ...	Jaunpur ...	13th March ...	Worship of Debi ...	Hindu and Muhammadan	25,000	1.
Bushwa-Mangal ...	Benares ...	1st or 2nd week after Holi in March.	......	Do. Ditto ...	100,000	7.
Hardwar ...	Saharanpur ...	April	Bathing ...	Hindus	400,000	8. After 1898, probably a falling off at Ganges bathing ghats, as the Nerbudda will then be the most sacred river.
Kushahri ...	Unao ...	Between 10th April and 10th May.	Worship of Debi ...	Do.	40,000	7 to 8.
Sikri Khurd ...	Meerut Division ...	May	Worship of Kalka Debi ...	Do.	20,000	14 days.
Madhopur ...	Farrukhabad ...	May and October ...	Bathing in the Bisnath ...	Do.	115,000	1.
Singi Rampur ...	Ditto ...	Ditto ...	Worship of Ram Krishn ...	Do.	80,000	1.
Mathura ...	Mathura ...	11th June ...	Jugal Jori Ka Parkarma ...	Do.	20,000	1.
Gobardhan ...	Ditto ...	June	Religious ...	Do.	20,000	1.
Imilia ...	Allahabad ...	June and July ...	Worship Debi ...	Do.	20,000	1.
Farhanpur ...	Ditto ...	Ditto ...	Worship Sitla Debi ...	Do.	30,000	1.
Jalbehar ...	Jhansi ...	September ...	Worship of Mahadeo ...	Do.	50,000	1.
Kakori ...	Rai Bareilly ...	July	Worship of Kakori ...	Do.	40,000	7.
Mariahu ...	Jaunpur ...	September ...	Worship of Debi ...	Hindu and Muhammadan	20,000	1.

Mathura ...	Mathura ...	8th August and September.	Birth day of Krishn ...	Hindus	21,000	1.
Ganga Nahan ...	Ramghat ...	October ...	Bathing Ganges ...	Ditto	100,000	1.
Kakorah ...	Etah district ...	October ...	Ditto ...	Ditto	30,000	8.
Ganga Nahan ...	Bijnor district ...	Do. ...	Ditto ...	Ditto	30,000	12. At Bithor also for 10 days.
Bansi Ghat ...	Gorakhpur ...	Do.	Bathing Gandak river ...	Ditto	25,000	3.
Mathura ...	Mathura ...	11th October ...	Religious ...	Ditto	30,000	1.
Ditto ...	Ditto ...	9th Kartik (October and November).	Ditto ...	Ditto	50,000	1.
Ditto ...	Ditto ...	10th Kartik ...	Representation of Ram being killed by Krishn and Bala Deo.	Ditto	20,000	1.
Ditto ...	Ditto ...	11th Kartik ...	Religious ...	Ditto	20,000	1.
Gobardhan ...	Ditto ...	10th Kartik ...	Dipmalika, illumination of the sacred Hill.	Ditto	80,000	1.
Kora ...	Fatehpur ...	October ...	Religious ...	Ditto	20,000	1.
Sheorajpur ...	Ditto ...	Ditto ...	Ditto ...	Ditto	50,000	1.
Durga puja ...	Benares ...	Ditto ...	Worship the Holy city ...	Ditto	50,000	7.
Set Barāh ...	Sultanpur ...	Kartik (October and November).	„ of Set Barāh ...	Ditto	25,000	1.
Paryar ...	Unao ...	Kartik ...	Bathing ...	Ditto	200,000	10 to 15 days.
Kathwagra ...	Do. ...	Ditto ...	Ditto ...	Ditto	200,000	7 to 10 days.
Saron ...	Etah district ...	November ...	Bathing in Bruh Ganga ..	Hindus and Muhammadans	50,000	8.
Dhanush Jugg ...	Baikunthpur, Gorakhpur.	November and December.	Commemoration of marriage of Ram.	Hindus	40,000	14.
Bhari ...	Rusalpur (Basti) ...	October and November	Bathing ...	Ditto	50,000	1.
Doba ...	Etawah ...	December ...	Worship of Debi ...	Ditto	30,000	17.
Bhigwasaram ...	Ballia ...	Kartik (October and November).	Ganges bathing ...	Ditto	30,000